HAGAR, SARAH, AND
THEIR CHILDREN

WITHDRAWN

WITHDRAWN

HAGAR, SARAH, AND THEIR CHILDREN

Jewish, Christian, and Muslim Perspectives

EDITED BY

Phyllis Trible
and
Letty M. Russell

St. Louis Community College
at Meramec
LIBRARY

WJK WESTMINSTER
JOHN KNOX PRESS
LOUISVILLE · KENTUCKY

© 2006 Westminster John Knox Press

All rights reserved. No part of this book may be reproduced or transmitted in any form or by any means, electronic or mechanical, including photocopying, recording, or by any information storage or retrieval system, without permission in writing from the publisher. For information, address Westminster John Knox Press, 100 Witherspoon Street, Louisville, Kentucky 40202-1396.

Scripture quotations from the New Revised Standard Version of the Bible are copyright © 1989 by the Division of Christian Education of the National Council of the Churches of Christ in the U.S.A. and are used by permission.

Portions of chapter 6, "Islamic Hagar and Her Family," were published by Exploration Press of Chicago Theological Seminary in Riffat Hassan, "Eid al-Adha (Feast of Sacrifice) in Islam: Abraham, Hagar, and Ishmael," in *Commitment and Commemoration: Jews, Christians, Muslims in Dialogue*, ed. André LaCocque (Chicago: Exploration Press, Chicago Theological Seminary, 1994), 131–50, and are used with permission.

The excerpts on 150–54, 165–67 are from *Sahih Al-Bukhari*, translated by Muhammad Muhsin Khan (Lahore: Kazi Publications, 1983). Reprinted by permission.

Book design by Sharon Adams
Cover design by Lisa Buckley
Cover art by Yisehak F. Sellassie. Scripture Inspired Art "Sarah & Hagar." Yisehak Fine Arts. www.yisehakfinearts.com. Isaacfs@sbcglobal.net. About the art: "Love worketh no ill to his neighbor: therefore love is the fulfilling of the law" (Romans 13:10).

First edition
Published by Westminster John Knox Press
Louisville, Kentucky

This book is printed on acid-free paper that meets the American National Standards Institute Z39.48 standard. ∞

PRINTED IN THE UNITED STATES OF AMERICA

06 07 08 09 10 11 12 13 14 15—10 9 8 7 6 5 4 3 2 1

Library of Congress Cataloging-in-Publication Data is on file at the Library of Congress, Washington, D.C.

ISBN-13: 978-0-664-22982-5
ISBN-10: 0-664-22982-4

For
Sarah Ryan
and
J. Shannon Clarkson

Contents

Preface

This book grows out of the 2004 Phyllis Trible Lecture Series held at the Divinity School of Wake Forest University. Founded the preceding year, the series explores feminist perspectives in the field of religious studies as these perspectives relate to the academy, diverse communities of faith, and society at large.

The 2004 event featured four lecturers on the subject "Children of Hagar and Sarah: Feminist Perspectives in Judaism, Christianity, and Islam." As adherents of the three religions, the lecturers spoke within their respective scholarly disciplines. Phyllis Trible interpreted narratives in the book of Genesis that pertain to Hagar and Sarah. Adele Reinhardt focused on Judaism and gender in the Gospel of John. Riffat Hassan reported on stories about Hagar in the traditions of Islam. Letty Russell considered Paul's allegory in the book of Galatians about Hagar and Sarah and reflected theologically on the larger subject.

For this book the lecturers have altered their presentations. Trible and Hassan expand theirs. Reinhardt, joined by her daughter Miriam-Simma Walfish, changes her subject to write about rabbinic interpretations of Hagar. Russell divides her material into two essays, the first on Paul's allegory and the second on theological and ethical ramifications of the Hagar and Sarah stories. Moreover, two scholars who did not participate in the lecture series offer essays. Elizabeth Clark investigates what the church fathers said about Hagar and Sarah; her study parallels Reinhardt and Walfish's on the rabbis. Delores Williams gives a womanist reading of the Hagar tradition for African American Christian communities; her study parallels Russell's reflections from the perspective of a white Christian feminist. As a whole, the book moves from ancient and medieval sources to contemporary appropriations of a story that haunts the centuries with unresolved problems and formidable challenges.

Special thanks for the success of the lecture series belong to the committee who oversaw the event. Specific thanks also belong to Sylva Billue, former member of the Board of Visitors at Wake Forest University, who originated the series. She remains its advocate and advisor. Lu Leake, retired associate vice president of academic affairs at the university, serves as liaison to the institution. She understands the hospitality of details. The Rev. Dr. Darla Dee Turlington, pastor of the First Baptist Church of Westfield, New Jersey, contributes generously to the series from year to year. Ever since she was a graduate student and biblical tutor at Union Theological Seminary, she has held a special place in my roster of the righteous.

In moving the 2004 Lecture Series and its sequels from oral deliveries and rough drafts to printed words, Letty Russell and I have benefitted from the time and talents of two friends, Sarah Ryan and Shannon Clarkson. With their assistance, delight has seasoned our work of editing. To them we dedicate the book.

—Phyllis Trible

Contributors

Elizabeth A. Clark is the John Carlisle Kilgo Professor of Religion at Duke University in Durham, North Carolina. Dr. Clark has been President of the American Academy of Religion, of the American Society of Church History, and of the North American Patristic Society. She teaches all phases of the history of Christianity.

Riffat Hassan is Professor of Religious Studies and Humanities at the University of Louisville, Kentucky. She is well known as a pioneer of feminist theology in the context of the Islamic tradition, an area in which she has been engaged since 1974.

Adele Reinhartz is a Canadian scholar, the Associate Vice President of Research at the University of Ottawa, in Ottawa, Ontario, where she also holds the position of Professor in the Department of Classics and Religious Studies. Her main areas of research are the Gospel of John, early Jewish-Christian relations, feminist criticism, and, most recently, the Bible and film.

Letty M. Russell is Professor Emerita of Theology at Yale Divinity School, in New Haven, Connecticut. Well known as a leading feminist theologian, she is also a leader in the ecumenical movement, having worked with the World Council of Churches and the YWCA both at the national and international levels.

Phyllis Trible, an internationally known biblical scholar and rhetorical critic, is University Professor of Biblical Studies at Wake Forest University Divinity School in Winston-Salem, North Carolina. A past president of the Society of Biblical Literature, she taught at Union Theological Seminary in New York where she was the Baldwin Professor of Sacred Literature.

Miriam-Simma Walfish holds a BA in Jewish Studies from McGill University, Montreal, Canada. She specializes in the study of rabbinic literature and is currently working towards the degree of Masters of Arts in Jewish Education at the Hebrew University of Jerusalem.

Delores S. Williams is the Paul Tillich Professor Emerita of Theology and Culture at Union Theological Seminary in New York. Her research and teaching focus on the emergence of Womanist Theology in addition to theological doctrines and the critique of popular and technological cultures.

Chapter 1

Unto the Thousandth Generation

Phyllis Trible and Letty M. Russell

The topics of family, faith, and interfaith relations hold a prominent place in public discourse as they have long held in the monotheistic religions of the world. In
different ways, Judaism, Christianity, and Islam all trace their beginnings to the
man Abraham whom they deem the founding father of an extended family of
believers. Though also pivotal in the story, his two wives—the founding mothers
Hagar and Sarah—receive less attention. This deficiency befits the patriarchal
milieus in which these familial faiths developed and continued to flourish.

Most contemporary studies of the three faiths keep the traditional focus on
Abraham.[1] But not this book. It focuses on Hagar, Sarah, and their children.[2]
The children include their respective sons Ishmael and Isaac as well as their many
descendants through the centuries. In particular, the descendants include the
women who contribute essays to this book. They see themselves as daughters of
Hagar and Sarah. They believe that understanding problems and opportunities
of the past and present among Jews, Christians, and Muslims, as well as envisioning a different future, resides more in studying the women Hagar and Sarah
than in stressing the putative unity located in Abraham. Further, they believe that
to the myriad children of Hagar and Sarah, now unto the thousandth generation
and beyond, comes the responsibility of seeking understanding, doing justice,

1

and walking humbly with one another in the diverse families of faith. These beliefs guide their essays.

To introduce the essays and set a context for reading them, we present in this chapter an overview of the three religions that includes previews of forthcoming chapters. The overview extends from scriptural beginnings through postscriptural developments and historical highlights to questions that linger. The previews give samples of texts that the authors will explore in depth. Our intention is to orient readers to the design and content of the book, offer a foretaste of what to expect, and so provide a comprehensive framework for a long and difficult story. In other words, overview and previews prepare the way for informed reading.

SCRIPTURAL BEGINNINGS

Before Judaism, Christianity, and Islam were Abraham, Sarah, and Hagar. Their story, itself a compilation of ancient and diverse sources, appears first in the Scripture common to Jews and Christians. Traditionally called Tanakh or the Bible by Jews and the Old Testament by Christians, this Scripture is also known as the Hebrew Bible or the First Testament. The story it tells about the founding families of these faiths reappears in the Scripture unique to Christians, traditionally called the New Testament but also known as the Second Testament. Later the story reappears in the Scripture unique to Muslims, the Qur'an (anglicized as Koran).[3] Through references, allusions, echoes, omissions, and additions, the two reappearances depend on and depart from the story given in the First Testament. They set forth new interpretations for new occasions. A brief report on each of these scriptural stories about Abraham, Sarah, and Hagar indicates similarities and differences in the beginnings of the faiths.

The First Testament

Genesis, the first book of the Bible, contains the foundational text for family, faith, and interfaith relations. It tells the story of Abraham, Sarah, and Hagar. The report presented here merely outlines the content to provide the base from which a look at the history of its interpretation can unfold. In chapter 2, Phyllis Trible exegetes the entire narrative.

The story begins with God's promise of blessing to the man Abraham (Gen. 11:27–25:18). The promise involves land, progeny, and inheritance (cf. Gen. 12:1–3). To claim it, Abraham must leave his native land for the unknown land that God has chosen for him. Accompanying him are his barren wife Sarah (Sarai) and his nephew Lot. In time, Sarah proposes that Abraham take Hagar, her Egyptian slave, as a second wife in order to have a child. Abraham consents. The child, in turn, would enhance Sarah and become the progeny that God promised. As property, Hagar herself plays no role in the decision. When she becomes pregnant, however, she acquires a different view of Sarah as well as of herself. The distance in status between the women begins to shrink. Resenting the change, Sarah afflicts Hagar, who then flees to the wilderness. There she receives divine assurances about the coming birth and future of her child, to be named Ishmael. She learns that he cannot be the child of promise even as she receives instructions to return to Sarah and suffer affliction.

Through speech and visitation (cf. Gen. 17–18), God continues to promise Abraham a son by Sarah. When Sarah herself hears the news, she laughs "in her heart," but the laugh is heard by God, who questions its meaning. Sarah then denies it altogether. Eventually the divine promise comes to pass. Sarah conceives and bears Isaac (Gen. 21:1–7). The family grows: one husband and two wives, each with a son. Some years later, Sarah, fearing for the inheritance of Isaac, orders Abraham to expel Hagar and Ishmael. Reluctantly he obeys. Sent away, the rejected wife and son face death in the wilderness until God rescues them. The deity promises Hagar that her child will become a great nation. The story concludes with Ishmael thriving in the wilderness and his mother finding him a wife from Egypt.

By the command of God, a single family has become two families, one living with the father, and the other, apart from him. The outcome settles the question of inheritance to favor Isaac over Ishmael, but it does not come to terms with the inequities between them. The putative unity of family and faith, located in the man Abraham, spawns disunity and disparity between his two wives and their respective children.

After Hagar finds Ishmael a wife, she disappears altogether from the biblical story (though her son does not). Sarah survives long enough for the narrative to guarantee the future of Isaac. Then she dies. Outside the book of Genesis, the Bible shared by Jews and Christians mentions Hagar not at all and Sarah but once more (Isa. 51:2). The difficulties buried in the relationship between these women—difficulties that embrace not just Abraham and his sons but also the God of the narrative and the ways of patriarchy—find neither outlet nor resolution.

The Second Testament

In the Scripture unique to Christians, the Second Testament, faith promotes yet more disunity and disparity within the families of Abraham. Not only does the old divide between the descendants of Hagar and Sarah persist, but new divisions also open among the children of Sarah. Jews by birth and faith believe that they, not Christians, are the only true descendants and so inheritors of the promise made to Abraham. But Jews by birth and faith who embrace the revelation of Jesus as the Messiah believe that they too are the true descendants and inheritors. (Christianity begins, then, as a movement within Judaism.) Unrelated to Judaism by faith or birth, Gentiles who embrace the revelation of Jesus as the Messiah believe that through adoption they are also true descendants and inheritors of the promise to Abraham.

Disputes between the last two groups, Jewish and Hellenistic Christians, wrestle with the question of promise and inheritance. Over and over the answer of the Second Testament resounds: We are all the true children of Abraham and Sarah. Through faith in Jesus Christ, all Christians are the children of the promise to the ancestors (cf., e.g., Acts 13:26–33; Rom. 9:6–8; Gal. 3:6–9).

In many ways and in many texts, the Second Testament connects Christians, both Jewish and Hellenistic, to Abraham and occasionally to Sarah. We consider, first, references in the Gospels and Acts. Matthew links Jesus to the Abrahamic narrative through a genealogy (1:1–6). It begins, "An account of the genealogy of Jesus the Messiah, the son of David, the son of Abraham."[4] The account ends with the figure Joseph, but it avoids saying that he is the father of Jesus. Instead, it identifies Joseph as "the husband of Mary, of whom Jesus was born, who is called the Messiah" (Matt. 1:16). Although Matthew includes four women from the First Testament in his otherwise male genealogy (Tamar, Rahab, Ruth, and "the wife of Uriah"), he does not list Sarah, wife of Abraham and founding mother of the ancestral line. Later, through the message of John the Baptist, Matthew again connects Christians to the family of Abraham but without reference to his wives. Condemning religious leaders for thinking that Jews alone are the true descendants, John claims that "God is able from these stones to raise up children to Abraham" (Matt. 3:9). Such a divine act of lapidary procreation requires neither Sarah nor Hagar, nor any other woman. Nor does it require Jewish identity.

Near its beginning, the Gospel of Luke connects Christians to Abraham's promise through the voice of Mary. In the Magnificat she, pregnant with the child Jesus, sings of fulfillment:

> [The Lord] has helped servant Israel,
> in remembrance of divine mercy,
> according to the promise made to our ancestors,
> to Abraham and his descendants forever.
> (Luke 1:54–55*)

After the baptism of Jesus, however, Luke uses Joseph's line to trace the sonship of Jesus not just to Abraham but to Adam and God (Luke 3:23–38). Though, unlike Matthew's, no women appear in his genealogy, elsewhere Luke depicts Jesus describing the bent-over woman, whom he has healed on the Sabbath, as a "daughter of Abraham" (Luke 13:16). Luke also includes a midrash about Father Abraham's welcoming to the joys of the afterlife Lazarus, the beggar at the rich man's gate, while refusing to welcome the rich man, who is tormented in Hades (Luke 16:19–31). In telling the story, for which there is no precedent in the First Testament, Luke appropriates Abraham to speak to a situation arising in the early Christian community. But nowhere does he appropriate Hagar and Sarah. Given Luke's interest in reporting on women contemporary with Jesus, his failure even to mention ancestral women merits note.

The Acts of the Apostles, the continuation of Luke's Gospel, frequently alludes to the story of Abraham. In a sermon preached in the Jerusalem Temple, Peter declares that "the God of Abraham . . . has glorified his servant Jesus. . . ." Further, he reminds his listeners that they are descendants of the covenant God gave to Abraham (Acts 3:13, 25). Similarly, the apostle Stephen preaches to the Jewish high priest and council in Jerusalem. His sermon begins with God's appearance to "our ancestor Abraham when he was in Mesopotamia," quotes God's call to Abraham, alludes to the barrenness of Sarah (though not by name), notes Abraham's eventual circumcision of Isaac, and moves on to Abraham's purchase of burial land in Shechem (Acts 7:1–16). Later in Antioch on the Sabbath, Paul addresses the men gathered there as "descendants of Abraham's family" (Acts 13:26). Repeatedly in Acts the question of who are the true inheritors of the promise presses itself upon Jewish and Hellenistic Christian communities. Though Sarah and Hagar are not named, their story continues to play itself out—in a new key.

In the Gospel of John, a lengthy dispute between Jesus and certain Jewish leaders hinges on who are the legitimate and illegitimate children of Abraham (John 8:31–58). As in the other Gospels, this one does not mention Sarah and Hagar. Claiming Abraham as their father, Jewish leaders question the veracity of Jesus. He retorts that "Abraham rejoiced that he would see my day" (v. 56) and concludes with the revelatory formula "Very truly, I tell you, before Abraham was, I am" (v. 58). Jesus appropriates ancient Scripture for a new occasion. In the Gospel of Mark he makes a similar interpretive move, using the formula "the God of Abraham" in chastising the Sadducees on questions about resurrection (Mark 12:26). By such interpretations and reinterpretations, the Christian community establishes itself as true heirs of Abraham.

The absence of Sarah and Hagar from the Gospels and Acts does not persist throughout the Second Testament. In the book of Romans, for instance, Paul says that the barrenness of Sarah's womb testifies to the firmness of Abraham's faith. Further, her eventual motherhood validates those who become true sons and daughters of God (Rom. 4:19). Paul also invokes the promise of God to Abraham that "Sarah shall have a son" to argue that Christians are Isaac's true descendants (Rom. 9:6–18). Similarly, the author of the letter to the Hebrews cites the barrenness of Sarah, along with the advanced age of Abraham, to talk about faith and faithfulness (Heb. 11:11). In contrast to the motif of barrenness, Sarah appears in the first letter of Peter as a model of faith because of her obedience to Abraham. The writer calls her "a holy woman" and deems all Christian women who submit to their husbands "her daughters" (1 Pet. 3:1–6). Speaking to problems and controversies in early Christian communities, the authors of Romans, Hebrews, and Peter manipulate the stories of Sarah and Abraham to fit their own needs.

Paul makes another interpretive move in the book of Galatians. It contains the only reference to Hagar in the Second Testament. By turning the story of Hagar and Sarah into an allegory, he turns the women into the covenants of law and promise (Gal. 4:21–31). In the move, he reverses the status of Hagar in the First Testament and co-opts Sarah for the Second. "Hagar is Mount Sinai," he says; she "bears children for slavery." But "the other woman [Sarah] corresponds to the Jerusalem above; she is free, and she is our mother." Through irony, genre, and theology Paul exacerbates negative images of Hagar as well as tensions between Jews and early Christians. Letty Russell explicates his allegory in chapter 3. The report presented here, joined with other texts, indicates that the disunity and disparity that mark the families of Abraham in the First Testament remain alive and well in the Second.

The Qur'an

In the Qur'an (the Scripture unique to Islam), Abraham, Ishmael, and Isaac make numerous appearances.[5] Sarah appears but once, and without her name. Hagar appears not at all, though some interpreters discern an allusion to her and Ishmael in a prayer by Abraham about settling "some of my offspring in a valley" without cultivation (Surah 14:37; cf. Gen. 21:14). For certain, the Qur'an, not unlike most of the Second Testament, pays little attention to the wives of Abraham even though they make the difference for the grand narrative and for relationships of Muslims to Jews and Christians.

Viewing Islam as the true heir to the monotheistic revelation that God gave Abraham (a revelation from which Jews and Christians have strayed),[6] the Qur'an draws on stories in the book of Genesis. One such story relates divine messengers visiting Abraham to announce the forthcoming birth of a son to him and Sarah in their old age (cf. Gen. 18:1–22). In the qur'anic version, the messengers bring "good news" to Abraham. He becomes suspicious when they do not "reach out" to eat the roasted calf he has prepared, and so they reassure him. The account continues:

> His wife was standing by, so she laughed. Thereupon We announced to her
> the good news of Isaac. . . . She said, "Woe is me, shall I bear a child while
> I am an old woman, and this, my husband, is an old man too? This is truly
> a very strange thing." (Surah 11:69–72)

Unlike the biblical account, this one does not give Sarah her name, does have the messengers speak directly to her, and does give the promised son his name Isaac.

Another story that the Qur'an appropriates from Genesis relates Abraham's near sacrifice of his son at the command of God (cf. Gen. 22:1–19). Like the Bible, this version underscores the radical obedience of Abraham while according the child's mother no role in the matter. But unlike the Bible, it leaves unspecified the name of the son to be sacrificed, Isaac or Ishmael. Immediately thereafter, however, it announces "the good news of Isaac as a Prophet, one of the righteous" (Surah 37:100–12).[7]

Besides drawing on stories from the Bible, the Qur'an relates other matters about Abraham and his sons. Following Jewish traditions, one of its stories reports that early on Abraham broke the idols of his people and then summoned them to worship the one true God. In retaliation, the people sought to destroy him by fire. But the fire turned cold, and Abraham survived as the prophet of God (Surah 21:68). Another story declares that God commanded Abraham and Ishmael to build and purify the Holy House (the Ka'bah) in the city of Mecca and also to initiate the obligatory pilgrimage (the hajj) to the sacred places of that city (Surah 41:120).

Repeatedly the Qur'an depicts Ishmael as a prophet, an apostle, and a just man favored over humankind (e.g., Surah 6:86; 19:54; 38:48). Likewise, it depicts Isaac as a prophet, a righteous man, and a recipient of blessing (e.g., Surah 19:49; 21:72; 37:112; 38:45). The attention that Hagar and Sarah do not receive in this Scripture, their children enjoy.

POSTSCRIPTURAL COMMENTARIES

In the ancient and medieval worlds, stories about Hagar, Sarah, Abraham, and their children appear outside the Scriptures of Judaism, Christianity, and Islam. Although they lack canonical authority in shaping faith and settling disputes, these postscriptural texts play major roles in the development of the three religions. Interpreting Scripture in multiple ways, they may clarify particular sections, add and remove content, or offer alternative points of view. By whatever strategy, they give new meanings to old stories placed in new settings. A brief examination of some of these texts as they relate to the founding families of the faiths shows similarities and differences from the scriptural beginnings.

Judaism

In chapter 4, Adele Reinhartz and Miriam-Simma Walfish examine at length the postscriptural literature of Judaism that pertains to Hagar and Sarah. This section offers but a few samples.[8]

The Book of Jubilees

Among ancient Jewish literature that did not become canonical is a work of the second century BCE entitled Jubilees.[9] Composed in the Hebrew language, it basically rewrites the book of Genesis to conform to Mosaic law. In the process, it alters the first of the Hagar and Sarah stories (Gen. 16) through omissions. It does not report, for example, either the tension between Hagar and Sarah or Hagar's flight to the wilderness. Jubilees does not have to return Hagar to Sarah because it does not allow her to leave. The second story about these women (Gen. 21:1–20) Jubilees alters through additions. They include surrounding the birth of Isaac with cultic activities, supplying jealousy as Sarah's motive for protecting the inheritance of Isaac, and giving Ishmael a son named Nabaioth. Whereas Jubilees slights Hagar in retelling the first biblical story, it expands her portrayal favorably in retelling the second. By contrast, Sarah remains a constant figure. As for Abraham, his virtue grows, in accordance with Mosaic law.

Midrashim

In the centuries following the composition of Jubilees, rabbinic interpretations of the Bible, known as *midrashim*, put imagination and invention at the service of the problems and perspectives of particular Jewish communities of faith. By the Middle Ages a vast corpus of this work had evolved. Included were stories about Abraham and his family.

One story, centered on the conception and birth of Ishmael, presents Sarah as a righteous woman who, without jealousy, gave Hagar to Abraham for a wife and continued to care for her in her pregnancy.[10] The story claims that Sarah's subsequent cruel treatment of Hagar, which involved casting an evil eye upon her, resulted from Hagar's own contemptuous treatment of barren Sarah. In other words, Hagar got what she deserved. Such an interpretation shows rabbinic discomfort with Sarah's behavior and seeks a convincing explanation for it.

Another story, this one centered on the birth of Isaac, supports the apotheosis of Sarah. It describes her as a new mother with sufficient milk in her breasts to suckle all the babies of the parents whom Abraham invited to the natal celebration. Both blessed and blesser, Sarah is the bearer and the giver of life. This tale undergirds her status as the mother of Judaism.

Yet another story tries to justify the (mis)treatment that Ishmael and his mother receive in the Bible. It faults Ishmael for insisting that he get a double portion of the inheritance from Abraham in contrast to Isaac's single portion. It claims that Ishmael aimed arrows at Isaac while pretending to be jesting. These matters (not jealousy about inheritance, as in Jubilees) lead Sarah to insist that Abraham divorce Hagar and send her and her son away. As the two leave, Sarah gives Ishmael the evil eye. It makes him sick unto death—so sick that Hagar has to carry her grown son.[11] Thanks to God's intervention, these two undeserving characters survive in the wilderness.

In all such stories the split between Hagar and Sarah (and so between their children) widens and deepens. Any putative unity within the families of Abraham diminishes, if not disappears. Rabbinic midrashim and commentaries use these texts to set Judaism over against its rivals, both Christian and Muslim.

Christianity

Postscriptural commentaries in Christianity employ exegetical strategies similar to rabbinic interpretation. The church fathers, writing between 100 and 600 CE, use the biblical stories about Hagar, Sarah, and Abraham to support and defend their own faith over against its rivals.[12] In chapter 5 Elizabeth Clark reports in full on these matters. The few samples given here address the topic of Jewish and Christian relationships.

The earliest church fathers do not use Paul's allegory in Galatians 4 to express anti-Jewish sentiments. Instead, a certain filial devotion to the parental faith marks their attitude. But by the middle of the third century that attitude changes. "Hagar" and "Sarah" become codes for "synagogue" and "church." To exalt the growth and superiority of Christianity, Origen of Alexandria (d. 251) cites God's promise to Abraham that his descendants will be as numerous as the stars (Gen. 15:5). And Cyprian, bishop of Carthage (d. 258), boasts about the church growing through the conversion of Gentiles whereas the synagogue shrinks in size.

Embracing that view more than a century later, John Chrysostom of Antioch (d. 407) disparages Christians who continue to practice Jewish rituals by remind- ing them that they belong to "free Jerusalem" (i.e., to mother Sarah and not to slave Hagar). He denounces Jews as "Christ killers." Jerome (d. 420) appropri- ates the motif of barren Sarah becoming the ancestor of multitudes to marvel at the growth of the church. Augustine of Hippo (d. 430) argues that Jews, contrary to their claim, descend from Hagar while Christians are the "seed of Abraham." Manipulating the adaptability of Scripture and thus its openness to multiple interpretations, the church fathers, from the mid-third century on, reinforce divi- sion between the children of Hagar and Sarah.

Islam

In Islam, postscriptural commentary on the family of Abraham comes from tra- ditions known as *hadith*, a term meaning "report" or "story."[13] These traditions claim to derive from the words or deeds of the prophet Muhammad as trans- mitted by his contemporaries. In general, the reports include guidance on mat- ters of life and law not provided in the Qur'an. Not unlike the midrashim and Christian commentaries, they often interpret by filling in gaps present in the sacred text.

Of varying authority, collections of hadith began to appear in the century after Muhammad's death (d. 632). Efforts to distinguish authentic from inauthentic traditions continued for another century or so. The particular hadith about Abra- ham's extended family drew on stories circulating in the city of Medina during Muhammad's time. Yet the beginnings of this process may have lain in Mecca, the birthplace of Muhammad in 570 CE. There he experienced the revelations that led to the founding of Islam, and there he first encountered Jews and Chris- tians. After he fled, under threat of assassination, from Mecca to Medina (622), his knowledge of those religions increased. A number of Jewish tribes lived in Medina. Although they refused to recognize Muhammad as a prophet in the tra- dition of Moses—a claim he made about himself—a few Jews remained friendly toward him. From them he learned about their Scriptures, in particular the sto- ries of Hagar, Sarah, Abraham, and their children. Some of that learning made its way into the hadith.

Although evidence is lacking that Muhammad believed Arabs to be the blood descendants of Ishmael, later generations of Jews and Christians and then Muslims developed this genealogy.[14] Tradition holds that after Abraham sent Hagar and Ish- mael into the wilderness (Gen. 21:14–21), the two made their way to Mecca and settled there. In time, Ishmael came to be regarded as the father of the Arabs.

In chapter 6 of this book, Riffat Hassan examines at length the hadith per- taining to Hagar. A brief summary here anticipates that record of her importance. Without doubt, Islamic tradition deems Hagar a woman of true faith, indeed a monotheist in a pagan world. As "the mother of Arabs," she not only gave birth to Ishmael but was herself a faithful messenger appointed by the one God. An attempt to promote this understanding associates her name with the Arabic verb *hajara*, meaning to separate from evil. Another attempt seeks to relate her name to the *hijara*, the journey she made in faith to the Arabian peninsula. Apart from their disputed accuracies, these etymological plays emphasize the worth of Hagar. Another tradition depicts her walking repeatedly between two mountains in the wilderness to find water for her dying child. On her seventh walk, the archangel Gabriel appeared to her and used his wing to stir up water from the dust. The water flowed in such abundance that Hagar built a dam to contain it. In time, her walk became a ritual for Muslims to emulate. Having received divine revelation and acted upon it, Hagar set forth the path of true devotion.

Respect for Hagar continued to her death. Tradition says that she was buried in Mecca near the Ka'bah where later Ishmael was buried. To this day their tombs belong to the holy places of Islam. Every Muslim who makes the required pilgrimage (the hajj) to Mecca, at least once in a lifetime, pays homage to this mother and her son. If the Qur'an itself fails to name Hagar in the family of faith, Islamic traditions establish her pivotal presence. In effect, they honor Hagar as the matriarch of monotheism.

HISTORICAL HIGHLIGHTS

The scriptural and postscriptural literatures of Judaism, Christianity, and Islam provide aetiologies for the extended families of Abraham, Sarah, and Hagar. Although the complex beginnings of each faith come with promise and sometimes fulfillment, they are hardly sanguine. Affection and affliction, cooperation and conflict, tenderness and terror, comfort and cruelty—all these and other matters not only contend in the early narratives but also continue in the tortuous and torturous histories of the three religions. Those histories cannot be covered here or in the chapters that follow. Suffice it to highlight instances, starting with antiquity and the Middle Ages, moving into the Reformation of the sixteenth century, and then jumping to the twentieth century. Along the way, we observe multiple variations on the foundational stories of Hagar, Sarah, and their children.

Antiquity

What the early literature of Judaism and Christianity discloses, historical events undergird. The religion of Judaism emerged shortly after the exilic period (587–536 BCE), the time when many of the children of Sarah and Abraham became captives in Babylon. As descendants of the tribe of Judah, but no longer an independent nation, these Jews began to reshape family and faith.[15] No matter where they lived in the ancient world or under whose rule, they focused on temple and Torah. With the defeat of the Babylonians, the Persian authorities permitted Jews who so wished to return to their homeland. There they rebuilt the temple (515 BCE). As for keeping the Law (Torah), it became the defining mark of the faithful. But obeying Torah raised interpretive questions that produced different answers. Diverse views emerged among diverse groups in diverse places; yet all belonged to this one family of faith.

By the second century BCE, a reforming party of the landowning aristocracy in Jerusalem sought to accommodate Jewish life to Hellenistic ways. The common folk of city and countryside opposed the attempt and, in time, rebelled. Their success led the Syrian ruler Antiochus IV to intervene. Among other measures, he replaced Jewish practices in the Jerusalem temple with the worship of the Greek god Zeus. Although the Jews recovered sufficiently to purify the temple and establish their own rule for about a century, continuing squabbles among themselves resulted in a takeover by Rome in 63 BCE.

During the first century CE, religious rivalries flourished in Judaism. Pharisees, Sadducees, and Essenes, plus other groups, advocated different, even incompatible, versions of the faith. Most especially, the advent of the Jesus movement exacerbated dissension. Jesus saw himself as a faithful child of Abraham, even though his message and deeds brought him into conflict with religious authorities (cf. stories in the Gospels). For his followers, the conflict increased after his death and resurrection. By the early second century, disputes about the inclusion of Gentiles into the community, the place and practice of Mosaic law, and the understanding of Jesus as Messiah resulted in the expulsion of Jewish Christians from the synagogue. Thereafter Christianity became a separate, yet related, religion with its own internal divisions.[16]

The separation of synagogue and church inaugurated a new religious environment. Two faiths, Judaism and Christianity, claimed the same ancestry but in different ways; worshiped the same God but with different theologies; and shared the same Scripture but with different interpretations. Sarah and her children acquired two identities. Sometimes the two families coexisted, but more often they lived in tension, if not hostility. Further, within each of the families divisions persisted. *In nuce,* the cruelty that Sarah once inflicted upon Hagar and her child, the children of Sarah came in time to inflict upon each other.

The Middle Ages

In the seventh century CE Islam joined Judaism and Christianity as the third monotheistic religion.[17] Its founder, Muhammad ibn Abdullah (c. 570–632 CE), was born in the city of Mecca on the Arabian peninsula. Almost from the beginning of his religious awakening, Muhammad understood himself as a prophet in the tradition of Abraham, Moses, and Jesus. (No doubt Arabs on the peninsula knew something of Judaism and Christianity through trading with the Byzantine and Persian empires.) That tradition Muhammad accepted as a valid revelation of monotheism. At first he did not seek to found a new religion but rather to proclaim to his own people the worship of the one God. Arabs who, in response to his preaching, practiced submission (the meaning of the word Islam) to God (Allah in Arabic) became known as "believers" (i.e., Muslims).

Twelve years after Muhammad began preaching in Mecca, his life under threat of death, he fled to the city Medina (622 CE). For the next forty years it was the center of Islam. Even though Muhammad viewed Judaism and Christianity as companions in monotheistic faith, Jewish tribes living in Medina rejected him and the faith he proclaimed. They mocked his versions of biblical stories; discredited his claim to be a prophet; resented his political ascendancy in the city; and joined forces with others of his enemies to destroy him. Not unlike the biblical narrative, the children of Sarah resented and spurned the children of Hagar.

Surprised and disappointed, Muhammad struck back. He came to believe that Jews had been unfaithful to the Tawrat (Torah) given to Moses, and Christians to the Injil (Gospels) given by Jesus. So Muhammad called his people to the pure form of monotheism as set forth in Islam. Couched in familial language, his stance reversed the biblical narrative. This child of Hagar faulted the children of Sarah for debasing the revelations God entrusted to them. Signaling his independence from both religions, Muhammad instructed his believers to pray in the direction of Mecca rather than Jerusalem. He also took on the rebellious Jewish tribes of Medina in bloody battle—expelling, enslaving, and killing them.

Though a horrendous act, this single incident did not signify hatred of all Jews or of Judaism. Instead, Muhammad sought to coexist with Jews and Christians. Referring to them as "people of the Book," one section of the Qur'an teaches conciliation (Surah 29:46):

> Do not dispute with the people of the Book save in the fairest way; except for those of them who are evildoers. And say: "We believe in what has been sent down to us and what has been sent down to you. Our God and your God are one and to Him we are submissive."

Another instance of Muhammad's tolerance toward Jews and Christians came in his offer of a contract or covenant (*dhimma*). If they submitted peaceably to Islamic authority, they would be permitted the freedom, though with certain restrictions, to practice their own faiths. As time passed, the relationship of Islam to Judaism and Christianity developed in ways ranging from tolerance to bloodshed.[18]

Tolerance in Spain

The exemplary story of tolerance among Muslims, Jews, and Christians in the medieval world comes from Spain. In 711 CE, less than a century after Muhammad's death (d. 632), Muslims from Africa crossed the Strait of Gilbraltar to settle in Iberia (called *al-Andalus* in Arabic). Some forty-four years later, a young Muslim from Damascus, named Abd al-Rahman, also arrived there, settling in the city Cordoba. He was a political refugee, the survivor of a massacre of his royal family by a rival Muslim group. (Not unlike Judaism and Christianity, Islam early on broke into competing groups; the two major groups, Sunnis and Shiites, split on the question of the source of authority within the community.) In a short time and by military means Abd al-Rahman usurped power from the resident emir to establish a kingdom that, with ups and downs, with expansion and shrinkage, lasted almost seven hundred years.

Even with occasions of conflict, this Muslim kingdom produced what the scholar María Rosa Menocal designates "a culture of tolerance" among Muslims, Jews, and Christians.[19] A prominent citizen of Cordoba named Hasdai exemplified Andalusian Jews who assimilated to Islamic culture and yet remained a practicing religious group. Living in the tenth century, he was not only prince of his own religious community but also became vizier to the ruler (the caliph) of the Muslim residents. The tolerance seen in his story extended to other areas of public discourse: government and diplomacy, art and architecture, literature and library, translation and theology, poetry and philosophy.[20] Overall, so splendid a culture of intellect and wealth developed in Cordoba that its glories were known throughout Europe. Indeed, the tenth-century Christian nun named Hroswitha, who herself lived in Saxon, declared Cordoba "the ornament of the world."

In the twelfth century, the city Toledo became another center of intellectual ferment and cooperation among Muslims, Jews, and Christians.[21] The Archbishop Raymund founded there a translation center to make available ancient Western classics, preserved in Arabic, to Latin Christian communities. Most particularly, the recovery of the works of Aristotle, indeed of the entire philosophical tradition of reason, brought a lively challenge to the three "revealed" religions. Two contemporaries, both natives of Cordoba, took up the challenge: the Muslim called Averroes and the Jew called Maimonides. Each in his way argued for the validity of both revelation and reason. Denounced in time by factions within their own peoples, these thinkers fled into exile: Averroes to Marrakech and Maimonides to Alexandria. But their ideas prevailed, to be cited approvingly, for example, by the Christian philosopher Thomas Aquinas in the thirteenth century.

Unlike their treatment of "pagans," the Muslim rulers of Andalusia, following the practice begun by Muhammad, instituted the special covenant of *dhimma* with the "People of the Book" (Jews and Christians). It protected religious freedom (no forced conversions), and it allowed for intermarriage and cultural exchanges among the faiths. Yet with this freedom came obligations and restrictions: an annual poll tax, no building of new churches or synagogues, and no public practice of their faiths. These restrictions Jews found less troublesome than Christians. After all, for centuries Jews had learned to survive as an ethnic and religious minority. But Christians had ruled Europe and the East since the fourth century. So the dominance of Muslims in medieval Spain posed for Christianity no small threat, especially because large numbers of Christians willingly converted to Islam. Others fled into exile. The once-dominant group shrank in size and influence.

Gradually the Christian struggle to keep Islam out of Europe overtook Andalusian Spain. By the thirteenth century Muslim rule had shrunk to just the city Granada; four weak Christian kingdoms controlled the rest of the country. Their strength grew in the next two centuries, culminating with the marriage of Ferdinand, the heir to the kingdom of Aragon, to Isabella, the heir to the kingdom of

Castile. To these Christian monarchs in 1492, Muhammad XII turned over the keys of his royal house in Granada. Thus ended the history of Muslim rule in Spain, a history that had begun in the eighth century. And though Muslims remained in the country for more than a century thereafter, they lived under suppression and bloodshed.[22] Jews, on the other hand, were expelled immediately in 1492, unless they converted to Christianity.

The events of 1492 and their aftermath echo the biblical accounts about Sarah and Hagar. Much as the Christian apostle Paul rejected Hagar, representing Jews, and embraced Sarah, representing Christians, so the Christian rulers Ferdinand and Isabella expelled all professed Jews from Spain and exalted Christianity. Much as Sarah afflicted Hagar in Canaan and later cast her out, so Christian rulers afflicted Muslims in Spain and later expelled them, the final expulsions coming in 1609 and 1615. In this history the allegory in Galatians and the story in Genesis live on.

Cruelty in the Crusades

If Muslim Spain provides the exemplary story of tolerance in the medieval world, the Christian Crusades provide the exemplary story of cruelty. In 1095 Pope Urban II preached a sermon in Clermont, France, urging Christians to undertake an armed pilgrimage to Jerusalem to rescue it from "infidel" Muslims and thereby achieve for themselves a place in paradise.[23] Rallying to the call, thousands of Christians—women, men, and children—turned their hostility first on the "aliens" in their midst, namely, Jews who for centuries had lived in peace among them. Thousands were killed. The crusaders then set out for the Holy Land. In Antioch they met strong resistance from Muslims, and their numbers shrank significantly. Nonetheless, a devout group reached Jerusalem in 1099. Sacking the city, they slaughtered thousands of Muslim women, men, and children.

The hostilities unleashed by Christians against Jews and Muslims in the First Crusade continued, with breaks, for two centuries. Lacking the fervor of the First, the Second Crusade (1147–49) ended in failure as Muslims struck back.[24] United under the Kurdish general Saladin, they regained Jerusalem in 1187. That reversal in power inspired Christians to launch the Third Crusade (1189–92). Though generously equipped for battle, with leaders like Richard the Lion-Heart, this venture failed to recapture Jerusalem from the Muslims.

The Fourth Crusade (1202–04) was the most disastrous for Christianity because it resulted in an internal split.[25] Working in concert with the Venetians and in disregard of the wishes of Pope Innocent III, these crusaders captured and plundered the Byzantine city of Constantinople, the seat of Greek Christian Orthodoxy. They raped women and girls, desecrated churches, and torched the city. They exiled the imperial government and set up a rival empire, which endured until 1261. From these events dates the age-old hatred between Greek and Latin Christians. The Christian branch of the children of Sarah experienced a devastating and virtually irreparable breach.

Depending on the judgments of historians, two or three more crusading ventures followed.[76] Between 1217 and 1221, a revived plan to enter the Holy Land via Egypt failed. Although in 1228 the German emperor Frederick II did succeed in repossessing Jerusalem, in fewer than twenty years it was lost again. By 1291 the Crusades as identifiable movements within Christianity were over—though the crusading spirit was not. In contrast to the relatively tolerant climate of Andalusian Spain that survived, in part, until 1492, hostilities prevailed elsewhere in Europe and in the East: among them, hostilities between Christians and Muslims, between Christians and Jews, and between Christians and Christians. As these hostilities moved into the next century, they found a locus in the Protestant Reformation.

The Reformation

With a Janus-like face, directed to the medieval and the modern worlds, the Reformation of the sixteenth century in northern Europe produced yet more perspectives on the three monotheistic faiths.[27] As Jewish and Christian commentators of earlier centuries used biblical stories to speak to their own times and situations, likewise did the Reformers interpret Scripture. They used the biblical accounts of Hagar, Sarah, Abraham, and their children to discourse on matters of church and state, to draw lessons against perceived enemies, to instruct their followers on personal morality and true faith, to exhort them to live virtuous lives, and, in general, to find comfort and vindication for their own points of view.

Regrettably, we do not include in this book a chapter on the Reformers. To compensate for that lacuna, we provide here an extended section on the writings of Martin Luther and John Calvin. Of all the Reformers, only they produced commentaries on both Genesis and Galatians. In the process, they had much to say about our particular texts in relationship to their particular interests.

Martin Luther (1483–1546)

The length of Martin Luther's commentaries on Genesis (some eight volumes in English translation), which he delivered as lectures between 1535 and 1545, is due in part to his many diatribes against papists, Jews, and Turks (Muslims).[28] His interpretation of Genesis 16 parades these hostilities.[29] Luther begins by praising matrimony and procreation over against lust, celibacy, and monasticism. He deems Sarah a "very wise woman," and he notes "the faith of this most saintly woman" in giving her maid Hagar to Abraham in order to have a child. He calls Abraham "the chaste husband of his very chaste wife" even when Abraham lies with Hagar. But Luther deems Hagar "haughty" and "ungrateful," with a heart that added "hate and anger to the haughtiness." Following this description, he condemns the Turks (Muslims) who, he claims, have mistreated the Christians they have captured in Luther's own era. Returning to Hagar, he calls her an "example of the carnal human being who cannot be improved by chastisement or by kindness." Luther judges Hagar's flight from Sarah while she [Hagar] is pregnant to be the "kidnapping" of Abraham's child. In sum, this Reformer faults Hagar as "the cause of all the sins of the family" and not infrequently links her faults to his view of Muslims.

The condemnation continues as Luther moves to the next part of the biblical story, when Hagar is in the wilderness with the divine messenger (Gen. 16:7–16). He denounces the Koran (so spelled in the English translation of his commentary) for "incorrectly" using the promise of descendants to Hagar to exalt the Saracens (i.e., Muslims).[30] He charges that the Koran "lies" when it says that God ordered Abraham to sacrifice Ishmael (rather than Isaac).[31] Thereby the Saracens, he deduces, want to transfer the divine promise to themselves. Even though he acknowledges the beauty of the name Ishmael in contrast to the names Abraham, Isaac, and Jacob, which are "not so glorious," he nonetheless finds that name "undoubtedly also a cause of the haughtiness of the Saracens." The descendants of Ishmael, he says, live "by plundering and robbery."[32]

After these harsh words about Muslims, Luther turns his vitriol against Jews. In general, he inveighs about "the prattle of the Jews" who "know nothing about sacred matters." Then he focuses on Hagar's return and submission to Sarah (Gen. 16:9), using that text against the Jews for the purpose of exalting Christians of his ilk. Jews do not understand, he asserts, "the universal statement of Holy Scripture that God wants all people of lower rank to be subject to their superiors." A contrast between rabbis and Christians follows. The rabbis do not know the "subject matter" of Scripture; they do not understand that, in returning to Sarah (a code for Christians), Hagar is giving thanks to God (a code for what Jews should do). The "only thing the rabbis have" is "grammar"; on sacred matters, "they should be completely disregarded."[33]

At the close of his exegesis on Genesis 16, Luther seemingly makes Hagar a model for conversion. He holds that after her theophany in the wilderness, she becomes a different character. "Haughty" Hagar becomes "saintly Hagar" who "honors God" (as Jews do not). So pleased is Abraham by this change in the woman that he allows the name Ishmael to remain for his son. Through this interpretation Luther coordinates the divine word that Hagar will name the child (Gen. 16:11) with the narrator's word that Abraham named him (Gen. 16:15). Luther concludes by commending Hagar for returning home to obey Sarah. From condemnation to commendation, Luther's views on Hagar shift to accommodate his own prejudices and pronouncements.

The type of exegesis Luther employs for Genesis 16 continues in his commentary on Genesis 18, the story about the divine visitation to Abraham and Sarah.[34] Luther praises Sarah profusely. Chauvinist that he is, he makes much of the fact that "Sarah is in the tent" when the visitors ask about her. These words, he writes, "should be inscribed on the veils of all matrons; for in this way they would be reminded of their duty to beware of inquisitiveness, gadding, and garrulousness, and to accustom themselves to managing the household with care."[35]

As for Sarah's laugh when she (over)hears the divine promise of a child, Luther interprets it as exemplary of her "extraordinary continence and chastity." Moreover, the "Holy Spirit," with words that constitute only "a cheerful and very friendly reproof," asks why she laughed in order to strengthen her and raise her to life lest she think "she is a corpse." And even though in her reply, "the saintly mother adds a little sin and says that she did not laugh," that sin is pardonable because Sarah fears God. To support his excessive praise of Sarah "the saintly mistress," Luther draws on the commendation of her uxorial obedience found in 1 Peter 3:1–6. He notes that when Peter instructed wives to honor their husbands, Peter cited Sarah as the model to be emulated.[36]

In reporting on Genesis 21, the second clash between Sarah and Hagar, Luther describes the "corpse" Sarah giving birth to "joy" (Isaac). Then he faults Hagar for causing trouble in the household.[37] This woman, whom earlier he commended for returning to Sarah, he now condemns as "contemptuous" and "insulting." Further, her son Ishmael he deems "a mocker," puffed up like his mother. He is "proud and smug and an antinomian Epicurean," comparable to the Turks, the pope, and Paul before his conversion. Although Luther acknowledges that Sarah may seem less than humble when she orders Abraham to cast out the slave woman and her son, he defends her as living by duty, as "imploring" rather than ordering, and as submitting to Abraham, the head of the house. Further, he believes that Abraham only appears to be cruel when he sends away Hagar and Ishmael. Actually, he "sacrifices conjugal and paternal love" in order to obey and love God alone. Despite the appearance of being "the murderer of his son and wife" (cf. Gen. 21:16), Abraham must risk everything to obey God.

According to Luther, in the wilderness Hagar and Ishmael learn that God alone is the author of life and that everything comes by grace and not by righteousness. When Ishmael confesses his unworthiness to be a son, God saves him. Growing up "in God" (Gen. 21:20), he becomes "a well-informed and learned preacher" and is rewarded with a wife because he heeded the authority of his mother.[38] Hagar herself learns grace again (cf. her theophanic experience in Gen. 16), particularly when "she lifts up her voice and weeps" (Gen. 21:16). In still another way Luther finds redemption for Hagar. Despite his many tirades against the Jews, he embraces the view of some rabbis that Abraham's third wife, Keturah (Gen. 25:1), was actually Hagar. She returned to Abraham after Sarah's death (cf. Gen. 23–24). For Luther, Hagar eventually becomes a mother of the church. He enfolds her and Ishmael within a theology of salvation by grace.[39]

Given this turn in interpretation, one might expect Luther to soften his views on Jews, papists, and Muslims. But that does not happen. He continues to call Jews "stubborn and obstinate," having been born according to the flesh and yet boasting to be alone the people of God. He condemns them for mocking Christians as idolaters and blasphemers. Similarly, he charges that "Turks" (Muslims) trust in the flesh and are smug to call themselves "people of God." Though their ancestor Ishmael reconciled with his father Abraham, "his descendants, as usually happens, gradually deteriorated."[40]

With vivid imagery, Luther dismisses the Turkish empire of his day, "whatever its extent," as "nothing but a morsel of bread which a rich head of household throws to his dogs." Although Turks do not know these things about themselves, he declares, Christians know because "they have a firm foundation, namely the promise of God which has been set before them in the Son of God while the Turks have their stinking Koran, their victories, and the temporal power on which they rely."[41]

Such hostile sentiments spill over into Luther's commentary on Galatians 4:21–31, Paul's allegory of Hagar and Sarah.[42] Here Luther focuses primarily on the distinction between Law and Gospel. He claims that the difference between the two "true sons" of Abraham, both born of the flesh, lies not in their mothers, one free and one slave, but rather in one son (Ishmael) being born apart from the promise and one (Isaac) being born of the promise. Nonetheless, for Luther interpreting Paul, Sarah, the mother of the promised child, comes in for great commendation whereas Hagar, the mother of the rejected child, is herself rejected.

Luther writes that, in making Sarah the mother of the promised child, God rewards this "saintly woman," for her "act of humility" toward Hagar when she gave Hagar to Abraham to bear a child. Correspondingly, in making Sarah the heavenly Jerusalem (above the law and free), Paul helps us to see that Sarah is "the church, the bride of Christ who gave birth to all." She is not, however, "the church triumphant in heaven" but "the church militant on earth." Introducing into this exposition Sarah's words about casting out Hagar and Ishmael, Luther applies them approvingly to those whom he deems enemies—beginning with the Ishmaelites (Muslims) and extending to "the Jews, the Greeks, the Romans . . . and the papists." They should all be cast out.

In general, Luther waxes eloquent about Paul's use of the genre allegory. It functions, he claims, "as a kind of ornament" after Paul has made his solid theological argument for gospel over law. The allegory "teaches in a beautiful way that the church should not do anything but preach the Gospel correctly and purely and thus give birth to children." But alas, according to Luther, the children of Hagar are excluded from this gospel.

The twisted thinking of Luther about Hagar, Sarah, and their children defies consistency to thrive on contradiction, ignorance, and prejudice as well as on a firm belief in the superior revelation of Jesus Christ. For this Reformer, the foundational family of three faiths is irrevocably and properly divided. Luther's views promote disunity and discord; they do not bless all the families of the earth. Although his position connotes but one witness to faith, its importance stretches across centuries, cultures, and religions. On a larger scale, yet just within Christianity itself, another division has emerged: Protestantism versus Roman Catholicism.

John Calvin (1509–1564)

Among other Reformers contributing to this division in sixteenth-century Europe, John Calvin of France and Switzerland merits attention. More than thirty years after Martin Luther concluded his lectures on Genesis (1545), Calvin produced his commentary on the book (1578).[43] In discussing Genesis 16, he draws a picture of Sarah quite different from Luther's "most saintly woman" and, in places, a somewhat less harsh picture of Hagar.[44] For Calvin, no matter how laudable was Sarah's desire to give Abraham "children," in her pursuit of it through Hagar "she was guilty of no light sin." He faults Sarah for despairing, not trusting God, and trying to do other than God's will. With a touch of misogyny, he cautions, "We know the vehemence of female jealousy."[45]

Whereas Luther excused the polygamy in the story as acceptable in biblical times for acquiring children, Calvin finds it totally reprehensible. Sarah, he claims, perverted the law, and by following her plan Abraham was also at fault. Both wife and husband had "defective faith." Holding fast to the rule of monogamy, Calvin thinks that Hagar was "improperly called a wife" (cf. Gen. 16:3). He cites her response after conceiving, when she "despised" her mistress, as "an instance of ingratitude." Yet he continues to put the chief blame on Sarah. Aroused to anger, she was so blinded that she used God's name "improperly" to demand that Abraham set the matter right (Gen. 16:4–5). Abraham himself bore her vehemence with "humility and modesty."

Calvin views Hagar's flight to the wilderness and its aftermath from several angles. He describes Hagar as being of "servile temper" and "indomitable ferocity." She fled not so much because of Sarah's cruelty as her own "contumacy." God extended favor to her even when she deserved punishment. That God ordered her to return to Sarah justifies servitude and its burdens. The divine order supports "the power of magistrates." So, by obeying, Hagar corrected her faults. Moreover, in the wilderness she of "wild and intractable temper" perceived God guiding all things. As she called the name of God, she "prayed" with words of "self-reproach." Similar to Luther, Calvin deems the name of Hagar's child "honorable" even as he designates Ishmael himself a future "reprobate." As for the two versions about who named Ishmael, Calvin does not try, as did Luther, to coordinate them. Rather, even while acknowledging that Hagar was to name her child, he asserts that "Moses [for him, the author of the story] follows the order of nature" that accords fathers power over sons. Fittingly, Abraham named Ishmael (Gen. 16:11,15).

Unlike Luther, Calvin does not insert Jews, papists, or Muslims into the story of Genesis 16.[46] His interests focus on personal morality, proper behavior, familial values, and matters of order and authority in nature, church, and state. He preaches about the virtues of Abraham as patriarchal ruler, the faults of Sarah as the wife who misguided him, and the role of Hagar as servant. Throughout he vindicates God.

In commenting on Genesis 18, the story of the divine visitation, Calvin again takes a tack different from Luther's.[47] For Calvin, Sarah's laugh when she heard the promise of a child signifies "incredulity" (not continence and chastity). Her laugh casts discredit upon God, even if not intentional. Sarah was too fixed on "the accustomed order of nature," on "carnal reason," to recognize the greatness of God's power. So the "angel" of God "chides" her by asking why she laughed. Her denial constitutes "another sin" (not just "a little sin," as Luther judged it). For sure, Calvin does not commend Sarah for uxorial virtue

The subject of laughter also enters Calvin's commentary on Genesis 21. He holds that Sarah saw Ishmael "laughing" at Isaac, not playing with him (v. 9).[48] This laughter he judges "a malignant expression of scorn" in contrast to the positive laughter embedded in the name Isaac. Accordingly, Sarah's angry response that Abraham cast out Hagar and her son (v. 10) was "not without cause." Sparing Ishmael not at all, Calvin calls upon Paul's allegory in Galatians 4:21–31 to support his interpretation. Paul, he claims, rightly understood the laugh of Ishmael, son of Hagar, as "persecution" of Isaac, son of Sarah. It is "the scorn of the virulent tongue piercing the soul."

Exasperated by Ishmael's laugh, Sarah in response exceeded the bounds of a "modest wife." This time the spirit guided her in telling Abraham to banish Hagar and Ishmael. Having granted Sarah a certain status in positing for her a direct and positive relationship with the divine, Calvin hastens to protect patriarchal prerogatives. He maintains that, in telling Abraham what to do, Sarah did not take power from him. Further, God's taking the side of Sarah did not mean approval of her "disposition." Instead, God again averted "the order of nature" to accomplish God's own plan. By commanding Abraham to do what Sarah wanted, God was testing Abraham's faith. Sarah herself, concludes Calvin, is not to be commended.

Calvin questions why Abraham sent Hagar and Ishmael away with only the meager provisions of bread and water (Gen. 21:14). He offers two answers: Either God shut Abraham's eyes to the pending danger or Abraham acted deliberately so that mother and son would not go far from "his home" and he could continue to help them. Again, Abraham becomes the benevolent patriarch. Calvin also believes that God decreed the banishment in order to "strike terror into their pride." The single reference to pride resonates with Luther's repeated emphasis on that problem for Hagar and Ishmael. Near the close of the story (Gen. 21:17), says Calvin, God heard the voice of Ishmael because he was the son of Abraham. In other words, patriarchy once more saved Ishmael and helped Hagar. "Stupefied by grief" that blurred her vision, she found no resources in the wilderness. But God restored her sight and so enabled her to see a well of water to nourish her child (Gen. 21:15–19).

Whereas Luther interprets Ishmael's acquiring a wife as the reward for obeying his mother, Calvin uses the information to promote his own views on marriage and monogamy. Having emphasized monogamy in faulting Sarah for giving Hagar to Abraham (Gen. 16), now he emphasizes marriage as "a principal part of human life." In the process, he makes a rare comment about the papacy. The pope, he says, is "a prodigious monster" for forbidding clergy to marry.

Calvin's views on the papacy and on Jews expand in his exegesis of the allegory in Galatians.[49] He sees Paul presenting two mothers in the "church of God": even as there were two mothers in "the house of Abraham." These mothers represent Doctrine, which itself is twofold, legal and evangelical. Hagar resembles the legal mother, giving birth to bondage, and Sarah the evangelical, giving birth to freedom. Though both their sons are born of the flesh, Ishmael (i.e., Jews) has nothing besides the flesh whereas Isaac (i.e., Christians) has election in addition to the flesh. Thereby Paul reproaches Jews who "haughtily boasted that they were the sons of Abraham."

Similar to Luther, Calvin understands the "Jerusalem above" not as an entity contained in heaven but rather as the church "spread over the whole world." It is called "heavenly" because of its origin, not its location. The church itself is "the mother of us all," but not as the Papists understand the phrase because "the Papists are fools." By comparison, even the synagogue of Jerusalem at the time of Paul had greater claim to being children of God than the Papists. And yet Paul himself stripped that distinction from the synagogue, consigning it to Hagar.

Continuing his diatribe, Calvin expresses relief that he and his followers "have escaped the tyranny of the Pope" and takes further cheer from this allegory that "the tyranny of the Ishmaelites will not last for ever." With these remarks, he alters his identification of the Ishmaelites (and the Hagarites). No longer are they Jews, as Paul intended, but rather they have become Papists. In other words, Calvin allegorizes Paul's allegory to fit his own context.

In writing about Galatians, Calvin boldly attacks the Papists, but in interpreting Genesis he rarely inserts them into the text. About the Jews he has less to say than Luther, and he does not take on the Muslims. Instead, his primary interests lie in patriarchal family values, accompanied by hints of misogyny, and in election and the sovereignty of God. For this Reformer, Hagar, Sarah, and their children might heed lessons on the propriety, indeed obligation under God, of servitude to husbands and magistrates.

The Modern Period

By the close of the sixteenth century, Europe had entered what we call the modern period. Rather than sketching historical highlights in Judaism, Christianity, and Islam from the seventeenth century to the present—a task that exceeds the limits of this study—we comment on each of the religions in the context of the West and then cite one specific series of events that involves them all. Further, rather than following historical sequence, we start with the least prominent religion in this volume, namely, Islam, and give it somewhat more attention. Next we move to Judaism and then conclude with the most prominent, Christianity.

Islam

The shrinkage and eventual expulsion of Muslims from Spain, beginning in the late fifteenth and continuing into the early seventeenth centuries, resulted in their relative absence from the West until the last decades of the twentieth century. Since the breakup in the early 1990s of the Soviet Union and the Republic of Yugoslavia, however, some of the large Muslim population of Eastern Europe, joined by Muslims coming from the Middle East and from Asia, have expanded to become a significant presence throughout the West. Turmoil and fighting under the horrific rubric of "ethnic cleansing" in such countries as Serbia, Bosnia, and Kosovo have also drawn attention to Muslims; indeed, these events have disclosed open hostility to them.[50] Muslims have been objects of not just discrimination but slaughter. The children of Hagar suffer.[51]

Over against distortions in the Western press and in Western scholarship, many Muslims have begun to tell their own stories. Writing in the context of Christian-Muslim encounters, Yvonne Haddad and Wadi Haddad observe that contemporary Muslims see Christians in Europe and the United States redefining themselves in relationship to Judaism. In turn, "Muslims are asking for the same kind of acceptance, pressing Christians to acknowledge Islam as a legitimate religion in the same way that Muslims have always accepted the validity of the faith of Christianity."[52]

With a similar interest, Richard Bulliet focuses on contributions of Muslims in the West.[53] Over against those who speak of irreconcilable differences between Christianity and Islam and hence of an inevitable "clash of civilizations," he argues the case for "Islamo-Christian civilization."[54] The argument holds that the Christian society of Western Europe and the Muslim society of the Middle East and North Africa belong to a single civilization that a master narrative has obscured through fourteen centuries of "fear and polemic." These societies "are historical twins whose resemblance did not cease when their paths parted."[55] Recovery of this hyphenated civilization is imperative if we are to hope for a future of tolerance and peace.

Judaism

Although Jews were expelled from Spain in the late fifteenth and the sixteenth centuries, they remained in the West and continued to contribute richly to all areas of the civilization—art, architecture, literature, philosophy, music, business, science, and other endeavors. At the same time, Jews have experienced a sad, troubled, and harsh history, often one of persecution at the behest and hands of Christians.[56] A random citing of events attests that past and present: the ghettos of Europe, which began in the Middle Ages and lasted in some quarters into the twentieth century; forced conversions to Christianity, also stretching from the Middle Ages into the twentieth century; l'affaire Dreyfus in late-nineteenth-century France; in the same century, the Marxist stereotyping of Jews as the devils of capitalism and greed; in the twentieth century the genocide of European Jews by the Nazi government of Germany followed by the anti-Semitism of Soviet Communism.

The role of Christianity, as perpetrator or accomplice, in many of these tragedies is well documented. David Wyman reports, for instance, that America's Christian churches were "almost inert in the face of the Holocaust and nearly silent too."[57] Commenting in a larger context, Marvin Wilson avers, "From the biblical period to the present day one would be hard-pressed to find a single century in which the Church has not in some significant way contributed to the anguish of the Jewish people."[58] The children of Sarah suffer.

Christianity

Since the Crusades, and so even before the expulsion of Jews and Muslims from Spain, Christianity has been the dominant religion of the West. Its power and influence have reached into all realms of rule, for weal and for woe. Not unlike Jewish contributions, yet with the chauvinism of the "masters," Christian contributions have benefited art, architecture, music, literature, philosophy, business, science, and other endeavors. At the same time, the ascendancy of Christianity has often resulted in disdain for other religions. It has fostered stereotypes, projected inferiority, and practiced hostility on them. In exercising enormous power, Christianity has resorted not infrequently to violence and persecution as well as to indifference about the plight of others. As a result, these children of Sarah have brought suffering to both the children of Hagar and other children of Sarah.[59]

Given momentous changes throughout the world since World War II and the later demise of the Soviet Union, Christianity's dominance in the West seems much less secure than in the past. This shifting scene compels a rethinking of the religion and its relationships to Judaism and Islam (as well as to other faiths). A series of events, already alluded to, focus the point; indeed, they haunt the three monotheistic religions.

A Series of Events

In 1933 the political party known as the National Socialist German Workers, led by Adolf Hitler, came to power in the heartland of the Protestant Reformation. Hoping to redeem Germany from the humiliation it suffered in World War I, this party sought to form a master race that would rule the world. Only Germans of "pure descent" qualified for admission. Jews were not only excluded, but some six million were exterminated through a program called the "final solution." All this happened in Christian Europe. Writing about Jewish-Catholic relationships then and now, Arthur Hertzberg asserts that the Roman Catholic Church "was the only institution that possessed the moral stature and strength to denounce and forbid the murder of the Jews. It did not do so." Later Pope John Paul II did pronounce "the murder of six million Jews by the Nazis an unspeakable crime, but a crime by some Catholics, not by the church."[60] Broadening the indictment to include Protestants, Wilson declares, "It is to the shame of Christians everywhere that the established Church did so little to prevent or protest the slaughter."[61]

Three years after the defeat of Nazi Germany in 1948, the United Nations, with the support of the international community, established for Jews a permanent homeland, to be called Israel, in the land of Palestine. No doubt forged out of guilt and the desire to make restitution, the decision brought yet more trouble to the children of Hagar and Sarah. Palestine was already inhabited by Arabs, most of whom were Muslims and a small percentage, Christians.[62] The founding of the state of Israel came at their expense and disposal; they lost their homeland to the Zionists. Even if unintended, many of the evils perpetrated in Christian Europe against the Jews reappeared against the Palestinians. Writing as "a freelance monotheist" (her self-description), Karen Armstrong observes, "The loss of Palestine became a potent symbol of the humiliation of the Muslim world at the hands of the Western powers, who seemed to feel no qualms about the dispossession and permanent exile of hundreds of thousands of Palestinians."[63]

Taking account of the guilt felt by Christians about the Holocaust, Rosemary Ruether and Herman Ruether comment as follows on Christian responsibility in the Israeli-Palestinian conflict: "One cannot care about Jews as fellow human beings, and as part of the family of Abrahamic faiths, and at the same time cover up a continuing ethnocide of the Palestinian people. . . ." They continue: Christians must "hold one another equally accountable, not silencing ourselves about today's evil to pay for yesterday's evil."[64]

Despite efforts throughout decades to solve the problems resulting from the establishment of Israel and the dispossession of the Palestinians, to this day peace does not prevail. Moreover, the injustice visited on the Palestinian people continues to rankle in the Arab world with its vast Muslim population. This unresolved situation played no small part in the tragic events of September 11, 2001, and afterwards in the United States. Unto the thousandth generation and beyond, disputes and divisions among all the families descended from Hagar and Sarah continue to breed violence.

QUESTIONS THE CHILDREN ASK

As heirs to so troubling a history of relationships among Jews, Christians, and Muslims, from biblical and qur'anic beginnings to contemporary events, what can the distaff authors of this little book hope to do? How might we as daughters of Hagar and Sarah contribute to the topics of family, faith, and interfaith relations—topics that occupy so prominent a place in public discourse as in the monotheistic religions of the world? At this juncture, a few answers surface; they lead, in turn, to more questions.

First, we can make available certain major sources from the past that shape the present and impinge on the future. Although these and other sources may be accessible in a variety of places, here they appear together in a planned sequence with an overarching purpose. That sequence and purpose focus not primarily on Abraham as the founding father of three religions but on Hagar and Sarah as the founding mothers. This shift in focus allows for shifts in meaning.

Second, we can interpret sources in ways different from the traditional approach. Not only do patriarchal worldviews reside in the sources, but conventional readings also perpetuate, even promote, those views. By contrast, our perspectives often yield new interpretations that can alter the use and authority of the sources. Sometimes these interpretations show that texts are less patriarchal than conventional readings have maintained; other times, that they are more patriarchal; and still other times, that ambiguities and gaps as well as diverse contexts compel continual wrestling rather than the certitude of single or set answers.

Third, we can advocate as women of diverse faiths who refuse to allow those faiths to be used against us or against outsiders. We work for the full humanity of all women, men, and children and for the integrity and goodness of God's creation. Advocacy compels us to expose dualistic structures of domination and subordination, of mastery and oppression, that warp individual lives and relationships among us. It also compels us to seek blessings even, perhaps especially, in the midst of curses.

Given these potential contributions, we conclude this chapter by raising questions to be wrestled with later in a contemporary context. Delores Williams and Letty Russell undertake that wrestling, respectively, in chapters 7 and 8. Meantime, the questions can prod and guide our explorations.

What new insights can we gain by reading our sources from the perspectives of Hagar and Sarah? For sure, their situations highlight issues of race, class, ethnicity, nationality, and religion that we have ignored for too long. To ask about the presence of women in the grand narrative is, by extension, to ask what the voices of all marginalized people can contribute to overcoming division and hostility.

How do competing claims for patriarchal and exclusive descent constrain God's blessing? This question relates to familial structures that promote hierarchical values and so not only demean certain members of a family but also lock God into the power dynamics of contending factions. The issue is not which family structure is correct or which parent is more important but rather how we come to see that God's blessing to one family signifies blessing to all nations.

Does God show partiality? On this matter, the overall biblical record is mixed. For instance, an exposition in the book of Deuteronomy on justice describes "the great God, mighty and awesome, who is not partial and takes no bribe" (Deut. 10:17). Peter in the book of Acts comes to understand "that God shows no partiality . . ." (Acts 10:34–35). Paul makes the identical claim in Galatians 2:6. In the stories at hand, however, God both cares for Hagar and orders her to suffer, promises Sarah a child but withholds the fulfillment until after problems arise, and rejects Ishmael as the child of promise but makes of him a great nation. If Scripture yields no single answer to God's preferences, it does show that human beings yearn above all else to be among God's chosen.

To these questions we shall return after our journey through many texts. The journey comes in three parts. The first part (chapters 2 and 3), entitled "Hagar and Sarah in Genesis and Galatians," explores the first and second generation of the biblical story. The second part (chapters 4, 5, and 6), entitled "Hagar and Sarah in Jewish, Christian, and Muslim Traditions," presents the early, postscriptural development of the story. The third part (chapters 7 and 8), entitled "Hagar and Sarah in Continuing Conversation," moves into a contemporary context with Christian witnesses from womanist and feminist perspectives.

Continuing the conversation calls for rethinking the relationship among our three religions. In this rethinking, the perspective of the character most marginal to the original story, namely, Hagar, may help us to create a different vision of human and gendered relations and of justice and mercy in familial and interfaith relations. After all, Hagar's vision of God enabled her to see in the wilderness the water of life. That vision endures for those who struggle for freedom and the flourishing of their children unto the thousandth generation.

Notes

1. Cf., e.g., the Abrahamic titles of the following books, all published within the past sixteen years: Marvin R. Wilson, *Our Father Abraham: Jewish Roots of the Christian Faith* (Grand Rapids: Wm. B. Eerdmans Publishing Co., 1989); Hershel Shanks, ed., *Abraham & Family: New Insights into the Patriarchal Narratives* (Washington, DC: Biblical Archaeology Society, 2000); Yvonne Yazbeck Haddad and John L. Esposito, eds., *Daughters of Abraham: Feminist Thought in Judaism, Christianity, and Islam* (Gainesville: University Press of Florida, 2001); Bruce Feiler, *Abraham; A Journey to the Heart of Three Faiths* (New York: William Morrow & Co., 2002); F. E. Peters, *The Children of Abraham: Judaism, Christianity, Islam* (Princeton, NJ: Princeton University Press, 2004); Michael Wyschogrod (ed. and introduced by R. Kendall Soulen), *Abraham's Promise: Judaism and Jewish-Christian Relations* (Grand Rapids: Wm. B. Eerdmans Publishing Co., 2004); Ronald Hendel, *Remembering Abraham: Culture, Memory, and History in the Hebrew Bible* (Oxford: Oxford University Press, 2005).
2. Cf. the observation by John L. Thompson in *Writing the Wrongs: Women of the Old Testament among Biblical Commentators from Philo through the Reformation* (Oxford: Oxford University Press, 2001), 17: "It is one thing to acknowledge the centrality of Abraham and his descendants in the overall plot of the book of Genesis, but there is something amiss when the center is allowed to fill or erase the margins, especially when some of these apparently marginal characters may fairly claim to be the focus of God's benevolent concern in ways that parallel or even rival the divine attention paid to other, seemingly more central characters."
3. See Michael Cook, *The Koran: A Very Short Introduction* (Oxford: Oxford University Press, 2000); for "a female inclusive reading of the Qur'an," see Amina Wadud, *Qur'an and Woman: Rereading the Sacred Text from a Woman's Perspective* (New York: Oxford University Press, 1999).
4. Biblical quotations in this chapter come from the New Revised Standard Version of the Bible (New York: Division of Christian Education of the National Council of Churches of Christ in the USA, 1989). Citations with an asterisk (*) after them indicate modifications of the NRSV.
5. Muslims hold that the Qur'an cannot be translated; it must be read and recited in Arabic. Therefore, any English text is an interpretation. The text used here, with English and Arabic in adjoining columns, is entitled *An Interpretation of the Qur'an: English Translation of the Meanings; A Bilingual Edition*, trans. Majid Fakhry (New York: New York University Press, 2004). *Surah* (also transliterated *sura*) is the Arabic word for a major division of the Qur'an. For a recent report on translations of the Qur'an and other texts relevant to Islam, see "Reading Islam" by Charles Kimball, *The Christian Century* (May 17, 2005): 44–52.
6. For an introduction to Islam, see Mahmoud M. Ayoub, *Islam: Faith and History* (Oxford: Oneworld Publications, 2005), and other texts cited by Kimball, "Reading Islam."
7. Early on, most Muslim scholars identified Isaac as the son in the sacrifice story; over time, the dominant view switched to Ishmael. On this and other matters, see John Kaltner, "Abraham's Sons: How the Bible and Qur'an See the Same Story

Differently," *Bible Review* (April 2002), 16–23, 45–46; cf. also the view of Riffat Hassan in chapter 6 of this book.

8. On the historical context, see James L. Kugel and Rowan A. Greer, *Early Biblical Interpretation* (Philadelphia: Westminster Press, 1986), 11–72. On Hagar in ancient and medieval Jewish writings, cf. Thompson, *Writing the Wrongs*, 24–28, 53–60.

9. For an introduction and translation, see O. S. Wintermute, "Jubilees," *The Old Testament Pseudepigrapha,* vol. 2, ed. James H. Charlesworth (Garden City, NY: Doubleday & Co., Inc., 1985), 35–142.

10. For the stories that follow, see Louis Ginzberg, *Legends of the Bible,* vol. 1, *From the Creation to Jacob,* trans. Henrietta Szold (Baltimore: John Hopkins University Press, 1998), 237–40; 261–63.

11. This explanation seeks to harmonize the information in Gen. 17:25 that Ishmael was thirteen years old when circumcised, with the depiction of him in Gen. 21:14–16 as a young child carried by his mother, who puts him under a bush.

12. On Hagar in ancient and medieval Christian writings, cf. Thompson, *Writing the Wrongs,* 29–53; 60–69.

13. Cf. Peters, *The Children of Abraham,* 77–82.

14. Cf. Feiler, *Abraham,* 75–81.

15. On the history of early Judaism, see James C. VanderKam, *An Introduction to Early Judaism* (Grand Rapids: Wm. B. Eerdmans Publishing Co., 2001), esp. 1–52, 175–217; for the history from the second century BCE through the second century CE, see Shaye J. D. Cohen, *From the Maccabees to the Mishnah* (Philadelphia: Westminster Press, 1987). For an overview, see Norman Solomon, *Judaism: A Very Short Introduction* (Oxford: Oxford University Press, 1996).

16. On the conflict that characterized Jewish-Christian relationships from the beginning, see Alan F. Segal, *Rebecca's Children: Judaism and Christianity in the Roman World* (Cambridge, MA: Harvard University Press, 1986).

17. For succinct histories of Islam, see, e.g., Karen Armstrong, *Islam* (New York: Modern Library, 2000); Peters, *The Children of Abraham*; Richard Fletcher, *The Cross and the Crescent: Christianity and Islam from Muhammad to the Reformation* (New York: Viking, 2003).

18. On the relationship of Islam and Christianity, see Fletcher (*The Cross and the Crescent*) who writes that "[A]loofness on the one side and hostility on the other were to prove remarkably pervasive and enduring over the centuries . . ." (19). On the many interactions in the period 750–1000, both violent and harmonious, the most striking absence is "any sense that either side of the cultural divide was remotely interested in the religion of the other . . . Christian and Muslim lived side by side in a state of mutual religious aversion" (65–66).

19. This discussion relies on María Rosa Menocal, *The Ornament of the World: How Muslims, Jews, and Christians Created a Culture of Tolerance in Medieval Spain* (Boston: Little, Brown and Co., 2002).

20. On literary and theological contributions of Jews in Spain (as well as in France and Italy), see Adele Berlin, *Biblical Poetry Through Medieval Jewish Eyes* (Bloomington: Indiana University Press, 1991).

21. See Richard E. Rubenstein, *Aristotle's Children: How Christians, Muslims, and Jews Rediscovered Ancient Wisdom and Illuminated the Dark Ages* (New York: Harcourt Brace Jovanovich, 2003), esp. 1–87.

22. On this complicated history of rebellion, suppression, and bloodshed, see L. P. Harvey, *Muslims in Spain: 1500 to 1614* (Chicago: University of Chicago Press, 2005).

23. See Thomas Asbridge, *The First Crusade: A New History* (Oxford: Oxford University Press, 2004).

24. See Fletcher, *The Cross and the Crescent,* 77–82.

25. See Jonathan Phillips, *The Fourth Crusade and the Sack of Constantinople* (New York: Viking Penguin, 2004).

26. See Fletcher, *The Cross and the Crescent*, 82–85.

27. As Fletcher points out, many contemporary scholars are skeptical of arranging the past with a period called the Middle Ages ending around 1500 (*The Cross and the Crescent*, 159). Despite that observation, we have used the traditional divisions for this overview. For background on the Reformation, we rely on the standard textbook by Williston Walker, Richard A. Norris, David W. Lotz, and Robert T. Handy, *A History of the Christian Church*, 4th ed. (New York: Charles Scribner's Sons, 1985), esp. 417–80; see also Diarmaid MacCulloch, *The Reformation* (New York: Penguin Books, 2005), esp. 115–57; 237–53.

28. *Luther's Works: Lectures on Genesis*, vols. 1–8, ed. Jaroslav Pelikan (St. Louis: Concordia Publishing House, 1958–1966). For background information, see the general introductions to each of these volumes.

29. *Luther's Works: Lectures on Genesis*, vol. 3, chaps. 15–20, 42–74.

30. In another context, Pelikan draws attention to Luther's statement that he read the Koran for the first time only in 1542. Before then, he knew of Muslim scholars solely from Italian writers. See *Luther's Works: Sermons on the Gospel of St. John*, vol. 22, chaps. 1–4, ed. Jaroslav Pelikan (St. Louis: Concordia Publishing House, 1957), 17–18.

31. The Qur'an does not say specifically that Ishmael is the son offered for sacrifice; on this matter, see n. 7 above.

32. *Luther's Works: Lectures on Genesis*, vol. 3, chaps. 15–20, 63–66.

33. Ibid., 67–72.

34. Ibid., 176–218.

35. Ibid., 201.

36. Ibid., 208–16.

37. Ibid., 10–73.

38. Ibid., 68–69.

39. On Luther's interpretation of Hagar, see Thompson, *Writing the Wrongs*, 87–92; for sixteenth-century interpretations of Hagar apart from those of Luther (and of Calvin), cf. Thompson, *Writing the Wrongs*, 69–83; 92–94. On the ways Luther contradicts himself in evaluating biblical women, especially Hagar and Sarah, see *Luther on Women: A Sourcebook*, ed. and trans. Susan C. Karant-Nunn and Merry E. Wiesner-Hanks (Cambridge: Cambridge University Press, 2003), esp. 58–65.

40. *Luther's Works*, vol. 3, 71.

41. Ibid., 29.

42. See *Luther's Works: Lectures on Galatians*, vol. 26, chaps. 1–4, ed. Jaroslav Pelikan (St. Louis: Concordia Publishing Company, 1963), 433–61.

43. See John Calvin, *Commentaries on the First Book of Moses called Genesis*, vol. 1, trans. John King (Grand Rapids: Wm. B. Eerdmans Publishing Co., 1948), 421–39.

44. On Calvin's overall interpretation of Hagar, see Thompson, *Writing the Wrongs*, 83–87.

45. See Calvin, *Commentaries*, vol. 1, 423.

46. See Jan Slomp, "Calvin and the Turks," in *Christian-Muslim Encounters*, ed. Yvonne Yazbeck Haddad and Wadi Zaydan Haddad (Gainesville: University Press of Florida, 1995), 126–42. She argues that Calvin shows little knowledge of Islamic religion. Following the stereotypes of his time, he lumps it with his criticisms of the papacy as well as of Jews and pagans. Yet his emphasis on the sovereignty of God might well have resonated with the tenets of Islam.

47. See Calvin, *Commentaries*, vol. l, 465–91.

48. See Ibid., 534–57.

49. See John Calvin, *Commentaries on the Epistles of Paul to the Galatians and Ephesians*, trans. William Pringle (Grand Rapids: Wm. B. Eerdmans Publishing Co., 1948), 134–45.

50. On the history of religious tolerance and intolerance among Jews, Christians, and Muslims in the Ottoman Empire (1453–1923) and since, see Mark Mazower, *The Balkans: A Short History* (New York: Modern Library, 2000), esp. 39–76.

51. But "a reverse ethnic cleansing" also occurred in Kosovo, with Muslim Albanians persecuting Orthodox (Christian) Serbs; see Alkman Granitsas, "Paradigm Slip," *The New Republic* (April 11, 2005), 14, 16, 18.

52. See Haddad and Haddad, *Christian-Muslim Encounters*, 2. (We assume that these editors of the volume are the authors of the unsigned introduction from which this quotation comes.) On self-critique within Islam about its use to promote violence in the world, see, e.g., "Massacre Draws Self-Criticism in Muslim Press," *The New York Times* (September 9, 2004).

53. See Richard W. Bulliet, *The Case for Islamo-Christian Civilization* (New York: Columbia University Press, 2004).

54. On similarities and differences between the well-known, if sometimes disputed, phrase "Judeo-Christian civilization" and the neologism "Islamo-Christian civilization," see ibid., 5–6, 10.

55. Bulliet overstates his case, however, when he asserts that "the scriptural and doctrinal linkages between Judaism and Christianity are no closer than those between Judaism and Islam, or between Christianity and Islam" (6). After all, even with differences, Judaism and Christianity share a Scripture with each other and not with Islam; moreover, the theological vocabulary of the Second Testament has its roots in the First.

56. For a comprehensive study of Christianity's role (in particular, Roman Catholicism's role) in the sad history of the Jews, see James Carroll, *Constantine's Sword: The Church and the Jews, A History* (Boston: Houghton Mifflin Co., 2001). Cf. Rosemary Radford Ruether, *Faith and Fratricide: The Theological Roots of Anti-Semitism* (New York: Seabury Press, 1974).

57. See David S. Wyman, *The Abandonment of the Jews: America and the Holocaust, 1941–1945* (New York: New Press, 1998), 317.

58. See Wilson, *Our Father Abraham*, 90–91. Cf. also "Faith and Holocaust" in Wyschograd, *Abraham's Promise*, 111–20; this essay reviews Emil L. Fackenheim's *God Presence in History: Jewish Affirmations and Philosophical Reflections* (New York: New York University Press, 1970).

59. For a poignant counter to the regrettable history of Christianity's relationship to Judaism, see the personal testimonies of prominent Christian scholars in John C. Merkle, ed., *Faith Transformed: Christian Encounters with Jews and Judaism* (Collegeville, MN: Liturgical Press, 2003).

60. See Arthur Hertzberg, "The Vatican's Sin of Omission," *The New York Times* (May 14, 2005).

61. See Wilson, *Our Father Abraham*, 101.

62. For theological reflections by one who belongs to the Christian minority and identifies himself as "an Arab, a Palestinian, a Christian, and a citizen of the State of Israel," see Naim Stifan Ateek, *Justice, and Only Justice: A Palestinian Theology of Liberation* (Maryknoll, NY: Orbis Books, 1989); see also Mitri Raheb, *I Am a Palestinian Christian*, trans. Ruth C. L. Gritsch, foreword by Rosemary Radford Ruether (Minneapolis: Fortress Press, 1995).

63. See Armstrong, *Islam*, 149.

64. Rosemary Radford Ruether and Herman J. Ruether, *The Wrath of Jonah: The Crisis of Religious Nationalism in the Israeli-Palestinian Conflict*, 2nd ed. (Minneapolis: Fortress Press, 2002), 246.

PART ONE
HAGAR AND SARAH IN GENESIS AND GALATIANS

Chapter 2

Ominous Beginnings for a Promise of Blessing

Phyllis Trible

Our story begins with a short genealogy, one of those records of male descendants that abound in the Bible (Gen. 11:27–32). For many people, such records do not arouse interest. Series of "begats," full of father and son names, hardly inspire us to read on or to live well. Yet, despite their gender and rhetorical limitations, genealogies testify to the ever-rolling stream of time, to the inescapable flow of past, present, and future. Moreover, here and there the "begats" give information or perspectives that make the difference for the stories they introduce, link, or conclude.[1] So it is with our genealogy. In introducing a family that God will bless, it discloses a seemingly insoluble problem.

This genealogy flows from a long one that it parallels through contrast. Following the story of the Tower of Babel (Gen. 11:1–9), the long genealogy (Gen. 11:10–26) reports on Shem, son of Noah, and his descendants through eight generations. The first seven follow a pattern. Each names a male and gives the age when he becomes the father of another male, also named. Next comes a statement of how long the father lived after the birth of the named son. At the close appears gendered information about "other sons and daughters," who are unnamed. The pattern establishes stability, order, continuity, and predictability

33

for the seven generations in the male line of the ancestor Shem. With patriarchal plodding,[2] it assures readers that what was in the beginning is now and ever more shall be so.

But the assurance does not last. The eighth generation breaks the pattern. To be sure, the report begins by naming the male character and giving the age when he becomes a father. "When Terah had lived seventy years," it says, "he became the father of . . ." (Gen. 11:26).[3] Instead of naming just one son, however, it names three: Abram, Nahor, and Haran. Further, it says nothing about the length of Terah's life or about "other sons and daughters." These departures from the pattern both conclude the long genealogy and preface the short one. They suggest that what was in the beginning and is now may not forever be so.

GENEALOGY WITH A FLAW

Just as the long list begins, "These are the descendants of Shem," so the short one begins, "These are the descendants of Terah" (Gen. 11:27). For a second time the three sons are named. Abram, Nahor, and Haran signify the largesse of genealogy. And even though Haran dies before his father, he leaves a son named Lot. He leaves a future. Abram and Nahor prepare futures for themselves through marriages. Abram's wife is Sarai; Nahor's is Milcah. The genealogy then gives the lineage of Milcah as "the daughter of Haran," but it fails to give the lineage of Sarai. Instead, the recital of names and relationships yields to a parenthesis of information that threatens genealogy: "Now Sarai was barren; she had no child" (Gen. 11:30).

This datum makes the difference. However we may view barrenness, within the biblical narrative it is a tragic flaw.[4] It robs a woman of her labor and her status. It undercuts patriarchy, upsets family values, and negates life. Coming at the close of the short genealogy of Terah, the news of Sarai's barrenness sounds ominous. It endangers the stability, order, continuity, and predictability that genealogy promotes. This seemingly insoluble problem forecasts the end to a family that is only beginning.

Terah takes the larger family from Ur of the Chaldeans to the city Haran. There he dies; his generation passes. If the next generation holds promise, it likewise harbors peril. The peril increases as the short genealogy leads into a narrative that focuses not on Nahor or Lot but rather on Abram whose wife Sarai is barren.[5]

A CALL WITH AMBIGUITIES

As we enter the narrative,[6] we encounter another threat to the family. Yhwh speaks to Abram with an uncompromising command:[7]

Go forth from your native land
    and from your clan
    and from your father's house
to a land that I will show you.
        (Gen. 12:1*)

The divine imperative requires Abram to break with all that identifies a man in his ancient world, from the large category of native land through clan to the small unit of "father's house." In effect, Abram must relinquish his past and his present and go forth to an unknown future in an unspecified land. Although the command does not require him to give up Sarai his wife, of what value for life, family, and future is barren property?

Following the uncompromising command comes the promise:

I will make of you a great nation.
    And I will bless you
    and I will make great your name
        that it will be a blessing.
I will bless those who bless you
    and the one despising you I will curse.[8]
And will bless themselves through you
    all the families of the earth.
        (Gen. 12:2–3*)

Blessing saturates the promise.[9] Five times the word occurs in contrast to a single occurrence of the word "curse." Blessing extends the strength, power, and vitality of Yhwh to Abram and through him to all the families of the earth.

Yet ambiguity attends the blessing. What constitutes a great nation remains unclear. The lack of explication and the absence of a specified historical context allow for an array of interpretations that scholars draw from almost the entire narrative of ancient Israel. Does the promise of blessing undergird the Davidic-Solomonic empire of the tenth century BCE with its nationalistic aspirations? Does it aid the reform efforts of King Hezekiah in the eighth century and King Josiah in the seventh? Does it give hope in the sixth century to Jewish exiles who have experienced the total destruction of their nation? Does it inspire Jewish nationalists of the fifth and fourth centuries? Does the promise promote imperialism, the extension of empire and power to all the families of the earth, or does it support universalism, the responsibility to extend blessing to all? In short, is the promise dangerous or comforting—and for whom? Different historical and sociological contexts, as well as indeterminate speech, shift the meanings of Abram's call.[10] But whatever the interpretation, the tragic flaw remains to undercut the promise. "Sarai is barren; she has no child."

Without a child there will be no great nation; without a child, no great name; without a child the blessings will be barren. Everything hinges on Sarai. Her condition threatens to negate the future, the continuation of genealogy, even while Yhwh calls Abram to relinquish his past and present. Let there be no misunderstanding: Sarai the barren wife is the human pivot in this patriarchal narrative. She counts.

CALCULATION IN EGYPT

For Abram the counting soon inspires calculation. At first, however, he silently obeys the divine command.[11] He "went, as the Lord had told him . . . and took Sarai his wife . . ." (Gen. 12:5*). They arrive in Canaan only to leave, in a time of famine, for a sojourn in Egypt. The land Yhwh promised holds death; the land Pharaoh rules holds life. As the couple approach Egypt, Abram speaks for the first time. He addresses Sarai who, so the narrator reminds us for now a fourth time, is "his wife" (Gen. 12:11; cf. 11:29, 31; 12:5). But as Abram sees it, that uxorial relationship may be a liability. To avoid the problem, he decides to replace the word.

"Now I know that you are a woman [or a wife] beautiful in appearance," says Abram to Sarai, "and when the Egyptians see you, they will say, 'His wife is this.' Then they will kill me, but you they will let live. Say then, my sister you are so that it may go well [ytb] with me for your sake [baʿabûrēk] and my life may be spared on your account" (Gen. 12:11–13*). "Sister" replaces "wife" in Abram's scheme.[12] With flattery he would manipulate Sarai to justify deception and save himself. He would have her lie on his behalf, ostensibly for her own good. She does not reply. Yet as the story unfolds, we find reason to think that she does not assent—even though she cannot thwart the plan.

After Abram's instructions, the narrator reports what happens when the couple reach Egypt (Gen. 12:14–16*). The officials see "the woman [the wife], how exceedingly beautiful she is."[13] They commend her to Pharaoh, and "the woman" (the wife) is taken into his house. At the place of betrayal Sarai has no name. Beauty and gender alone describe her. The object of her husband's calculation and Pharaoh's pleasure, she serves male desires. Although she is central to the story, patriarchy marginalizes this manhandled woman.

Abram's plan works. The narrator underscores his achievement in a sentence that puts his name first and appropriates his earlier phrase of self-concern that he couched as concern for Sarai (cf. Gen. 12:13). "And for-Abram, he [Pharaoh] treated well [ytb] for her sake [baʿabûrâ]" (Gen. 12:16*; cf. 12:13). Indeed, so well does Pharaoh treat Abram that he acquires "sheep and cattle and male donkeys and male slaves and female slaves and female donkeys and male camels." (In the Hebrew syntax, the gendered people appear between the gendered donkeys.) Abram the pimp becomes a wealthy man.

But the situation changes when Yhwh enters the story. The deity "struck [ngʿ] Pharaoh with serious diseases, and also his household . . ." (Gen. 12:17*). In completing this sentence, the narrator accounts for the divine action with a phrase that allows different interpretations. Literally, the Hebrew reads, "on account of the word [ʿl dbr] of [or about] Sarai." Most translations drop the term *word* to give the meaning "on account of" or "because of Sarai."[14] An alternative keeps the phrase "because of the deed [or matter] concerning Sarai." Both renderings present Sarai as the object of divine solicitude. But a third translation stays close to the Hebrew: "because of the word of Sarai."[15] In contrast to the other choices, it presents Sarai not just as object but as subject with speech (even if the text does not give her particular word). Accordingly, the full sentence reads, "But Yhwh struck Pharaoh with serious diseases, and also his household, because of the word of Sarai, Abram's wife."[16]

This third translation may suggest that from the beginning Sarai did not assent to Abram's plan, though she was unable to thwart it.[17] Now her own "word" effects her release as Yhwh sides with her against her male lords. Yet the appositive "Abram's wife" at the end of the sentence shows the limits under which she lives. Yhwh saves Sarai as Abram's possession. For a divine purpose, the deity protects this patriarchal marriage.

Alerted to Abram's deceit, Pharaoh reprimands him. "What is this you have done to me?" Minus the phrase "to me," the language repeats the accusatory question that Yhwh asks the primal woman after her disobedience in the garden of Eden (Gen. 3:13; cf. also 4:10). The repetition commences a number of parallels between these two narratives.[18] In this one Pharaoh takes the moral high ground as he calls Abram to account. "Why did you not tell me that your wife is she? Why did you say, 'my sister is she,' so that I took her to me for a wife?" (Gen. 12:19a*). For certain, Pharaoh respects another man's property. Moreover, he discloses, contrary to Abram's stated plan (Gen. 12:13), that Abram himself (not Sarai) spoke the deceptive words about her. The disclosure reinforces the view that Sarai's lack of a reply to Abram's plan did not mean assent. Upon their arrival in Egypt, she did not speak as Abram instructed. Though trapped by his words to Pharaoh, her "word" (*dbr*; to Yhwh?) sounded a different message (cf. Gen. 12:17). That Yhwh acted "because of the word of Sarai, Abram's wife" signals both her protest and her powerlessness.

Continuing to take the moral high ground within patriarchy, Pharaoh expels Abram and Sarai from Egypt even as Yhwh expelled the primal man and woman from the garden of Eden. Four words in Hebrew report the decisive order: "Behold, your-wife; take and-go" (Gen. 12:19b*).[19] In confirming Pharaoh's command, the narrator reports on the present while alluding to the past and the future. "And Pharaoh gave the men orders about him. And they sent him away, and his wife and all that he had" (Gen. 12:20*). The verb "send away" (*šlḥ*), with the meaning of expulsion, appeared at the close of the garden story (Gen. 3:23) and will reappear in a story about the Egyptian slave woman Hagar (Gen. 21:14). The phrase "all that he had" may well include Hagar, who in time will clash with "his wife."[20] Expelled from Egypt, Abram carries Egypt with him.

EGYPT IN CANAAN

Upon his return to Canaan (cf. Gen. 13:1), Abram begins to struggle with the divine promises of land and offspring. Strife and threats about the possession of the land he resolves (Gen. 13–14), but the need for descendants he cannot meet. Yhwh continues, however, to reiterate the promise, even making a covenant with Abram that links abundant land with progeny numerous as the stars (Gen. 15). Yet nothing happens until barren Sarai takes charge.

An artfully arranged sentence begins the story of her action.[21] Reversing the usual order of Hebrew syntax for emphasis, the sentence places the subject Sarai before the verb. "Now Sarai, wife of Abram, did not bear [a child] to him, but to her [was] an Egyptian maid whose name [was] Hagar" (Gen. 16:1*). Beginning with Sarai and ending with Hagar, the sentence opposes the two women around the man Abram. Sarai the Hebrew is married, rich, and free but also old and barren. Hagar the Egyptian is single, poor, and slave but also young and fertile. Power belongs to Sarai; powerlessness marks Hagar. Abram mediates between them.

Sarai proposes a plan to acquire a child.

> And Sarai said to Abram:
> 'Behold, God has prevented me from bearing children.
> Go, then, to my maid.
> Perhaps I shall be built up from her.'
>
> (Gen. 16:2*)

To enhance her own status, Sarai would make Hagar a surrogate mother. The fertility that God has denied Sarai, she can achieve through the maid whose name she never utters and to whom she never speaks.

Even though Sarai's plan for Hagar is legitimate in the culture,[22] it evokes disturbing parallels to Abram's illegitimate plan for Sarai in Egypt. In that story, Abram's first words ever addressed Sarai; now Sarai's first words ever address Abram. As Abram schemed to save himself by manipulating Sarai and Pharaoh, so Sarai schemes to promote herself by manipulating Abram and Hagar. As Abram tricked Pharaoh into manhandling Sarai, so Sarai would persuade Abram to manhandle Hagar. Like husband, like wife. Altogether, Sarai would treat Hagar in Canaan much as she herself was treated in Egypt: the object of use for the desires of others. Like oppressor, like oppressed.

Abram, mediator between the women, makes no attempt to halt Sarai's plan. Instead, the narrator reports that he "heard her voice" (Gen. 16:2). The phrase recalls Yhwh's accusation to the disobedient man in the garden: "Because you heard the voice of your woman . . ." (Gen. 3:17). Like the first man, Abram obeys his wife. The obedience signals trouble, which the narrator reinforces through repeated use of relational language (Gen. 16:3*):

> Sarai, *wife* of Abram, took [*lqḥ*] Hagar the Egyptian, *her maid* (after Abram had dwelt ten years in the land of Canaan) and gave [*ntn*] her to Abram, *her husband*, to him for a *wife*

This language promotes tension between Hagar as maid and Hagar as wife and between Sarai as wife and Hagar as second wife. The vocabulary also recalls the story of the garden. The primal woman "took" (*lqḥ*) the forbidden fruit, ate it, and "gave" (*ntn*) it to her man (Gen. 3:6). Hagar becomes, in effect, the for-bidden fruit. Like the primal man, Abram "eats" what is offered, without ques-tion or objection. Succinctly, the narrator says, "He went in to Hagar" (Gen. 16:4). Like Sarai, Abram never calls Hagar by name and never speaks to her. No mighty patriarch is he but rather the silent and acquiescent figure in this drama between two women.

As the story moves into a crowded marriage of three, the focus rests on Hagar. "She conceived" (Gen. 16:4). The news is precisely what Sarai wants, but it leads to an insight on Hagar's part that her mistress has not anticipated. "And [when] she [Hagar] saw that she had conceived, her mistress became slight in her eyes" (Gen. 16:4*). In the Hebrew syntax, words of sight, connoting understanding, begin and end this sentence: the verb "see" and the phrase "in her eyes." Struc-turally and substantively, new understanding encircles Hagar's view of herself and her mistress. Hierarchical blinders drop. The exalted mistress decreases; the lowly slave increases. Not hatred or contempt but a reordering of the relationship emerges.[23] Unintentionally, Sarai prepared for the insight. In giving Hagar to Abram for a *wife* (Gen. 16:3), she enhanced the status of the slave woman to become herself correspondingly lowered in the eyes of Hagar. The arrangement models well-documented tension between mistresses and their maids.[24]

Yet the arrangement also offers an occasion for mutuality and equality. The two women, caught in a patriarchal bind, might draw closer together. But that is not to be. If Hagar sees anew, Sarai sees within the old structures. They give her security even as they enslave her. As the wife of a rich patriarch, Sarai is both pow-erful and powerless. Rather than speaking directly to Hagar about what disturbs her, she speaks to Abram. She faults him for the outcome of her plan and appeals to Yhwh for judgment and vindication.

> And Sarai said to Abram:
> "May the wrong done to me be upon you.
> I [*anōkî*] gave my maid to your embrace,
> but when she saw that she had conceived,
> then I was slight in her eyes.
> May the Lord judge between you and me."
> (Gen. 16:5*)

Once again, echoes of the garden story surface. Dissension between the pri-mal man and primal woman followed their joint participation in deviating from the divine plan. He betrayed, even blamed, her when accounting for his eating of the forbidden fruit (Gen. 3:11–12). Similarly, Sarai blames Abram for the con-sequences of their "eating" of the "forbidden fruit." Sarai wants returned the superior status that she unwittingly relinquished in using Hagar. She demands that her husband rectify the wrong because, as also the husband of Hagar, he holds authority over her. This time Abram finds his voice but retains his passive role. Appropriating the vocabulary of vision, with the phrase "in your eyes" (cf. Gen. 16:4, 5), he concedes power to Sarai:

And Abram said to Sarai,
"Behold, your maid is in your hand.
Do to her the good in your eyes."
[i.e., do to her what you deem right.]
(Gen. 16:6*)

Despite his authority within the family, the patriarch will not mediate between his uxorial possessions. He ducks responsibility.

Immediately the narrator reports, "And Sarai afflicts her [Hagar]." The verb "afflict" (ʿnh) connotes harsh treatment. It characterizes, for example, the sufferings of the entire Hebrew population in Egypt, the land of their bondage to Pharaoh (Exod. 1:11, 12; Deut. 26:6). Ironically, the verb depicts here the suffering of a lone Egyptian woman in Canaan, the land of her bondage to the Hebrews. Sarai afflicts Hagar.[25]

In conceiving a child for her mistress, Hagar sees a new reality that challenges the power structure. Her vision leads not to a softening but to an intensification of the system. In "the hand" (i.e., power) of Sarai, with the consent of Abram, Hagar becomes the suffering servant, indeed the precursor of Israel's plight under Pharaoh. Yet no deity delivers Hagar from bondage. Nor does she beseech one. Instead, this tortured woman claims her own exodus, thereby becoming the first person in the Bible to flee oppression, indeed the first runaway slave. The power to flee counters the power to afflict. "Sarai afflicts her, and so she flees [brḥ] from her"—even as Israel will flee (brḥ) from Pharaoh (Exod. 14:5a).

EGYPTIAN EXODUS FROM HEBREW BONDAGE

Pregnant Hagar enters the wilderness. For her it is a hospitable place, symbolized by a spring on the way to Shur, a region near the Egyptian border. The Hebrew word "spring" (ʿayn) also means "eye." The association resonates with Hagar's having acquired a new vision of Sarai, and it anticipates the new vision of God that she will soon acquire.[26] By this spring, a messenger of God finds Hagar. She, an Egyptian and a slave, is the first person in the Bible whom such a messenger visits.[27] Moreover, for the first time in the narrative a character speaks to Hagar (rather than about her) and uses her name. "Hagar, slave of Sarai, where have you come from and where are you going?" (Gen. 16:8*). The questions embody origin and destiny. Hagar answers the first question by naming a person, not a place. Using the emphatic first-person singular, she asserts the power of flight: "From the face of Sarai, my mistress, I [ʾanōkî] am fleeing" (Gen. 16:8*). The second question, about destiny, Hagar seems not to answer. Perhaps she does not know or perhaps wilderness itself is her destiny.

The messenger's reply to Hagar yields desolation and consolation (Gen. 16:9–12*). First, the messenger orders Hagar to return to Sarai and "suffer affliction [ʿnh] under her hand," even as earlier Abram placed Hagar in the "hand" of Sarai (Gen. 16:6). The human power of flight yields to the divine command of return. Hagar's unbearable past becomes her future; her origin in suffering becomes her destiny in suffering. Second, the messenger promises Hagar innumerable descendants, thereby according her the special status of being the only woman in the Bible to receive such a promise.[28] Beyond her destiny of suffering, then, lies a future of progeny. Third, the messenger affirms Hagar's conceiving. She will bear a son and will name him Ishmael. Hagar becomes the first woman in the Bible to receive an annunciation. Fourth, the messenger specifies the meaning of the name Ishmael (God hears): "For God has heard your affliction." And yet the messenger has ordered her to return to affliction.[29] Rather than dispelling suffering, divine hearing affirms it. The comforting name attends affliction. Fifth, the messenger describes Ishmael in contrasting ways. He will be "a wild ass of a man;[30] his hand against everyone and everyone's hand against him." Ishmael will be a free man and a strong man. But the description harbors a negative side. He will live in perpetual strife with all his brothers. Desolation and consolation contend throughout the messenger's speech. Hagar and her son live on the boundary of affliction and release, a boundary decreed by God.

Hagar's next words bypass the messenger's words. She does not comment on her continuing affliction, the promise of descendants, the naming of her son, the meaning of his name, or his future. Nor does she comment on the God who hears. Instead, she names the Lord who sees. The narrator introduces her words with a striking expression that accords her a power attributed to no one else in the Bible. Hagar "calls the name of the Lord who spoke to her" (Gen. 16:13*). She does not invoke the Lord; she names the Lord. She calls the name; she does not call *upon* the name. "You are El-roi [God of seeing]," she says. And she continues, "Have I really seen God and remained alive after seeing him?" At a spring ("eye") on the way to Shur, Hagar the theologian sees God and lives.[31] Uniting the God who sees and the God who is seen, Hagar's insights move from life under affliction to life after theophany. Fittingly, they conclude the divine-human encounter in the wilderness.

Of Hagar's return and affliction under Sarai the narrator says nothing. Instead, the story ends with a formulaic statement about the birth of Ishmael. Its opening sentence counters the opening sentence of the entire story to form an inclusio. At the beginning, "Sarai, wife of Abram, did not bear [*yld*] [a child] to him . . ." (Gen. 16:1); now, at the end, "And bore [*yld*] Hagar to Abram a son . . ." (Gen. 16:15a). The limitation of the first wife accords the second wife a special distinction. Hagar becomes the first woman in the ancestor stories to bear a child.

> And Hagar bore Abram a son; and Abram called the name of his son, whom Hagar bore, Ishmael. Abram was eighty-six years old when Hagar bore Ishmael to Abram. (Gen. 16:15–16*)

Despite Hagar's distinction as first mother, the report undermines her in two ways. First, it stresses the fatherhood of Abram, whom the messenger of the Lord never mentioned. Second, it declares that Abram names the child Ishmael and so denies Hagar the power the messenger gave her. The report also undermines

Sarai, who spoke of building up herself, not Abram, through Hagar's child. With a jarring twist, this conclusion to a story focused on women exalts Abram, as his own name ("exalted father") testifies. Nonetheless, Abram's story continues to pivot on Sarai and Hagar.

THE PLIGHT OF SARAH

Another clash looms. For a time Hagar leaves the story while the deity lets Abram know that the divine plan remains a child through Sarai, no one else (Gen. 17:1–23). Reaffirming and revising the covenant made earlier (Gen. 15), before the episode with Hagar, God again underscores the promise of numerous descendants, including nations and kings, as well as the gift of the land of Canaan. On this occasion God adds that it is to be an "everlasting covenant" sealed by male circumcision (Gen. 17:7, 13).[32] To mark the reaffirmed relationship, God changes Abram's name to Abraham and Sarai's to Sarah.[33]

Still using royal language, the deity underscores the singular role of Sarah in the covenant.

> I will bless her
> and will give from her to you a son.
> I will bless her
> and she will become nations.
> Royal people from her will be.
> (Gen. 17:16*)

God is adamant. Only Sarah can bear the legitimate heir; only Sarah can keep genealogy alive; only Sarah can give birth to the child of the covenant. Elect among women, Sarah is the princess (the meaning of her name) placed, in effect, on the pedestal. By contrast, Hagar is the slave placed, in effect, in the pit. Both women dwell where patriarchy puts them.

Abraham laughs (*ṣḥq*) at the divine words about Sarah as he notes (*ʾmr*) "in his heart" (i.e., to himself) the advanced ages of himself (one hundred years) and of her (ninety years). His proleptic laughter signals the forthcoming name of the child of promise. This veiled anticipation of Isaac (*yiṣḥaq* = he-laughs; cf. Gen. 17:21) adds poignancy to his subsequent words, which, unlike the speech "in his heart," he addresses (*ʾmr*) "to God." Abraham pleads for the legitimacy of Ishmael: "O that Ishmael might live in your sight!"(Gen. 17:18*). But that is not to be. From God's perspective Ishmael has the wrong mother. To be sure, he will be blessed, becoming the father of twelve princes and a great nation, but he will not be the child of the covenant. Not even Ishmael circumcised qualifies (Gen. 17:23–27).

God's reply to Abraham's plea begins with an asseverative particle (*ʾabal*) that holds both positive and negative meaning. It affirms and it refutes. Translations capture the nuance with phrases such as "No, but" and "Yes, but."[34] However the particle is rendered, the divine word holds: "Sarah your wife will bear to you a son, and you will call his name Isaac" (Gen. 17:19). Only Sarah, not Hagar, can bear the promised child.

Blessed Sarah remains, however, barren Sarah. Indeed, her condition worsens. "It has ceased to be with Sarah after the manner of women" (Gen. 18:11). Then, upon a day, mysterious strangers (divine messengers) visit Abraham and announce to him that in the spring they will return and Sarah will have a child. Unlike Hagar the slave, Sarah the mistress does not receive an annunciation. Hers went to Abraham. Nonetheless, she overhears it as she stands surreptitiously outside the tent. Understandably, she "laughs to herself, saying, 'After I have grown old and my husband is old, shall I have pleasure?'" (Gen. 18:12). As with Abraham on the earlier occasion (Gen. 17:15–17), after hearing God's promise, Sarah first laughs (*ṣḥq*) and then speaks (*ʾmr*). And as with Abraham's laughing, Sarah's signals the coming of Isaac.

Yet striking differences emerge between these parallel laughs and speeches. In the earlier event, the text does not indicate that God heard Abraham's laugh. In fact, it follows the clause "he laughed" with a report about what Abraham said "in his heart" and does not indicate that God heard those words. Only after these two responses apart from God does the text have Abraham speaking to God and God answering. By contrast, the account of Sarah's laugh "to herself" followed by her speech elicits an explicit response from God. In her case, internal laughter reaches divine ears.

Yhwh hears Sarah and asks not her, but Abraham, why she has laughed. Abraham says nothing. Sarah, fueled perhaps by fear, answers with denial: "I did not laugh." Then for the first and only time God speaks to her. Not unlike the asseverative particle that began the divine reply to Abraham, the particle that begins this reply inspires both negative and positive nuances. Translations vary accordingly. Here the negative is preferred, for it reiterates and counters the negative in Sarah's own denial. "I did not [*lōʾ*] laugh," she says. "Not [*lōʾ*]? But you did laugh," says God (Gen. 18:15*).[35] The divine response is a curt reprimand for disbelief.[36]

At long last the promise comes to pass. "The Lord visited Sarah . . . and did to Sarah as the Lord had promised" (Gen. 21:1*). She bears a son. Having named his first son "God hears" (Ishmael), Abraham names this one "he laughs" (*yiṣḥaq* = Isaac, Gen. 21:3). Although the sound of the name recalls both Abraham's and Sarah's laughs of disbelief when told they would have a child in their old age (Gen. 17:17; 18:12), now at the birth of the child, Sarah gives a different interpretation.

> Laughter God has made for me (*lî*).
> All who hear will laugh for me (*lî*).
>   (Gen. 21:6*)

Her words hold ambiguity because the Hebrew preposition (*l*) that follows the verb "laugh" carries positive and negative connotations: laugh *with* or *at*. It may be that "all who hear" join Sarah in rejoicing in the birth of her child *or* that they make fun of her giving birth in her old age. "All who hear will laugh with me," or "all who hear will laugh at me." A single preposition governs contrasting meanings of her words. Further, her use of the verb "hear" ("all who hear . . .") carries irony, for it echoes the name Ishmael (God hears). As hearing yields to laughter, so Ishmael will yield to Isaac. For sure, Sarah's words say more than at first we hear.

EXILE FROM CANAAN

Arriving after decades of barrenness for Sarah, Isaac fulfills his mother's wish to be built up (cf. Gen. 16:2). Through him—her one and only child, the promised child of the covenant—she fulfills herself, completes her role as wife, and obtains the status she sought. As for Abraham, he circumcises "his son Isaac" when he is eight days old and makes a great feast when later the child is weaned (Gen. 21:1–8).

Sarah's Problem

Yet all does not remain well for Sarah. Ironically, laughter becomes the problem.[37] It occasions a second story about Sarah, Hagar, and their children (Gen. 21:9–21).[38] We read that "Sarah saw the son of Hagar the Egyptian, whom she had borne to Abraham, laughing" (Gen. 21:9*). With Sarah as subject and Hagar and her son as objects, every word in the sentence counts. The verb "see" ($r^{>}h$), used earlier to describe Hagar's awareness of her pregnancy (Gen. 16:4), now describes Sarah's awareness of the threat that the child of that pregnancy poses to her own son. Both women see, but differently. The phrase "the son of Hagar the Egyptian" signals the unresolved problem between the women, both of whose names appear in the sentence, whereas the name of Hagar's son does not. The designation "Egyptian" also highlights the ethnic "otherness" of Hagar and her son. Immediately, however, the phrase "whom she had borne to Abraham" counters otherness to vouch for the legitimacy of the son of Hagar. As Abraham's son, he threatens Sarah's son. The verb translated "laughing" (*meṣaḥeq*) puns on the name Isaac (*yiṣḥaq*).[39] In the Hebrew syntax the verb sits at the end of the sentence with no object specified for it. As one of but two sounds attributed to Ishmael in the Bible (cf. Gen. 21:17), it implies a voice for him.

Lacking an object or clarifying phrase, the laughing may indicate simply the happiness of Ishmael. Given its link to the name Isaac, it may also indicate that Ishmael was playing happily with his half-brother. But for Sarah such meanings do not hold. She "sees" trouble in the laughing. From that perspective, the word may indicate mocking.[40] In laughing, the son of Hagar the Egyptian ridicules or mimics the son of Sarah the Hebrew. The son of the slave mocks the son of the mistress; the older child, son of a young woman, mocks the younger child, son of an old woman; the child outside the covenant mocks the child of the covenant. If Sarah's words at the time of Isaac's birth mean "all who hear [the same verb as in Ishmael's name] will laugh *at* me," then she may have anticipated the mockery. Consonant with mocking, the "laughing" may suggest usurpation. For Sarah, Ishmael's laughing poses a threat because, by word association, Ishmael is "Isaac-ing."[41] The son of Hagar plays the role of the son of Sarah. Thereby Ishmael signals his legitimacy as heir. This situation Sarah cannot tolerate.

Once again Sarah asserts her power within patriarchal limits. Concerned about Isaac's inheritance, she commands Abraham to get rid of the rivals.[42]

> Cast out this slave woman and her son,
> for the son of this slave woman
>> will not inherit with my son, with Isaac.
>> (Gen. 21:10*)

Sarah's language of contrast achieves several effects. The single phrase "her son" and the double phrase "with my son, with Isaac" accent the absence of equality between the sons of Abraham. That difference resides in their mothers. Further, the use of the name Isaac accords Sarah's son dignity and power in contrast to the lack of names, and hence of power, of both "this slave woman and her son." Again, the combination "my son Isaac" bespeaks possession, intimacy, exclusivity, and attachment in Sarah's relationship to her child. Tellingly, the combination foreshadows words that in the succeeding story of the near sacrifice of Isaac will apply to Abraham rather than to Sarah (cf. Gen. 22:2).

But in the story at hand Abraham has no exclusive relationship with Isaac. He uses no language of intimacy for either son. The narrator and God, however, attach him to Ishmael.

> The matter was very distressing *in the eyes* of Abraham
>> on account of his son.
> But God said to Abraham,
>> "Do not be distressed *in your eyes* on account of the lad
>> and on account of your slave woman."
>> (Gen. 21:11–12a*)

In the narrator's report, the possessive language "his son" links Abraham and Ishmael, a paternal-filial bond that will endure through Abraham's death (cf. Gen. 25:9). Though Sarah has only "my son Isaac," Abraham has "his son Ishmael" as well as "his son Isaac" (Gen. 21:4, 5). In God's speech to Abraham, however, the paternal bond with Ishmael yields to the impersonal language of "the lad" (na⁽ar), not even "your lad." Further, the reference to "your slave woman" shifts ownership of Hagar from Sarah to Abraham, and it ignores the uxorial relationship Hagar has with Abraham (cf. Gen. 16:2). Speaking to Abraham, God adopts Sarah's way of using descriptive nouns ("the lad" . . . "your slave woman"), rather than names, for Hagar and Ishmael. Similarly, God adopts the narrator's language of vision with the phrase "in your eyes," thereby continuing the accent on sight and insight that enlightens these narratives.[43]

In rejecting Abraham's distress about "the lad and your slave woman," God sides with the chosen mother and son, whose names God does use.

> Everything that Sarah says to you, hear her voice;
> for in Isaac will be named to you descendants.
>
> (Gen. 21:12b)

Sarah, the chosen vessel of the legitimate heir, remains secure on the pedestal that patriarchal religion has built for her. The divine command "hear her voice" harks back to Abram's first obeying Sarai when she bade him "go" to her maid (Gen. 16:2). Abram "heard her voice." Used here by God, the phrase echoes the garden story, though with striking reversal. The God who faulted the primal man for "hearing the voice" of his woman (Gen. 3:17) now orders the man Abraham to "hear the voice" of his woman. If in the first setting the divine charge suggested idolatry of the woman,[44] in this setting the divine command supports the apotheosis of Sarah. For God to put Sarah on the pedestal saves her from a threat but nonetheless deprives her of healing and freedom. And it damages those whom she encounters.

To protect the inheritance of her one and only son, Sarah has commanded Abraham, "Cast out [*grs*] this slave woman and her son. . . ." Supporting Sarah, God commands Abraham to obey. The verb "cast out" resonates with both past and future. The Lord God "cast out" the primal man and woman from Eden (Gen. 3:24). Sarah would now have Abraham "cast out" mother and child from the household. Her instructions also foreshadow the Exodus story but with terrifying differences. In time, Pharaoh will "cast out" (*grs*) the Hebrew slaves to save the life of his firstborn son, but God will take their side to bring salvation from expulsion (Exod. 12:39). By contrast, God identifies here not with the suffering slave Hagar and her son but with their oppressor Sarah. In being cast out, Hagar knows not exodus but exile.

Abraham's Acquiescence

Abraham, again the compliant one, obeys Sarah and God. Yet the narrator uses for his obedience the verb "send away" (*šlḥ*), seemingly softer than the verb "cast out" (*grs*) that Sarah used (Gen. 21:10).[45] Abraham "rose early in the morning and took bread and a skin of water and gave it to Hagar, putting it on her shoulder, along with the child, and he sent her away" (Gen. 21:14). Deplorable in motivation and consequence, Abraham's action accords Hagar, along with her child, another distinction. She is the first slave in Scripture to be freed. At the same time, she becomes the first divorced wife—banished by her husband at the command of his first wife and God.

The relationship between the two verbs of expulsion, "cast out" and "send away," varies in the Bible by context. At the conclusion of the garden story, the narrator says that God "sends out" (*šlḥ*) and "casts out" (*grs*) the disobedient couple (Gen. 3:23, 24). There the verbs appear to overlap in meaning. In this story, Sarah says to Abraham, "Cast out . . . ," and the narrator says that Abraham "sent away. . . ." Here the verbs appear to carry different meanings. Despite the difference, the uncompromising work of the verbs—"cast out" at the beginning and "send away" at the end—surround Hagar and Ishmael to seal their destiny. In the garden story the Lord God expelled the primal man and woman from the home that Yhwh had given them because they disobeyed authority. In this story Abraham (at the command of Sarah and God) expels Hagar and Ishmael from his home because they threaten authority. (Whether the threat is deliberate, as was the disobedience, remains a moot question.)

In addition to its links with the garden story, the verb "send away" connects with Abraham's expulsion from Egypt (cf. Gen. 12:20). At the command of Pharaoh, his men "sent away" (*šlḥ*) Abraham the Hebrew; now at the command of Sarah the Hebrew, Abraham "sends away" (*šlḥ*) Hagar the Egyptian. What Pharaoh did to him, Abraham does to Hagar. In each case an alien has become persona non grata to the powers that be—but for different reasons and with different outcomes. Having deceived Pharaoh, Abraham was sent away discredited. Pharaoh held the moral high ground. Having upset Sarah, Hagar is sent away abused. Sarah holds the tyrannical stance. Abraham left Egypt with Sarah and all his other possessions intact; he departed a wealthy man of stature. Hagar leaves Abraham's house with Ishmael and meager nourishment; she departs a poor woman of nonstature. In these two stories, the verb "send away" reverberates with dissonance.

Although Abraham may have been distressed about the matter, the few provisions he gives Hagar and Ishmael stand in marked contrast to his wealth. Hagar's rich husband uses none of his vast resources to support her and their son. Nor does he seek a new home for them. Over against his sheep, oxen, donkeys, camels, and slaves male and female (Gen. 12:16), plus silver and gold (Gen. 13:2), he sends them away with only bread and water. Paltry alimony it is. Over against his now-secure residence in Canaan, he sends them away with no specified destination. Homelessness he courts for them.

Abraham's giving Hagar and Ishmael bread and water to sustain themselves outside his house evokes through contrast Yhwh God's giving the primal couple garments of skin to protect themselves outside the garden (Gen. 3:21). Meager food for the mistreated contrasts with sturdy clothes for the disobedient. But Hagar and Ishmael are not Eve and Adam. They have not disobeyed God. To the contrary, Sarah and Abraham have disobeyed God, and in the process they have wronged Hagar and Ishmael. Yet this time around, Yhwh reverses the divine judgment. The disobedient couple stay in the "garden" while the "fruits" of their unfaithfulness are expelled. Within their "garden," Sarah and Abraham claim life with Isaac; outside in the wilderness, Hagar and "the child" face death. For certain, the designs of God do not conform to the logic of justice.

Reference to "the child" (*yeled*) being "sent away" (Gen. 21:14) belongs to a pattern for the common nouns used for Ishmael in the story. Heretofore he has been repeatedly called *ben* (son)—by the narrator (Gen. 21:9, 11), Sarah (v. 10), and God (v. 13)—and once called *naʿar* (lad) by God (v. 13). With his expulsion, those nouns cease and the word *yeled* takes over. Twice the narrator uses it: the *yeled* is sent away; the *yeled* is put under a bush (vv. 14, 15). And once Hagar uses the word: "Let me not see the death of the *yeled*" (v. 16). These three uses provide a poignant contrast to a single, earlier use of *yeled* for *Isaac*: "The child [*yeled*] grew and was weaned and Abraham held a great feast on that day" (Gen. 21:8). Isaac is the *yeled* in prosperity and safety; Ishmael, the *yeled* in poverty and danger. As the story unfolds, however, the vocabulary changes yet again.

Hagar's Struggle

The danger that begins when Abraham sends away Hagar and the child increases as they wander (*tʿh*) in the wilderness of Beersheba. Unlike the wilderness of Shur, where a spring of water nourished Hagar (Gen. 16:7), Beersheba provides no water (even though the word means "well of seven" or "well of oath"). Receiving Hagar in forced exile rather than voluntary flight, this second wilderness is an arid and alien place. Once the water that Hagar brought is gone, mother and child face death.

Sensing the nearness of his death, Hagar "puts the child" under a shrub (Gen. 21:15). Of various uses in Scripture for the verb "put" (*šlk*), one describes lowering a body into a grave (cf. 2 Sam. 18:17; 2 Kgs. 13:21; Jer. 41:9). That meaning suits well this context. Contrary to some translations, Hagar does not cast away, throw out, or abandon her son; instead, she prepares a deathbed for "the child" (*yeled*).[46] This occurrence of the noun *yeled* for Ishmael underscores the contrast with Isaac. Isaac is the *yeled* thriving; Ishmael the *yeled* dying. Powerless to save "the child," Hagar would give him a proper burial.

A collection of small words, subject to varied interpretations, continues to underline Hagar's ministrations to Ishmael (Gen. 21:16). Literally, the text begins, "She went and sat by herself. . . ." The phrase "by herself," a single word in Hebrew (*lāh*), accents helplessness and loneliness. The word following it (*min-neged*), sometimes translated "from in front of" or "near," can also mean "across from" or "opposite." It specifies Hagar's presence with the child. After this single word of proximity comes the phrase "to be away like the shooting of a bow;" that is, "about a bowshot away." The reference to a "bowshot" hints at Ishmael's future (cf. Gen. 21:20). Contrary to translations that place Hagar at a distance from the child, the entire sentence can be rendered, "She went and sat by herself in front of him, about a bowshot away."[47] Having put the child on his deathbed, Hagar awaits his dreaded ending.

Her compassionate actions lead to her only words in the episode, which are also her last words in the Bible: "Let me not look on the death of the child" (*yeled*; Gen. 21:16). Constructed in the cohortative form,[48] these words would deny death as they indirectly long for life. They would deny death even as they acknowledge its inevitability. That acknowledgment embraces psychic and physical distancing. Accordingly, Hagar refers to "the child," not to "my child" or "my son" or even "Ishmael." The separation that death brings has begun for mother and child.

Continuing the rhetoric of separation, the narrator reports Hagar's grief (Gen. 21:16): "As Hagar sat in front of him, she lifted up her voice and she wept" (*bkh*).

In this touching portrayal Hagar becomes the first character in the Bible to weep.[49] She becomes the mother of all weepers. Yet she does not cry out to God. Instead, her voice sounds and resounds in the desolate wilderness of exile and despair. A madonna alone, she laments the approaching death of her only child.

Immediately the narrator shifts the focus to Ishmael and changes the vocabulary that identifies him (Gen. 21:17).[50] "God heard the voice of the lad (na'ar)" responds to the report that "she lifted up her voice and she wept." The response indicates that the danger of death is passing. The word yeled, used as death approaches, yields to the word na'ar. Earlier God assured Abraham not to be distressed but rather to "hear the voice" of Sarah and banish "the lad (na'ar) and your slave woman" (Gen. 21:12). Now, in the wilderness of banishment, God "hears the voice of the lad."[51]

The divine hearing signals hope and help over against death. Indeed, the return of the word na'ar secures the pattern that governs the common nouns used for Ishmael. Before expulsion and wilderness, the nouns "son" (ben) and "lad" (na'ar) identify him. In the danger of death only the noun "child" (yeled) identifies him, and it is not used for him outside this setting. After the danger passes, the noun "lad" reappears five times (see below). The weeping of Hagar leads, then, not to the death of "the child," for "God heard the voice of the lad."[52] What Ishmael's voice sounded remains unknown. For sure, he is no longer laughing; he is no longer "Isaac-ing" (cf. Gen. 21:9).

In replying, the messenger of God speaks from heaven to Hagar. So the messenger heeds her voice as well as the voice of the lad. Comforting words unfold.

> What troubles you, Hagar?
> Do not be afraid,
> > for [kî] God has heard the voice of the lad [na'ar] where he is.
> Arise, lift up the lad [na'ar] and hold him by your hand,
> > for [kî] into a great nation I shall make him.
> > > (Gen. 21:17b–18*)

As the narrator first appropriated the noun na'ar to indicate Ishmael's change from death to life (Gen. 21:17), so now a second and third time God uses it. Unlike the revelation in Shur (Gen. 16:7–14), this one in Beersheba does not promise to Hagar innumerable descendants. Instead, within the words to her, the promise shifts to "the lad." If in effect the difference seems slight, the shift nonetheless diminishes Hagar. Having lived under the hand (yād) of her mistress Sarah, this woman must now lift up the hand (yād) of "the lad."

Following the divine words, the narrator completes the story. Hagar's weeping ceases. The God whom she saw (r'h) long ago in Shur opens her eyes, enabling her to see (r'h) a well of water at the site of the "well of seven" (Beersheba). She fills the skin and gives a drink to "the lad" (na'ar), the fourth occurrence of that word (Gen. 21:19).[53] The water of weeping yields to the water of life. Then, for the fifth and last time (Gen. 21:20), the noun na'ar identifies Ishmael after the danger of death has passed. "God was with the lad." The God who sided with Sarah to expel Hagar and Ishmael continues nonetheless to provide for them and remains with them.

God's presence with Ishmael leads to reassuring glimpses of his future, glimpses that ironically recall his precarious past. He "grew up, lived in the wilderness, and became a bow-shooter" (Gen. 21:20). The verb "grow up" or "become great" was last used for Isaac (Gen. 21:8), whose presence in the family led to the expulsion of Ishmael. The wilderness, which has just threatened Ishmael's life, becomes his home.[54] And he whose mother sat "about a bowshot away" from him in the danger of death becomes himself a bow-shooter. A concluding report enhances the reassurances. By his mother's action Ishmael acquires the indispensable possession for a future. "His mother took for him a wife from the land of Egypt" (Gen. 21:21).

Hagar's action highlights tension in the larger narrative. Early on, God promised her innumerable descendants (Gen. 16:10). Later, God transferred that promise, through Abraham, to Ishmael (Gen. 17:20). Now God reiterates the transferred promise, telling Hagar that Ishmael will be a great nation (Gen. 21:18). The male line prevails. Yet Hagar redirects the divine promise her way. In finding for Ishmael an Egyptian wife, she seeks for herself a future that God has diminished.[55] For the last time Hagar appears in the Hebrew Bible, and for the first time she is called "mother."

THE PROBLEM OF IDOLATRY

Following the near sacrifice of Ishmael, the narrative soon moves to the near sacrifice of Isaac (Gen. 22:1–19). In both stories, children are objects; God orders their abuse; Abraham acquiesces to the orders; God stops the abuse only in time to prevent their deaths. But differences between the stories contend with the similarities. Most significantly, Sarah is absent from the second story. She who demanded the expulsion of her surrogate son plays no role in the departure of her natural son. God, who supported her cruel treatment of Ishmael, does not even tell her what is to happen to Isaac.[56]

Instead, God tests Abraham.[57] First comes the calling of his name, "Abraham," with the obedient response, "Behold, I [*hinnēnî*]."[58] Next God issues a series of commands: take, go, and offer. Heavy-laden language—not a simple object but a multiplicity of words—accompanies the first command. The words move from the generic term of kinship, "your son," through the exclusivity of relationship, "your only son," through the intimacy of bonding, "whom you love," to climax in the name that fulfills promise, the name of laughter and joy, the name "*yiṣḥaq*" (Isaac).[59]

> Take your son
>   your only son
>   whom you love. . . .
>   Isaac
>   (Gen. 22:2)

The accumulation of these particular words indicates a deep attachment on Abraham's part to Isaac.[60] Their exclusivity discounts the banished Ishmael as well as Abraham's paternal ties to him, ties that nevertheless endure (cf. Gen. 25:9). But here divine words suggest Abraham's idolatry of his son Isaac.

The second command follows: "Go you" (*lek lekâ*). The verb is familiar, having appeared in the call of Abraham: "Go you (*lek lekâ*) from your country and your clan and your father's house" (Gen. 12:1). That command required a break with the past as it led to the promise of a future. Now in Isaac the future resides. Yet this time the verb "go you" joins the third command, namely, "offer," to destroy that future. "Go you to the land of Moriah and offer him ["your son, your only son, Isaac whom you love"] as a sacrifice on one of the mountains that I shall show you." The father who, by an act of expulsion, has lost one son, must now, by an act of sacrifice, lose the other. The divine promise and its fulfillment begin to unravel.

No resistance does Abraham offer. Silently he begins to obey. Two of the divine imperatives, "take" and "go," become human indicatives.

> So Abraham rose early in the morning
>> and saddled his ass
>> and <u>took</u> two of his young men with him
>>> and *Isaac his son;*
>> and he cut wood for a burnt-offering
>> and arose
> and <u>went</u> to the place that God, indeed God, told him.
>> (Gen. 22:3)

Six verbs (rose, saddled, took; cut, arose, went) with Abraham as obedient subject surround the phrase "Isaac his son." Rather than protecting Isaac, this paternal embrace traps him. Having sent away Ishmael to face death in the wilderness, Abraham takes Isaac to face death on the mountain.

Three days later father and son approach the appointed place. Abraham attends to the necessary provisions. Once he provides bread and a skin of water for the survival of Hagar and Ishmael; now he produces burnt wood, fire, and a knife for the sacrifice of Isaac. But Isaac sees what is missing. Invoking the intimacy of the paternal vocative "father," he asks where is the lamb for a burnt offering (Gen. 22:7). Invoking the intimacy of parent to child, Abraham replies with words reassuring and terrifying, truthful and deceptive: "God will provide the lamb for a burnt offering, my son" (Gen. 22:8). The phrase "my son" functions as vocative and appositive. It is speech to and speech about Isaac. God will provide; Isaac is the provision.

Arriving at the place of sacrifice, Abraham continues to embrace Isaac in the structure and content of the narrator's report.

> Abraham built there the altar,
>> arranged the wood,
>>> and bound *Isaac his son.*

> He laid him on the altar, from upon the wood.
>   Abraham put forth his hand
>   and took the knife to slay *his son.*
>   (Gen. 22:9–10)

In this section Isaac receives center-stress and end-stress. He is trapped; there is no exit. The moment, not just the hour, is at hand. In obedience to the divine command, Abraham, who "took" his son to the mountain (Gen. 22:3), now "takes" the knife to kill his son. As he stands poised to plunge it, the suspense becomes unbearable. The reader wants to scream, "Stop!"

God does precisely that. God stops the sacrifice. As the divine messenger intervened to save Ishmael from death, so the messenger intervenes to save Isaac. "Do not put forth your hand to the lad" (Gen. 22:12). Tellingly, the messenger does not say "to Isaac your son" but rather "to the lad" (*naʿar*). That description, used repeatedly for Ishmael after the danger of death passed (see above), here applies to Isaac as the danger of death passes. The change in vocabulary to "lad" suggests that Abraham's willingness to sacrifice his "son" has dissolved his attachment to Isaac.

The next words from the messenger confirm the change. Introduced by the deictic phrase, "For now I know that . . . ," they clarify the point of the test.[61] "For now I know that you worship God [not Isaac] because you have not withheld your son, your only son, from me" (Gen. 22:12). The reiteration of the possessive phrases "your son, your only son" from the beginning of the story (Gen. 22:2) underscores the problem even as the verbal construction "have not withheld" eliminates it. In his willingness to obey God, Abraham relinquishes attachment to Isaac. Looking around, Abraham sees (*rʾh*) a ram to sacrifice instead of his endangered son, much as Hagar saw (*rʾh*) a well of water to save her dying son. Fittingly, when Abraham leaves the mountain, the text does not say that Isaac accompanies him. Alone Abraham returns to his young men. The bonds of idolatry are broken. What happens to Isaac haunts the story in silence.

The last sentences give yet more tantalizing information. Abraham returns to live in Beersheba (Gen. 22:19). That location marks the region where Hagar and Ishmael wandered before settling in Paran as well as the region from which Abraham went forth to the mountain with Isaac (cf. Gen. 21:14 and 22–34).[62] But meanwhile, Sarah has moved to Hebron (Gen. 23:2). What the text does not say about a separation between Abraham and Sarah—between husband and wife and between father and mother—and what it does not say about a separation between father and son and between mother and son, the reader can surmise.[63] All continues not well in this troubled family.

Other consequences follow. Never again do Abraham and Isaac talk to each other. It falls to the narrator and Abraham's servant to link them (cf. Gen. 24). Similarly, never again do God and Abraham talk to each other. They too depend on the narrator.[64] Perhaps these characters dare not speak among themselves after participating in so terrifying an event of near sacrifice. For awhile, the story turns away altogether from Isaac and God.[65] Though God eventually reappears with vigor, we can wonder if Isaac ever recovers.

AGAIN, THE PLIGHT OF SARAH

If Genesis 22 is a story about idolatry, we might ask if Abraham had that problem. For sure, a different view of him and his wives begins to emerge when we compare the near sacrifices of Ishmael and Isaac. Ishmael in the wilderness with his mother Hagar comes close to death; a messenger of God saves him. Isaac on the mountain with his father Abraham comes close to death; a messenger of God saves him. Thus are paired the children and the divine representatives. Similarly are paired the parents Hagar and Abraham. Although this arrangement elevates Hagar, who is slave, second wife, and mother, to the status of Abraham, who is patriarch, husband, and father, it also skews relationships in their crowded marriage. The appropriate pairing of parents would be Sarah and Hagar, the mothers of the children of Abraham. Unlike him, each of them has only one son.

The stress on one single son moves the sacrifice story toward Sarah. That move fits the larger narrative, which itself promotes a close bond between Sarah and Isaac rather than between Abraham and Isaac. Before Genesis 22:7, Abraham himself never utters the possessive "my son" for Isaac.[66] The phrase belongs exclusively to Sarah's speech. She contrasts "her son" (i.e., Hagar's) with "my son Isaac" (Gen. 21:10). Given the status of Sarah as the legitimate mother of the promised child, her affliction of Hagar and Ishmael, and her attachment to Isaac, she, not Abraham, qualified for the test on the mountain (even as Hagar faced her trial in the wilderness). The dynamic of the larger narrative, from its genealogical preface on, suggests that Sarah learn the meaning of obedience to God, find liberation from attachment, free Isaac from maternal ties, and emerge herself shorn of idolatry. But patriarchy denies Sarah the story she needs. It denies her the possibility for reconciliation with Hagar and Ishmael.[67]

And patriarchy does not stop with these things. After securing the safety of Isaac by a substitute sacrifice (a ram) and by another genealogy—this one (Gen. 22:20–24) preparing for Isaac's future as it drops into the list the name of Rebekah, soon to become his wife—patriarchy needs Sarah no more. So it eliminates her. Whereas it has dropped Hagar from the narrative and yet left her alive in the wilderness, it brings Sarah to her death. Immediately following the sparing of Isaac and the genealogy leading to Rebekah, we read, "Sarah lived a hundred and twenty-seven years . . . and Sarah died at . . . Hebron in the land of Canaan" (Gen. 23:1).

From Beersheba Abraham "went [to Hebron] to mourn for Sarah and to weep for her" (Gen. 23:2*). If the near-sacrifice of Isaac resulted in the separation of this parental couple, Sarah's death now brings Abraham to her in mourning. Purchasing land from the Hittites, he buries her in Hebron.[68] Her one and only son Isaac figures not at all in the account. He whom she idolized, whose inheritance she protected, but to whom she never spoke recedes for a time. Saved from his own death on the mountain, Isaac neither witnesses the death of his mother nor participates in her burial. Later we learn of his grieving in less than a healthy way. When he takes Rebekah as his wife, he is "comforted after [the death of] his mother" (Gen. 24:67*). If Sarah's death ended her attachment to Isaac, his attachment to her perdures.

Sarah, mother of the chosen heir, dies without being healed of her possessive and exclusionist ways. The last words the Bible allows this matriarch are harsh: "Cast out this slave woman and her son, for the son of this slave woman will not inherit with my son Isaac" (Gen. 21:10). These words set the stage for Hagar's last words, words of weeping for life. "Let me not see the death of the child." In their final discourses, both women speak on behalf of their children. Yet the children hold contrasting places in the departures of their mothers. Hagar, alive in the wilderness, finds an Egyptian wife for her son Ishmael; Sarah, dead in Hebron, remains apart from her son Isaac. In different ways, these women pay the price of patriarchy. Having used them, it abandons through silence the woman it put in the pit and dismisses through death the woman it put on the pedestal. But then, patriarchy devises ways to replenish itself. After all, there *are* other women.

NARRATIVE ENDINGS WITHOUT END

The recent experiences of Abraham—banishing Hagar and Ishmael, almost killing Isaac, and now burying Sarah—hardly seem to mark a happy life. Nonetheless, just after Abraham buys the land in which he buries Sarah (Gen. 23:3–20), the narrator declares that "the Lord had blessed" this old man "in *all* things" (Gen. 24:1; ital. added). The leitmotif of blessing, with which the story began (Gen. 12:2–3), persists through all its twists and turns. Although God and Abraham no longer talk to each other, God continues to bless him.

For almost forty years after the death of Sarah,[69] Abraham prospers. First, he reconnects with his past for the sake of his future. Even as Hagar got a wife for Ishmael from her people, now Abraham sends a servant to his kin to get a wife for Isaac (Gen. 24). Rebekah, the chosen woman, makes possible a third generation and so the continuation of genealogy. Patriarchy replenishes itself. Second, Abraham remarries. The aged man takes a third wife, named Keturah.[70] She bears him six sons who, in time to come, will father tribes in Arabia and Transjordan (Gen. 25:1–6). The older Abraham grows, the more fertile he becomes. For certain, the divine promise that he would be "the ancestor of a multitude of nations" moves toward fulfillment (Gen. 17:5*; cf. Gen. 15:5). The patriarch thrives. Third, Abraham, rich in goods and offspring, settles his affairs. He deeds "all that he has" to Isaac and gives gifts to his other sons, whom he then "sends away" (*šlḥ*) from "his son Isaac" as earlier he "sent away" (*šlḥ*) Ishmael (Gen. 25:6). Dying at the age of 175 years, Abraham has lived a long and full life. The narrator who reported that Yhwh "had blessed Abraham in all things" (Gen. 24:1*) concludes, "Abraham breathed his last and died . . . and was gathered to his people" (Gen. 25:7–8).

His burial is no less blessed. In a precise arrangement of words, the narrator reports that "Isaac and Ishmael his sons" come to honor their father. Both are called "sons," but the order of the nouns puts the younger son, the child of the covenant, ahead of the older, not the child of the covenant. Inequality and equality contend when the brothers meet for the first time since their separation in childhood. The poignancy of their presence as well as their joint action bespeaks reconciliation. Together they bury their father in the cave of Machpelah "with Sarah his wife" (Gen. 25:9–10). Yet even in reconciliation they are divided. The narrator reports, "After the death of Abraham, God blessed Isaac his son" (Gen. 25:11). Nothing is said about a blessing for Ishmael his son (but cf. Gen. 17:20).

Genealogies in Tandem

The story is not ended. The blessing God gives Isaac precedes a list of the descendants of Ishmael, which in turn precedes a report about the descendants of Isaac. Mutatis mutandis, two genealogies conclude this grand narrative (Gen. 25:12–18 and 25:19–20) much as two introduced it (Gen. 11:10–26 and 11:27–32). As the following comparisons show, symmetry with variety marks the relationship between the boundaries.

1. Although not as extensive in content and length, the concluding set corresponds to the opening in its overall presentation. In the opening, the relatively long genealogy of Shem, with its repetitive account of names, led to the short genealogy of Terah, which in turn led into the narrative. In the conclusion, the relatively long genealogy of Ishmael, with its recital of names, leads to the short genealogy of Isaac, which in turn leads into narrative.

2. The first set of genealogies opened with only the names of the founding fathers; they were not identified otherwise. The long one began, "These are the descendants of Shem . . ."; the short one, "These are the descendants of Terah . . ." (Gen. 11:10, 27). One generation flowed smoothly into the next. By contrast, the concluding set of genealogies identifies each founder through his paternal line. The long one begins, "These are the descendants of Ishmael, Abraham's son . . ."; the short one, "These are the descendants of Isaac, Abraham's son . . ." (Gen. 25:12, 19). Staying within a single generation, this second set juxtaposes two distinct lines stemming from Abraham. Unlike the first set, they do not flow one into the other. The difference between them lies with the mothers Hagar and Sarah, whose names and relationships will soon surface.

3. In the first set, the genealogy of Terah contained the crucial information of Sarai's barrenness. In the second set, the genealogy of Ishmael contains information crucial to his treatment. It begins with a description of both his legitimacy and his otherness:

> These are the descendants of Ishmael, son of Abraham, whom Hagar the Egyptian, the slave of Sarah, bore to Abraham. (Gen. 25:12*)

The description recognizes Ishmael as Abraham's legitimate son but in two ways underscores his subordinate status: His mother is both foreigner and slave. Ignored altogether is Hagar's status as second wife to Abraham (cf. Gen. 16:3).

From another perspective, however, the reference to Hagar as Egyptian holds promise. It evokes her role in finding an Egyptian wife for her son (cf. Gen. 21:21) and so makes possible his genealogy.

Promises Fulfilled

The names of Ishmael's sons follow the reference to his mother and father (Gen. 25:13–16). Twelve princes are they, according to their tribes. This information recalls God's promise long ago to Abraham when God rejected Ishmael as the son of the covenant.

> As for Ishmael [i.e., God hears], I have heard you.
> Behold, I will bless him and I will make him fruitful;
> and I will increase him in the much of muchness.
> Twelve princes he will father;
> and I will give [make] him into a nation great.
> (Gen. 17:20*)

The emphatic particle "behold" (*hinnēh*) calls attention to the blessing. The three verbs that follow (bless, make, increase), each in the first-person singular of the deity and each with the independent pronoun "him" (*ôtô*) as object, accent the magnitude of the blessing and Ishmael as its recipient. The phrase "the much of muchness" heightens the accent. It leads into the report of the twelve princes whom Ishmael will father. Then, returning to the first-person singular of the deity ("I will give"), the last line reiterates the blessing in a striking way. God uses for Ishmael the phrase "a nation great" (*gôy gādôl*), the same phrase that Yhwh used in the call and promise of blessing to Abraham (Gen. 12:2).

What God promised long ago to Abraham has now come to pass. Twelve princes fathered by Ishmael give stability, order, continuity, and status to his line. Even though the verb "bless" does not attend Ishmael (unlike Isaac) here in the narrative of Abraham's death (Gen. 25:11), its earlier use for Ishmael reverberates in his many descendants (cf. Gen. 17:20). God has kept faith with the promise.

Having reported the fulfillment of God's promise, the genealogy of Ishmael yields to his obituary. It employs the formula used for his father's death (cf. Gen. 25:7–8). "This is the length of Ishmael's life, one hundred and thirty-seven years; he breathed his last and died and was gathered unto his people" (Gen. 25:17). Although the place of his burial is unrecorded, surely the wilderness, which provided him a deathbed in his youth and a home in his adult life, now receives this aged man unto itself. Abundant progeny, long life, a good death, and an assured future through descendants: Ishmael, rejected as the son of the covenant, is nonetheless blessed.[71]

His sons mirror the blessing. They "settled from Havilah to Shur that is near the border of Egypt . . ." (Gen. 25:18).[72] The latter site links them to Hagar, their grandmother, who reached a spring on the way to Shur in her flight from Sarai (Gen. 16:7). With an Egyptian grandmother and a Hebrew grandfather, the grandsons, eponymous ancestors of the Arabians, live on the boundaries of settled nations and peoples. This tantalizing detail about their location evokes the past and promises the future as it ends the genealogy of Ishmael.

The parallel yet contrasting genealogy of Isaac follows (Gen. 25:19–20). Unlike Ishmael, he is not identified by both father and mother. Instead, through redundancy and the use of anadiplosis (i.e., the last word of one clause beginning the following clause), the report accents only his paternal line. "These are the descendants of Isaac, son of Abraham. Abraham begot Isaac" (Gen. 25:19*). The omission of Sarah is noteworthy because the legitimacy of Isaac as the chosen heir depended on her. She who embodied the tragic flaw at the beginning here at the end receives no recognition in the happy outcome. The indispensable mother is disposable. Indeed, her daughter-in-law replaces her as the genealogy moves into narrative: "Isaac was forty when he took Rebekah . . ." (Gen. 25:20).

In content and length the genealogies of the sons of Abraham yield different messages. The first and long genealogy finishes Ishmael's story; the second and short one but begins Isaac's. So the text follows its bias, but not without nuances and nods in other directions.

CONCLUSION AND CONTINUATION

In twists and turns a narrator has told stories about blessing. The divine character God (sometimes as a messenger) and five human characters (Hagar, Sarah, Abraham, Ishmael, and Isaac), plus a supporting cast, populate these stories. Within them, manipulations, machinations, and malice abound alongside suffering, compassion, and faithfulness. In conclusion, from the distance of centuries, cultures, and perspectives, we comment on four topics: the narrator's purview, portrayals of God, portrayals of humans, and complexities of relationships.[73]

The Narrator's Purview

With economy of language, the narrator weaves multiple and diverse traditions into a coherent story of surprise and suspense. With little attention to psychological analysis, the narrator presents the characters as types and individuals. With a variety of techniques, the narrator stands apart from the characters in places and in other places adopts their viewpoints.[74] With forthright honesty, the narrator depicts a panorama of portraits, from the horrendous to the honorable.

Throughout this multifaceted narrative, the intertwined, though not inseparable, mandates of patriarchy and covenant prevail. As a general worldview, patriarchy surrounds and permeates the text.[75] The narrator does not invent this androcentric bias but rather is captive to it, along with all the characters. As a distinctive worldview, covenant marks the particularities of the story. The narrator shapes, controls, and promotes covenant. If patriarchy is given, covenant is chosen.

Although focused on the special relationship God makes with Abraham, the narrator limits use of the word "covenant." The first use comes at the close of the vision (Gen. 15:1–21) in which Yhwh reassures Abraham that his descendants will be as numerous as the stars. "On that day," we read, "the Lord made a covenant with Abraham" (Gen. 15:18). The second use constitutes a cluster of twelve references, three of them with the adjective "everlasting" preceding the noun (Gen. 17:1–27).[76] All twelve occur in a lengthy speech by God. Apart from introducing sections of the speech, the narrator remains silent, providing no commentary. After this cluster, the narrator never again uses the word "covenant" to describe the special relationship between God and Abraham.[77] Instead, the narrator anchors the stories with blessing.

Within blessing the narrator allows the problems of patriarchy and covenant to unfold. The components include a chosen man (Abraham, not Nahor or Haran); the right wife as property (Sarah, not Hagar); pure progeny (Isaac, not Ishmael); the promised land (Canaan, not Mesopotamia or Egypt); and restricted inheritance (to Isaac, not Ishmael). Patriarchy and covenant produce the outsider and the insider, the superior and the inferior, the accepted and the rejected. In exposing the problems of the mandates, the point of view of the narrator shifts. Sympathetic portrayals of Pharaoh, Hagar, and Ishmael, for instance, feed the ambiguities of the narrative to suggest meanings in tension with the dominant story line.

Portrayals of God

Within the narrator's story, framed by genealogies, the character God initiates and directs much of the action. The deity's modes of communication vary: direct speech to the human characters, mediated speech through messengers, and indirect speech reported through third-person narration. The deity's purpose (not fully achieved) is blessing for Abraham (Gen. 12:1–3) and Sarah (Gen. 17:15–16) that extends to all the families of the earth. With divine blessing come the promise of land and the making of covenant.

In pursuing the divine purpose, God behaves in diverse, indeed conflicted, ways toward both the chosen and the other. This deity afflicts innocent Pharaoh and lets guilty Abraham go free (Gen. 12:17–20); consigns Hagar to affliction while heeding her affliction (Gen. 16:7–12); excludes Ishmael from the covenant while blessing him (Gen. 17:18–21); reprimands Sarah for disbelief while designating her the only woman who can bear the son of the covenant (Gen. 18:13–15); favors the rich (Abraham and Sarah) over the poor (Hagar and Ishmael), the masters over the slaves, while giving comfort, care, and life to these outcasts; allows Ishmael almost to die before rescuing him with water (Gen. 21:15–20); abuses the chosen-child Isaac and then spares him (Gen. 22). Truly, compassion and cruelty contend within the character God. These "competing impulses" go unresolved, even if the overall tilt is toward blessing.[78]

Portrayals of Humans

Although God is the controlling character, the human characters also initiate and direct action. Abraham proposes the ruse to protect himself when he and Sarah enter Egypt; much later, he alone negotiates with the Hittites to purchase a family burial place (Gen. 12:10–13; 23:3–18). Sarai proposes the scheme to get a son by Hagar; she positions herself at the tent entrance to eavesdrop on the conversation between her husband and strangers (Gen. 16:1–2; 18:9–15). Hagar makes her own exodus from oppression; she even names God in direct address; and she secures a wife for her son (Gen. 16:6, 13; 21:21). Ishmael and Isaac, often the objects of actions by others, nonetheless appear on their own to bury Abraham (Gen. 25:9).

Individually and collectively, these characters, male and female, model diversity. Coming from Mesopotamia and Egypt, but focused on Canaan, they belong to different ethnic groups, social classes, ages, and professions. As individuals, they represent types.[79] The exalted father Abraham is also the compliant husband. He acts as wimp and pimp. He is the conniving husband, abuser husband and father, solicitous father, shrewd businessman, and faithful worshiper.[80] The princess Sarah is both tool and tyrant. She is the object of patriarchy, abused wife, afflicter of slaves, possessive mother, cruel matriarch, indispensable and disposable woman.

Like Sarah, Hagar is the object of patriarchy, but, unlike Sarah, she is also the object of matriarchy. Suffering slave, surrogate mother, expelled wife, freed slave, single mother, resident alien, tenacious survivor, and astute planner, she is woman of strength and theologian of insight. Ishmael, heard by God, is beloved son, expelled son, and dying child. He becomes a mighty huntsman, prince and chieftain, successful father, and faithful son to the father who abandoned him. Isaac of laughter is the pampered, abused, and compliant child; the faithful son to the father who almost killed him; the mother's boy who becomes the loving husband (cf. Gen. 24:67). Various combinations of roles and qualities result in complex characters who, given the conventional constraints of biblical narratives, are never fully developed.

Complexities of Relationships

Relationships among the characters of this extended family work in diverse ways. Abraham abuses his wife Sarah and also obeys her. Sarah models the patriarchal wife and orders her husband around. Sarah uses and abuses her slave Hagar. Abraham marries Hagar and has a son by her, only to divorce her at the command of Sarah and expel her and their son from the household. Hagar suffers under Sarah, seeks freedom, returns to captivity, and then recaptures freedom in expulsion. Although rejected in the dominant narrative, Hagar and Ishmael find fulfilling life in the wilderness. She chooses her son's wife; he produces abundant offspring. In addition, Ishmael eventually reconciles with his father; he joins his half-brother to bury Abraham. And the report of Ishmael's own death indicates that his offspring continue the legacy of his mother in the land of Shur (cf. Gen. 16:7; 25:18).

By contrast, Sarah dies apart from the son she so fiercely protected. She is also separated from the husband who abused her in Egypt, the husband whom she dominated, and the husband who did not return to her just after he nearly sacrificed their son. Sarah dies unhealed of jealousy, envy, rivalry, and malice toward Hagar and Ishmael. Yet, with her death, whatever distance developed between her and Abraham fades for him. He comes to Hebron to mourn and weep for her. Then, arising "from beside his dead," he debates at length the purchase of a burial site. At last, Abraham "buries Sarah his wife . . ." (Gen. 23). Thereafter he cares for her one and only son. He orders his servant to find a wife for Isaac among his kinfolk. In so doing, he reclaims Isaac as his own, referring five times to "my son."[81] As Abraham made peace with Sarah in death, so in life he makes peace with Isaac.

A happy resolution for Isaac, however, comes but gradually. After his sparing on the mountain, he drops from the narrative. He does not return with Abraham (Gen. 22:19). Nor is he present at the death and burial of his mother. His absence suggests estrangement from both parents. Further, Isaac plays no role in the finding of Rebekah as a wife for him. At the conclusion of that search, his responses, which come only through the narrator, signal danger as well as tenderness. If bringing Rebekah "into the tent of Sarah his mother" (Gen. 24:67) signifies Rebekah's new role as the matriarch in the family,[82] it also echoes the old attachment between Sarah and Isaac. Simply and eloquently, the narrator says, Isaac "loved [ʾhb] her [Rebekah]."[83] Yet that sentiment evokes the language of attachment in the near-sacrifice of Isaac (Gen. 22:2): "your son, your only son, whom you love [ʾhb]." Only in these two texts does the verb "love" appear in the narrative of this family. The closing sentence about Isaac's marriage reinforces the problem: "So Isaac was comforted after [the death of] his mother" (Gen. 24:67). If this story heals the hurts between Isaac and his parents, it likewise suggests a less-than-healthy beginning for his marriage.

How that marriage, including the subsequent arrival of twin sons, unfolds lies beyond the scope of this study (cf. Gen. 25:19–35:29). Suffice it to say that familial conflicts continue unabated until in Hebron (where his mother had died and was buried and where he and his father had resided as aliens) Isaac, at the age of 180 years, "breathed his last and died and was gathered to his people, old and full of days" (Gen. 35:27–29). This obituary follows the formula used for Abraham and for Ishmael. Moreover, as Isaac and Ishmael, sons of Abraham, buried their father, so Esau and Jacob, sons of Isaac, bury their father. From generation to generation patriarchy cares for its own.

Although as children Isaac and Ishmael play together (cf. Gen. 21:9), their lives diverge thereafter. Not until the death of their father do they reunite. Though together they bury him, they do not speak to each other. For Ishmael, the occasion signifies reunion with the father who abandoned him to the wilderness; for Isaac, reunion with the father who raised the knife to kill him on the mountain. Accordingly, the story joins other narratives to offer tenderness, comfort, and even reconciliation.[84] But it also revives painful memories.

Completely unresolved throughout the entire account is the conflict between Sarah and Hagar. This troubling and haunting situation involves nationality, ethnicity, class, gender, progeny, and the struggle for inheritance and land. Unlike their husband and their sons and unlike their relationships to their husband and sons, these women have no place in the text *as it stands* for resolving their plight. Both are caught within patriarchy but in different places. Both are covenant controlled but with different outcomes. Both exercise power but in different degrees and different contexts. Both "see" but from different perspectives. Living in similar yet different worlds, they struggle with each other—and that struggle persists throughout centuries to this day.

Sarah's harsh, last words hover in the air of hatred. "Cast out this slave woman and her son, for the son of this slave woman will not inherit with my son Isaac" (Gen. 21:10). Soon thereafter this embittered and triumphal woman dies. Hagar's poignant, last words hover in the air of lament: "Let me not look on the death of the child" (Gen. 21:16). Of the five human characters, she is the only one for whom God does not use the word "bless" and the only one not carried through to death. Scripture accords her no blessed life and no resting place.

Yet strikingly, Scripture gives Hagar a host of other distinctions. She is the first person in the Bible to flee oppression; the first runaway slave; the first person whom a messenger of God visits; the first woman to receive an annunciation; the only woman to receive a divine promise of descendants; the only person to name God; the first woman in the ancestor stories to bear a child; the first surrogate mother; the first slave to be freed; the first divorced wife; the first single parent; and the first person to weep. Given all these distinctions, Hagar haunts the biblical narrative and its afterlife in ways that the other characters do not.[85]

Patriarchy, promise, covenant; manipulation, machinations, malice; blessing, compassion, and faithfulness. Coming from an ancient past to our contemporary world, these weighty matters press in upon us. The stories we have explored are not finished, as we know and fear daily. All the children of Abraham and of Sarah and Hagar—Jews, Christians, and Muslims—find themselves afflicted with the iniquities and sufferings of their parents, well beyond the third and fourth generations. To say that we have the same father does not settle our relationships but rather commences our problems. Our different mothers offset the putative unity of our one father. Yet reckoning with the stories of these women has hardly begun.

The reckoning embraces familial and interfaith relationships. The biblical narrative shows that the former are fraught with peril—for both the nuclear family (Abraham, Sarah, and Isaac) and those whom it rejects (Hagar and Ishmael).[86] Likewise, the narrative shows that interfaith relationships are difficult to achieve. To value one partner over another (e.g., Sarah and Isaac over Hagar and Ishmael), conformity over difference, and privilege over responsibility produces counterfeit dialogue. It risks turning blessing into curse.

Who will deliver Sarah from the pedestal and Hagar from the pit? Who will save them, Abraham, and God from patriarchy? Who will redeem their children Ishmael and Isaac? When will the blessing for all the families of the earth overturn the curse? From ominous beginnings in the biblical narrative, the questions persist. The answers may come, at least in part, through our wrestling with this ancient text. For certain, these things we know: Only we, the children of Hagar and Sarah, can undo the mess wrought by God and our parents. Only we can appropriate the glimpses of grace offered by God and our parents. Only we can make the blessing work. But the hour is late, and we are not saved.

Notes

1. On the place of genealogies in the Bible, see Robert R. Wilson, *Genealogy and History in the Biblical World* (New Haven, CT: Yale Near Eastern Researches, 1977); Marshall D. Johnson, *The Purpose of the Biblical Genealogies*, 2nd ed. (Cambridge: Cambridge University Press, 1988). On "the idiom of genealogy" as representing the past in the present and pointing toward the future, see Ronald Hendel, *Remembering Abraham: Culture, Memory, and History in the Hebrew Bible* (Oxford: Oxford University Press, 2005), 33–43.
2. Despite the anthropological critique of the use of the word "patriarchy" by Carol Meyers, feminist writers continue to employ it to describe a male-centered and male-dominated society. Cf. Meyers, *Discovering Eve: Ancient Israelite Women in Context* (New York: Oxford University Press, 1988), 24–46. Note that older generations of male scholars used the word to identify the stories of the founding fathers in Gen. 12–36; see, e.g., "The Age of the Patriarchs" in John Bright, *A History of Israel*, 3rd ed. (Philadelphia: Westminster Press, 1981), 45–103.
3. Unless indicated otherwise, biblical quotations come from the New Revised Standard Version. My own translations, often modifications of the NRSV in order to adhere to Hebrew syntax, are marked by an asterisk (*).
4. Cf., e.g., Gen. 25:21; 30:1–2; Judg. 13:2–3; 1 Sam. 1:1–8.
5. For Abram's dealings with Lot, see Gen. 12:4; 13:1–13; 14:12–14; 19:1–38; for Abram's connections to Nahor, see Gen. 22:20; 24:15, 24. Bethuel, the son of Nahor and Milcah, becomes the father of Rebekah, who marries Abraham's son Isaac (Gen. 24:45–47).
6. This essay develops a literary reading of the narrative as it now appears. Yet the narrative itself is a compilation of sources usually designated J, E, D, P. These diverse sources may well account for inconsistencies and contradictions throughout the whole. The primary interest here is to interpret such phenomena within the integrity of the final form as editors and canonizers have shaped it. For a recent literary reading that pays attention to the sources behind the text, see, e.g., Jon Levenson, *The Death and Resurrection of the Beloved Son* (New Haven, CT: Yale University Press, 1993), esp. 55–142.
7. For a classic study, see James Muilenburg, "Abraham and the Nations," *Interpretation* 19 (October 1965): 387–98; also Hans Walter Wolff, "The Kerygma of the Yahwist," in *The Vitality of Old Testament Traditions*, ed. Walter Brueggemann and Hans Walter Wolff (Atlanta: John Knox Press, 1975), 41–66.
8. On this translation, see Patrick D. Miller Jr., "Syntax and Theology in Genesis XII 3a," *Vetus Testamentum* 24 (October 1984): 472–75. Theologically, the move from the plural, "I will bless those who bless you," to the singular, "the one despis-

ing you I will curse," (a move present in the Masoretic Text) is striking. It exalts blessing over curse in envisioning responses to the call of Abram. Further, the use of two different verbs—"despise" (or "hold in low esteem") (*qll*) and "curse" (*ʾrr*)—in this second line (not recognized in the NRSV) does not constitute a curse formula and so again softens the message in contrast to the blessing of the first line. On the curse formula, see Josef Scharbert, "*ʾrr*," *Theological Dictionary of the Old Testament*, vol. 1, ed. G. Johannes Botterweck and Helmer Ringgren (Grand Rapids: Wm. B. Eerdmans Publishing Co., 1974), esp. 408–13. In his recent translation, Robert Alter, though acknowledging that the MT has the singular pronoun, nonetheless renders the second line "and *those* [ital. mine] who damn you I will curse." Noting that the plural form occurs in some ancient texts, he argues literarily that it "makes better sense as parallelism" to the first line, which he renders, "and I will bless those who bless you." But the parallelism of contrast between the plural and singular pronoun objects, with their attendant theological message, Alter seems not to consider. See *The Five Books of Moses* (New York: W. W. Norton & Co., 2004), 62–63. By contrast, Everett Fox adheres to the Masoretic Text: "I will bless those who bless you;// he who curses you, I will damn." See *The Five Books of Moses* (New York: Schocken Books, 1995), 55. (Hereafter in referring to these translations, as distinct from the commentaries that accompany them, I shall use only the names of the translators, Alter and Fox, and not cite the page numbers on which the translations appear.)

9. On blessing, see the classic treatment by Johannes Pedersen, *Israel: Its Life and Culture, I and II* (London: Geoffrey Cumberlege, 1926), 182–212; cf. Claus Westermann, *Blessing: In the Bible and the Life of the Church* (Philadelphia: Fortress Press, 1978); C. W. Mitchell, *The Meaning of BRK "To Bless" in the Old Testament* (Atlanta: SBL Dissertation Series, 1987).

10. For a date in the tenth century BCE, see Wolff, *The Vitality of Old Testament Traditions*, 43–45; Robert B. Coote and David Robert Ord, *The Bible's First History* (Philadelphia: Fortress Press, 1989), 1–7; for the eighth and seventh centuries, see Israel Finkelstein and Neil Asher Silberman, *The Bible Unearthed* (New York: Free Press, 2001), 33–38; William M. Schniedewind, *How the Bible Became a Book: The Textualization of Ancient Israel* (New York: Cambridge University Press, 2004), esp. 81–84; for the sixth century, see John Van Seters, *Abraham in History and Tradition* (New Haven, CT: Yale University Press, 1975), esp. 269–78; 309–12; for the fifth and fourth centuries, see Philip R. Davies, *In Search of 'Ancient Israel'* (Sheffield: Sheffield Academic Press, 1995), 72–89; cf. Finkelstein and Silberman, *The Bible Unearthed*, 310–12. Most recently, Ronald Hendel projects that some (few) parts of the Abrahamic traditions may date from the midsecond millennium BCE; that the traditions crystallized in the tenth century; and that they were written down in the eighth century (*Remembering Abraham: Culture, Memory and History in the Hebrew Bible* [Oxford: Oxford University Press, 2005], 45–55; 131 n. 14).

11. Abram's silent and obedient response is often viewed as a model of faith. See Hebrews 6:13–15; 11:8–12 (which also cites Sarah as a model of faith); cf. B. Davie Napier, *From Faith to Faith* (New York: Harper & Row, 1955), 60–71. A contrary reading views the response as nonassertive, even "wimpish." For certain, it contrasts with later responses by Moses (Exod. 3 and 4), Jeremiah (Jer. 1:4–10), and Jonah (Jon. 1:1–3), even as it may resonate with the eagerness of Isaiah of Jerusalem (Isa. 6:8).

12. The contrast between "woman" and "wife" (cf. translations of Gen. 12:11) is more stable in English than in Hebrew. The latter uses only the one word *ʾissa* for both meanings. The distinction between "woman" and "wife" depends, then, on context and is subject also to the judgments of translators. But the distinction

between "woman" or "wife," on the one hand, and "sister" (*ʾaḥot*), on the other, holds fast in Hebrew.

13. Given both meanings of the word *ʾissa* (woman and wife), one finds irony in exactly whom the Egyptian officials see.

14. Cf., e.g., NRSV, NAB, REB, NJB, and Fox and Alter (cited above, n. 8).

15. See Fokkelien van Dijk-Hemmes, "Sarai's Exile: A Gender-Motivated Reading of Genesis 12.10–13.2," in *A Feminist Companion to Genesis*, ed. Althalya Brenner (Sheffield: Sheffield Academic Press, 1993), esp. 230–33. The essay is reprinted under the title "Sarai in Exile: A Gender-Specific Reading of Genesis 12:10–13:2" in *The Double Voice of Her Desire*, ed. J. Bekkenkamp and F. Droes; trans. D. E. Orton (Leiden: Deo, 2004), 136–45.

16. Note that the same phrase occurs in the parallel story of Abraham and Sarah in Gerar: God closed the wombs of the house of Abimelech "because of the word [*l dbr*] of Sarah his wife" (Gen. 20:18*).

17. Although Alter drops the term *dbr* in his translation, he considers the possibility of "a tense exchange between Pharoah [*sic*] and Sarai ending in a confession by Sarai of her status as Abram's wife" (Alter, *The Five Books of Moses*, 65 n. 17). Rather than "a confession," however, her *dbr* might signal a scream or cry for help to Yhwh (so van Dijk-Hemmes, "Sarai's Exile," 231–32) or a speaking out against the situation (cf. the next paragraph in the text).

18. On parallels between the story of Sarah and Abraham and the story of Eve and Adam (Gen. 2–3), see Joel Rosenberg, *King and Kin: Political Allegory in the Hebrew Bible* (Bloomington: Indiana University Press, 1986), 93–98. He proposes that the story of Sarah and Abraham "has the character of a transgression." See also Levenson, *The Death and Resurrection of the Beloved Son*, 91–110. Further, for parallels between Gen. 12 and the narrative of the exodus, see Michael Fishbane, *Biblical Interpretation in Ancient Israel* (Oxford: Clarendon Press, 1985), 375–76.

19. So abrupt is Pharoah's order that it omits the direct object "her" after the imperative "take." The omission contrasts with Pharoah's use of the same verb with an object in the preceding sentence: "I took her" (Gen. 12:19). On this "impatient brusqueness," see Alter, *The Five Books of Moses*, 65 n. 19. For a parallel construction, also involving an abused woman, see Judg. 19:25b.

20. Jewish legend says that Hagar was the daughter of Pharoah (royalty, no less). He gave her to Sarai (who herself bears the royal name "princess") when she was in Egypt; see Louis Ginzberg, *Legends of the Bible* (Philadelphia: Jewish Publication Society of America, 1968), 108. Though not specifically relating Hagar to Pharoah, contemporary scholars also suggest that she came out of Egypt with Abram and Sarai; see, e.g., Terence E. Fretheim, "The Book of Genesis," *The New Interpreter's Bible*, vol. 1, ed. Leander E. Keck (Nashville: Abingdon Press, 1994), 454.

21. Parts of this discussion draw on my essay "Hagar: The Desolation of Rejection," in Trible, *Texts of Terror* (Philadelphia: Fortress Press, 1984), 9–20. Since its publication, women from diverse ethnic, religious, and cultural contexts have written about Hagar and Sarai. Varying in quality and point of view, these essays include the following: Elsa Tamez, "The Woman Who Complicated the History of Salvation," in *New Eyes for Reading: Biblical and Theological Reflections by Women from the Third World*, ed. John S. Pobee and Barbel von Wartenberg-Potter (Geneva: World Council of Churches, 1986), 5–17; Renita J. Weems, "A Mistress, a Maid, and No Mercy," in *Just a Sister Away* (San Diego, CA: Lura-Media, 1988), 1–21; Jo Ann Hackett, "Rehabilitating Hagar: Fragments of an Epic Pattern," in *Gender and Difference in Ancient Israel*, ed. Peggy L. Day (Minneapolis: Fortress Press, 1989), 12–27; Katheryn Pfisterer Darr, "More than the

Stars of Heaven: Critical, Rabbinical, and Feminist Perspectives on Sarah" and "More than a Possession: Critical, Rabbinical, and Feminist Perspectives on Hagar," in *Far More Precious than Jewels: Perspectives on Biblical Women* (Louisville, KY: Westminster/John Knox Press, 1991), 85–131 and 132–63; Devora Steinmetz, *From Father to Son: Literary Currents in Biblical Interpretation* (Louisville, KY: Westminster/John Knox Press, 1991), 72–78; Dora R. Mbuwayesango, "Childlessness and Woman-To-Woman Relationships in Genesis and African Patriarchal Society: Sarah and Hagar from a Zimbabwean Woman's Perspective (Gen. 16:1–16; 21:8–21)," in *Semeia* 78, ed. Phyllis A. Bird (Society of Biblical Literature, 1997), 27–36; Wilma Ann Bailey, "Black and Jewish Women Consider Hagar," *Encounter* 63 (2002): 37–44; Tikva Frymer-Kensky, "Hagar, My Other, My Self," in *Reading the Women of the Bible* (New York: Schocken Books, 2002), 225–37; Amy-Jill Levine, "Settling at Beer-lahai-roi," in *Daughters of Abraham: Feminist Thought in Judaism, Christianity, and Islam*, ed. Yvonne Yazbeck Haddad and John L. Esposito (Gainesville: University of Florida Press, 2002), 12–34; Katharine Doob Sakenfeld, "Sarah and Hagar: Power and Privileges," in *Just Wives? Stories of Power & Survival in the Old Testament & Today* (Louisville, KY: Westminster John Knox Press, 2003), 7–25.

22. See, e.g., Claus Westermann, *Genesis 12–36: A Commentary* (Minneapolis: Augsburg Publishing House, 1981), 238–39.

23. The verb translated "became slight" (*qll*) connotes loss of esteem or status. Cf. Westermann, *Genesis*, 240. For translations similar to the one offered here, see, e.g., the NJB, Fox, Alter, and Levenson, *The Death and Birth of the Beloved Son*, 92. These translations follow closely the Hebrew vocabulary and syntax. Other translations modify both, seemingly to disparage Hagar and justify Sarai's response. For example, the NRSV reads, "[W]hen she [Hagar] saw that she had conceived, she looked with contempt on her mistress." Cf. also the NEB, NAB.

24. See, e.g., the stories reported in Sakenfeld, *Just Wives?* 7–25.

25. For a defense of Sarai as following law in the Mesopotamian Code of Hammurapi, see Savina J. Teubel, *Sarah the Priestess: The First Matriarch of Genesis* (Athens, OH: Swallow Press, 1984), 33–36.

26. See W. Sibley Towner, *Genesis* (Louisville, KY: Westminster John Knox Press, 2001), 160. Towner proposes that the significance of the place name Shur may be "its similarity to a Hebrew verb *shur*, meaning to see."

27. For this observation, see Martin Buber, *On the Bible* (New York: Schocken Books, 1969), 39.

28. The promise "I will so greatly multiply . . ." (*harbâ 'arbeh*, Gen. 16:10) appears in only two other places: Yhwh's judgment to the primal woman (Gen. 3:16) and Yhwh's promise to Abraham after the near-sacrifice of Isaac (Gen. 22:17). Levenson suggests that here Hagar becomes a counterpart to Eve (*The Death and Resurrection of the Beloved Son*, 93–94).

29. For Levenson, the command to "suffer affliction" (Gen. 16:9) counters the generalization that God has "a preferential option for the poor." Yet in the divine words that follow (Gen. 16:10ff.) he does detect "something not altogether dissimilar to the 'preferential option for the poor . . .'" (*The Death and Resurrection of the Beloved Son*, 93–94).

30. In discussing secondary meanings of words, Shimon Bar-Efrat takes the phrase "wild ass of a man" (*pere' 'adam*) to mean in this context "that the son would be a free man, independent like the nomadic tribes of the desert, not a slave like his mother" (cf. Job 39:5–8); see Shimon Bar-Efrat, *Narrative Art in the Bible* (Sheffield: Almond, 1989), 206–7.

31. The Bible speaks with ambivalence about "seeing" God. Relevant passages include Jacob's declaration of seeing God face to face, but in the darkness of night

(Gen. 32:30); the report that Moses, Aaron, Nadab, and Abihu "see" (*r'h*) and "behold" (*ḥzh*) God in dazzling light (Exod. 24:9–11); God's warning to Moses that "you cannot see [*r'h*] my face, for no one shall see me and live" (Exod. 33:20); prophetic proclamations of seeing (*r'h*) the Lord by Isaiah (in the temple filled with smoke, Isa. 6:1, 5) and by Micaiah (1 Kgs. 22:19); Job's affirmation contrasting the hearing of God with "now my eye sees [*r'h*] you" (Job 42:5). On this subject, see (!), *inter alia*, Samuel Terrien, *The Elusive Presence: Toward a New Biblical Theology* (New York: Harper & Row, 1978), 106–60, 227–77.

32. Source critics assign Gen. 17 to the priestly tradition; see, e.g. Westermann, *Genesis*, 256. As an external sign of the covenant, circumcision would restrict the relationship to males who bond with God. But the sign and so the restriction are absent from the report in Gen. 15 about the Abrahamic covenant, a report that belongs to the Jahwist source. Placed after the birth of Ishmael (Gen. 16) and before the birth of Isaac (Gen. 21), Abraham's circumcision in Gen. 17 makes a difference for his two sons. Ishmael (who himself is circumcised at the age of thirteen, Gen. 17:25) is conceived and born outside the circumcised covenant, and Isaac, within it. Abraham's circumcision would appear to introduce, if not induce, the fertility of Sarah, who will bear the child of the covenant.

33. The names Abram and Abraham and Sarai and Sarah are but dialectical variants. Although their appearance indicates diverse sources behind the text, the change from one to the other serves theological import within the final form. By making an everlasting covenant, God establishes a new relationship with Abraham and Sarah; hence, their names change.

34. Cf. "no, but" (NRSV) and "yes, but" (Victor P. Hamilton, *The Book of Genesis: Chapters 1–17* [Grand Rapids: Wm. B. Eerdmans Publishing Co., 1990], 476; cf. also "nevertheless" (NJB, NAB, Fox); "truly" (Fisher); "yet" (Alter).

35. For this translation, see Loren Fisher, *Genesis, A Royal Epic: Introduction, Translation and Notes* (Bridgewater, NJ: Replica Books, 2001), 115; cf. Fox, *The Five Books of Moses*, 77, which reads, "No, indeed you laughed." Other translations convert the Hebrew particle *lō'* (not) into the positive, thereby losing Yhwh's repetition of Sarah's speech; e.g., the NRSV, "Oh yes, you did laugh;" similarly, NJB, NAB, and Alter.

36. On the meaning of Sarah's laugh and God's response, scholars differ. Traditional (male) interpreters have read it as human disbelief and divine rebuke: e.g., Brueggemann, *Genesis*, 158–59; Westermann, *Genesis*, 281; Victor P. Hamilton, *The Book of Genesis: Chapters 18–50* (Grand Rapids: Wm. B. Eerdmans Publishing Co., 1995), 12–13 (though he does allow for a more benign rendering); Alter, *The Five Books of Moses*, 12. With such interpretations I agree. On the other hand, positive readings have surfaced among male and female scholars: e.g., Fretheim, who, without commenting on the differences between the two accounts, finds "it unlikely that God would be critical of Sarah if not of Abraham in 17:19" ("Genesis," 463–65); also van Dijk-Hemmes, who finds hope in the laugh ("And Sarah Laughed: Exegetical Thoughts on the Biblical Story of Sarah," in Bekkenkamp and Droes, eds., *The Double Voice of Her Desire*, 45–51).

37. For theological reflections on the biblical motif of laughter as focused on the Isaac stories, see Joel S. Kaminsky, "Humor and the Theology of Hope: Isaac as a Humorous Figure," *Interpretation* 54 (October 2000): 363–75.

38. Parts of this discussion draw on my essay "Hagar: The Desolation of Rejection," in Trible, *Texts of Terror*, 20–29.

39. The verb also means "playing." Using this meaning, certain translations, beginning with the Greek Bible and the Vulgate, add the phrase "with her son Isaac." That addition, plus the alternative meaning of "fondle" for the verb (cf. Gen. 26:8), leads some interpreters to find here "an incident of incestuous child

molestation" and so account for the harsh command of Sarah; see Jonathan Kirsch, "What Did Sarah See?" *Bible Review* (October 1998): 2, 49. On the many interpretations of the phrase, see Trible, *Texts of Terror*, 33 n. 44, and Alter, *The Five Books of Moses*, 103. See also Hamilton, *The Book of Genesis: Chapters 18–50*, 78–79.

40. Cf. Gen. 19:14, where this word (*mesaheq*) connotes mocking, joking, or jesting.

41. So Alter, *The Five Books of Moses*, 103.

42. For a positive interpretation of Sarah's "severity" that views her as granting freedom to a slave woman and child (an act that conforms to the ancient Mesopotamian Code of Lipit Ishtar), see Teubal, *Sarah the Priestess*, 37–40.

43. Cf. the use of "eyes" in Gen. 16:4, 5, 6.

44. See Phyllis Trible, *God and the Rhetoric of Sexuality* (Philadelphia: Fortress Press, 1978), 128–29.

45. See Hamilton, *Genesis: Chapters 18–50*, 82–83.

46. NRSV and Fox translate "cast"; Alter, "flung"; NJB, "left"; and Fisher, "abandoned." On the proposal offered here, see Hamilton, 83.

47. See Hamilton, 76, 83; cf. NIV, "sat down nearby, about a bowshot away." For translations accenting distance, see, e.g., NRSV, NJB, Alter and Fox.

48. The word "cohortative" means the first-person indirect imperative; in this case, "Let me not look. . . ."

49. The second character is Abraham, who weeps (*bkh*) at the death of Sarah (Gen. 23:2). The third is Esau, who "lifts up his voice and weeps [*bkh*]" when cheated out of his birthright. On parallels between Esau and Hagar, see Phyllis Trible, "Beholding Esau," in *Hineini in Our Lives*, ed. Norman J. Cohen (Woodstock, VT: Jewish Lights Publishing, 2003), 169–74.

50. The abrupt shift has led some translators (e.g., RSV, NAB) to alter the text to read, "The child lifted up his voice and wept." For this alteration there is no warrant.

51. Cf. above on Gen. 21:9 for another possible "voice" of Ishmael.

52. For "son" and "lad" before the danger, see Gen. 21:9, 10, 11, 12, 13; for "child" in the danger, see Gen. 21:14, 15, 16; for "lad" after the danger, see Gen. 21:17, 18, 19, 20.

53. In noting that biblical storytellers prefer reporting actions to probing feelings, Hermann Gunkel says, "How could a mother's love be better shown than in the story of Hagar?—she gave her son a drink (Gen. 21:19), it is not said that she herself drank." See *The Stories of Genesis*, trans. John J. Scullion (Vallejo, CA: BIBAL Press, 1994, originally published in German in 1910), 42–44.

54. Identified in Gen. 21:21 as "the wilderness of Paran," this site probably lay south of the kingdom Judah and north of the wilderness of Sinai (cf. Num. 10:11–12). See n. 62.

55. According to the genealogy of Gen. 25:12–13, however, the descendants of Ishmael are not limited to Egyptians. This list suggests yet more tension in Hagar's story.

56. For early Jewish and Christian traditions about Sarah's role, see S. P. Brock, "Sarah and the Aqedah," in *Le Muséon: Revue D'Etudes Orientales* vol. 87; fasc. 1–2 (Louvain, 1974), 67–77; cf. also Brock, "Two Syriac Verse Homilies on the Binding of Isaac," in *Le Museon: Revue D'Etudes Orientales*, vol. 99, fasc. 1–2 (Louvain, 1986), 61–129. Drawing on this research, Burton L. Visotzky comments on classical Jewish, Christian, and Muslim readings of Gen. 22 in "Binding Isaac," in *Reading the Book: Making the Bible a Timeless Text* (New York: Doubleday, 1991), 76–99.

57. For a fuller version of the interpretation given here, see Phyllis Trible, "Genesis 22: The Sacrifice of Sarah," in *"Not in Heaven": Coherence and Complexity in Biblical Narrative*, ed. Jason P. Rosenblatt and Joseph C. Sitterson Jr. (Bloomington:

Indiana University Press, 1991), 170–91. For classical interpretations, see, e.g., Shalom Spiegel, *The Last Trial* (New York: Pantheon Books, 1967); Søren Kierkegaard, *Fear and Trembling* (Garden City, NY: Doubleday, 1954; original date, 1843). For an eloquent and positive recent reading, see Levenson, *The Death and Resurrection of the Beloved Son*, 111–42. For a well-researched and negative reading that takes account of Christian, Jewish, Muslim, and Freudian interpretations, see Carol Delaney, *Abraham on Trial: The Social Legacy of Biblical Myth* (Princeton, NJ: Princeton University Press, 1998). For other discussions on child abuse and the role of God in this story, see Terence E. Fretheim, "God, Abraham, and the Abuse of Isaac," *Word & World* 15 (1995): 49–57; John J. Collins, "Faith without Works: Biblical Ethics and the Sacrifice of Isaac," *Recht und Ethos im Alten Testament*, ed. Stefan Beyerle et al. (Neukirchen-Vluyn: Neukirchener Verlag, 1999), 115–31. Cf. Edward Kessler, *Bound by the Bible: Jews, Christians and the Sacrifice of Isaac* (New York: Cambridge University Press, 2004).

58. On varieties of meaning for *hinneh*, traditionally translated "behold," see Thomas O. Lambdin, *Introduction to Biblical Hebrew* (New York: Charles Scribner's, 1971), 168–71; Adele Berlin, *Poetics and Interpretation of Biblical Narrative* (Sheffield: Almond Press, 1983), 62–63; Cohen, *Hineini in Our Lives*, 21–28.

59. Cf. Napier, *From Faith to Faith*, 69.

60. The word "attachment" plays on three concepts: attachment, detachment, and nonattachment. The first two designate human relationships, each of which may be both positive and negative. The third, nonattachment, posits a transcendent perspective that saves human relationships from mutual bondage. As used here, the terms are appropriated from Zen Buddhism; see Venerable Gyomay M. Kubose, "Non-attachment," *Zen Koans* (Chicago: Henry Regnery Co., 1973), 65–126.

61. On the use of this deictic phrase to signal climactic utterances, cf. Exod. 18:11; 1 Kgs. 17:24; Jon. 4:2.

62. Beersheba lies in the northern Negev. Paran is a wilderness beyond Beersheba, south of Canaan, west of Edom, and north of Sinai. Hebron lies about twenty miles south(west) of Jerusalem.

63. For Jewish legends about this separation, see Ginzberg, *Legends of the Bible*, 135–38.

64. Cf. Howard Moltz, "God and Abraham in the Binding of Isaac," *JSOT* 96 (December 2001): 59–69.

65. For Isaac's next appearance, see Gen. 24:62. Not until Gen. 25:23 does the Lord speak again, though references to the deity occur earlier (e.g., Gen. 24:3, 7, 12, etc.).

66. Although in a cluster of references (Gen. 21:2, 3, 4, 5) the narrator does connect Abraham and "his son Isaac," thereby preparing the way for Gen. 22, Abraham himself does not speak this language. Further, in Gen. 21:11 narrated discourse connects the phrase "his son" to Ishmael.

67. This proposal does not assume that there was ever a story in which Sarah was tested. Coming from outside the text, the proposal wrestles with the inner dynamics of the text.

68. On this story, see Meir Sternberg, "Double Cave, Double Talk: The Indirections of Biblical Dialogue," in Rosenblatt and Sitterson, ed., *"Not in Heaven,"* 28–57.

69. For this figure, cf. the chronologies given in Gen. 17:17, 21; 23:1; and 25:7.

70. A midrashic tradition, in *Genesis Rabbah* 61.4, equates Keturah with Hagar; see Alan Cooper, "Hagar in and out of Context," *Union Seminary Quarterly Review* 55, nos. 1–2 (2001): 46. On the possible confusion in the text between Keturah (and also Hagar? cf. Gen. 25:6) as wife and as concubine (cf. Gen. 16:3; 25:1, 6; 1 Chr. 1:32), see the comments by Hamilton, *Genesis: Chapters 18–50*, 164–65, and the references given there.

71. On the death of Isaac, see below on Gen. 35:29.
72. The precise location of Havilah, somewhere in Arabia, is difficult to identify; on the possibilities, see the commentaries.
73. These comments draw on numerous studies of biblical narratives: In addition to Gunkel, *The Stories of Genesis* and Bar-Efrat, *Narrative Art in the Bible*, see Robert Alter, *The Art of Biblical Narrative* (New York: Basic Books, 1981); J. P. Fokkelman, *Narrative Art in Genesis: Specimens of Stylistic and Structural Analysis* (Amsterdam: Van Gorcum, Assen, 1975); J. P. Fokkelman, *Reading Biblical Narratives: An Introductory Guide* (Louisville, KY: Westminster John Knox Press, 1999); Yairah Amit, *Reading Biblical Narratives: Literary Criticism and the Hebrew Bible* (Minneapolis: Fortress Press, 2001).
74. Bar-Efrat notes, e.g., that in Gen. 21:9–21 the narrator does not name Ishmael but instead uses descriptions such as "son," "child," and "lad" that reflect the attitude of other characters toward him (*Narrative Art in the Bible*, 36–37).
75. On the (mis)use of the word "patriarchy" as shorthand for male-centered and male-dominated cultures, see n. 2 above.
76. The single reference in Gen. 15:18 belongs to the J source; the cluster in Gen. 17 belongs to P.
77. But cf. the use of the word "covenant" in Gen. 21:27, 32 for the agreement between Abraham and Abimelech.
78. The phrase "competing impulses" comes from James L. Crenshaw, *A Whirlpool of Torment: Israelite Traditions of God as an Oppressive Presence* (Philadelphia: Fortress Press, 1984), 28. His poignant analysis of Gen. 22 (9–29), entitled "A Monstrous Test," raises many disturbing questions about the character of God. For a comprehensive study of the conflicted character of the biblical God, see Walter Brueggemann, *Theology of the Old Testament: Testimony, Dispute, Advocacy* (Minneapolis: Fortress Press, 1997).
79. Gunkel sees biblical storytellers grasping the individuality of a character through the construction of types (*The Stories of Genesis*, 38–41).
80. On differing representations of Abraham, see Hendel, *Remembering Abraham*, 37–43.
81. See Gen. 24:3, 4, 6, 7, 8; cf. 22:7–8.
82. See Fretheim, "Genesis," 512.
83. See Samuel Terrien, *Till the Heart Sings* (Grand Rapids: Wm. B. Eerdmans Publishing Co., 2004), 31–33.
84. Hamilton speculates on a period of "some forty years of shalom between Isaac and Ishmael after the demise of their father" (*Genesis: Chapters 18–50*, 170).
85. For a helpful overview of modern analyses and uses of Hagar, which also includes references to medieval Jewish interpretations, see Cooper, "Hagar in and out of Context," 35–46.
86. On familial relationships, with some attention to the "Abrahamic" family, see David L. Petersen, "Genesis and Family Values," *Journal of Biblical Literature* 124 (Spring 2005): 5–23.

Chapter 3

Twists and Turns in Paul's Allegory

Letty M. Russell

In chapter 1 of this book we saw the trajectory of the Hagar and Sarah story and followed the ways it has continued to be expounded and reinterpreted in all ages, including our own. In this chapter I will look at the twists and turns of Paul's allegory in Galatians, as well as at the many different turns used by modern interpreters of the text. I will examine the way Paul uses the Genesis account to make his point about Gentile Christian freedom from certain provisions of Jewish law, in opposition to his Jewish Christian or Judaizing opponents. The focus is on the Pauline text itself and the trajectory of its interpretation in contemporary commentaries by male scholars as well as in feminist, womanist, and postcolonial readings by female scholars. The readings twist and turn in many different directions and reveal the contradictions in Paul's theology as he struggles to bring new communities of Christ to life.

In Galatians 4:21–31 we have the only reference to Hagar in the Second Testament, along with implied references to Sarah without the use of her name. The names themselves are not important in this allegorical reading of the Genesis account because both women are used to represent the different sides in Paul's argument against either the Jewish Christians or the Judaizing Gentiles who are asking Gentile Christians to follow the teachings of the Torah, including the rite of circumcision. This already-twisted story is twisted again to suit its allegorical use by Paul. Not only the meaning but also the naming is turned around. Whereas Sarah refuses to call Hagar by name in Genesis 16 and 21, here Paul does not use Sarah's name and only speaks about her as the "other woman," the free mother of Christians (Gal. 4:26). In contrast, Hagar is named as the "slave woman," who is in slavery with her Jewish Christian or Judaizing children (Gal. 4:21, 25).

TWISTED ALLEGORY

Our journey with Hagar and Sarah takes us to Galatians 4:21–31, where Paul complicates the story of Hagar and Sarah even further. Paul does not help us move away from the conflict and enmity between the two women, but instead moves straight into it with an allegory that represents the two women as opposing covenants of law and promise. Paul also wants Hagar and the slavery to the law that she represents driven out of the Galatian church (4:30).

Hagar's Double Rejection

In his new version of Genesis 16 and 21 Paul doubles Hagar's rejection through the use of allegory. In Genesis she is a foreigner, a slave, and a threat to Sarah. In Galatians she is all of these, and also a Jewish Christian opponent, a slave to the Jewish law, and a threat to Gentile Christian freedom in Christ. Thus, in verses 24–26, Paul says,

> Now this is an allegory: these women are two covenants. One woman, in fact, is Hagar, from Mount Sinai, bearing children for slavery. Now Hagar is Mount Sinai in Arabia and corresponds to the present Jerusalem, for she is in slavery with her children. But the other woman corresponds to the Jerusalem above; she is free, and she is our mother.

The two women no longer represent themselves but are used figuratively to represent Paul's hidden meaning in his argument against other Jewish Christians who are trying to influence the gathered assembly. Paul opposes the claims of his opponents that they represent the mother church in Jerusalem in teaching that Gentiles must first become circumcised as Jews and follow certain provisions of the law in order to enter new life in Christ. He contends that in Christ baptism is the only ritual requirement for Gentile entrance into the Israel of God (Gal. 2:7–10; 6:15–16).

There is considerable discussion about the details of Paul's rhetoric in Galatians and about the divisions between his arguments, as we shall see. However, scholars generally agree that the letter is divided into three sections, along with an introduction and conclusion. Chapters 1:11–2:21 are a narrative defense of Paul's gospel based on his own conversion and commission as an apostle to the Gentiles. Chapters 3:1–5:1 are the center of Paul's arguments against his Jewish Christian and Judaizing opponents, who claim that following Jewish customs is essential to receiving the promised blessing offered by God to Abraham and his descendants. Chapters 5:2–8:18 are concerned with the promise of freedom and how this can be lived out in the new communities of Christ.

Paul uses the allegory as a rhetorical flourish at the end of his argument in chapters 3 and 4 against the necessity of keeping the Jewish law in order to live in Christ. The argument of the allegory also appears to be divided into three parts although there is a great deal of debate about how to "untwist the text" and order these parts. In verses 21–27 Paul proposes his new interpretation of the Hagar/Sarah story. He reinforces this new truth with a second proof from Scripture in verses 28–30, and then closes with a direct address to his listeners concerning their freedom in Christ in verses 4:31 and, probably, 5:1.

According to Elizabeth A. Castelli, an allegory is "a rendering of truth that asserts the truth is always somewhere else, something other than where or what appears."[1] It is used to persuade the reader to reimagine the meanings of a familiar tradition. Paul's allegory follows an accepted pattern of allegory in Hellenistic culture. To show that pattern Castelli focuses on the verses devoted to the allegory pattern and leaves off the verses that appear to be Paul's introduction (4:21) and ending (4:31–5:1). First, the story is reduced to the two women as representations of two missions and two covenants, those of Torah and of Christ.[2] Thus in verses 22–23 he speaks of Sarah as the free woman whose son Isaac is born according to the promise. Paul calls Hagar the slave woman whose son was born according to the flesh. Isaac has a miraculous birth according to the promise of God to Abraham and Sarah in their old age while Ishmael is born through the human attempt to fulfill God's promise without God's help.

Second, in verses 24–27, the story receives a new meaning hidden beneath the surface as Paul uses a typology to retell the familiar story of the two women.[3] Sarah now represents the covenant of promise symbolized by the eschatological vision of the promised heavenly Jerusalem familiar to us from Revelation 3:12 (Heb. 12:22). Hagar represents the covenant of the law given on Mount Sinai and practiced in the present Jerusalem church. Finally, in verse 27, Paul uses a proof text from Isaiah 54:1 confirming that in the end times the children of the barren woman (Sarah) will have many more children (Gentile Christians) than the woman (Hagar), whose son symbolizes those advocating the following of Jewish law (Jewish Christians).[4]

In verses 28–31 Paul reinforces this allegorical meaning by presenting a second proof. He uses the typology of the two mothers and an appeal to Christian birth through Christ's Spirit to establish this new meaning as the only true interpretation. He seeks to displace the authority of his opponents by alluding to a Jewish interpretation that describes Ishmael's playing with Isaac as a form of persecution. He then quotes Sarah's words as Scripture, with a new ending that highlights his theme of freedom by adding the words "of the free woman."

> Drive out the slave and her child; for the child of the slave will not share the inheritance with the child of the free woman. (Gal. 4:30; Gen. 21:9–10)

By appealing to a familiar story that might have been used as a proof of Abrahamic descent by his opponents, Paul seeks to establish a new truth in the story: Hagar, already the castaway, becomes the ancestor of his opponents who want Gentile Christians to follow the law. In Paul's new truth Sarah moves from being the Mother of Israel to the free Mother of Christians, and Hagar moves from being a cast-out Egyptian slave to the cast-out slave Mother of Israel and its Torah. We can only imagine how offended his Jewish Christian or Judaizing Gentile Christian opponents would have been by this rhetoric of rejection.[5]

Paul's Dangerous Rhetoric

The immediate goal of Paul's letter to the Galatian churches seems to be to interrupt the Gentile adoption of some of the observances inscribed in Jewish law.[6] In one of his many twists, Paul uses the story of Hagar and Sarah from the Jewish law to argue his point. In his relentlessly dualistic arguments Paul is fighting for his mission to the Gentiles, arguing that they can be included in the new community by faith and without observance of the law. He is afraid that those who want to require circumcision and other Jewish practices will win, and his distinctive Gentile mission will fail. This shows in his either-or rhetoric, which argues that salvation is a free gift from God offered through the life, death, and resurrection of Jesus Christ. For the sake of his mission to the Gentiles he seems to reinscribe the divisions that he had declared overcome in Christ a chapter earlier in Galatians 3:28. Here there are divisions of Jew and Greek, slave and free, and male and female. All are not "one in Christ Jesus."

Paul is so carried away by his rhetorical arguments that he relies on the accepted social norms of his day, in which one is born into subordination as a slave and/or as a woman. According to Sheila Briggs, Paul's understanding of slavery and gender contradicts the baptismal declaration in Galatians 3:28. In chapter 4:21, a few verses after 3:28, Paul's allegory uses the socially accepted understanding of slavery, with freedom as its opposite. His rhetoric reinforces the custom of sexual abuse of female slaves as a negative metaphor for slavery to the law. It interprets motherhood as only serving to establish paternity, in this case through Abraham, and. also uses women's biological role to define the boundaries of Christian community.

It is important to recall, however, that Paul is not only a missionary writing letters to put out fires of dissension in churches he has founded; he is also a firm believer in Jesus' immanent return. It seems that he pays little attention to the need for social transformation because he believes that this world is passing away (1 Cor. 7:25–31). Paul was using the allegory as a form of resistence to the opposing view, but its dangerous rhetoric about Hagar and Sarah has taken on a life of its own in subsequent Christian tradition. As we see in this book, his rhetoric has not only fueled anti-Jewish and anti-Islamic rhetoric but also given theological justification for racial and gender discrimination.

One of the reasons Paul contradicts himself by using this allegory of law and gospel in a way that reinforces slavery and the sexual use of women in slavery is that Paul, like many of us in contemporary society, is a hybrid and comes from a mixture of cultures and traditions in a globalized context. According to R. S. Sugirtharajah, hybrid identity is ". . . a complex web of cultural negotiation and interaction, forged imaginatively by redeploying the local and imported elements."[7] Certainly this fits Paul. He was born a Jew in exile; he lived among the Diaspora; he spoke Greek; and he became a fighter for Judaism who was "zealous for the traditions" of his ancestors and opposed their erosion by the religious, cultural, and political pressures of the Roman Empire (Gal. 1:13–17).[8] After his call, living in exile, Paul became a zealous advocate for Gentile Christian mission.[9]

Paul was a Hellenized Jewish writer who wrote in Greek, cited the Greek translation of the Scriptures, and used a wide range of interpretative practices that were part of first-century Judaism as well as the Greco-Roman world.[10] Although Luke says that Paul is a Roman citizen, he fashioned much of his rhetoric against Roman rule to establish that Jesus Christ is Lord, not Caesar (Acts 22:27–29; Phlm. 2:9–11). He spoke of an alternative empire of Christ using the same rhetoric of unity and rule employed by the Roman empire in worshiping Caesar Augustus as God and Father of the people. Such words as "gospel," "faith," "justice," "peace," and "Lord" were all part of the Roman political theology enacted in public ceremonies in the Hellenized cities of Asia Minor. According to Richard Horsley, Paul claimed that the new order had begun with the resurrection of Jesus Christ and the Roman imperial order was passing away.[11]

Paul was ministering to congregations that were hybrid as well, including mixtures of Jew and Gentile, male and female, slave and free, and people of different classes. In the changing social and political context of the Roman Empire, membership and customs in the Jewish assemblies were fluid and often led to intra-Jewish conflicts over interpretation of tradition, such as the one in Galatians.[12] At the time of Paul's letter to the Galatians, around 50 CE, Judaism and Christianity were both evolving together in the Roman imperial context. They did not emerge as separate entities until Emperor Hadrian's destruction of Jerusalem and expulsion of all Jews, including Jewish Christians, after the Bar Kochba revolt in 135 CE.[13]

In his attempt to forge a new Gentile Christian identity, Paul writes different letters to different struggling congregations—to reprimand those who go astray and to put forward his own interpretation of the gospel in each situation without regard to consistency. He is writing letters and not doctrinal statements. Yet some Christian interpreters insist that Paul's theology is consistent and that careful exegesis of his letters will reconcile the contradictions and discern the true meaning. The cautionary tale is that we need to avoid thinking that either Paul or we have the Truth, and seek to weave together the parts of our traditions that help us to overcome the contradictions and enmity in our own lives.

Straightening Up the Mess

The twists and turns in Paul's letter present a continuing challenge to all who are concerned with his teachings. He has a privileged place in the traditions of the church because the Second Testament contains seven letters, including Galatians, written in the early beginnings of the church and for whom Pauline authorship is undisputed. In addition, other writings are attributed to Paul, as is Luke's account of Paul's conversion and missionary journeys in Acts.[14] In a way we can characterize the continuing studies of Pauline scholars as an attempt to "straighten up the mess" of the various contradictions in his writings and to find out what Paul was teaching churches about Christian faith and life.

There are so many different views of Paul's teachings and life that Wayne Meeks has characterized Paul as a "Christian Proteus," making an analogy to Robert Jay Lifton's description of modern men (and women) who seem to have a constantly changing identity in a fast-changing society.[15]

However, what Meeks shows in his historical survey of writings about Paul is that the scholarship itself is also protean, changing as history changes.[16] In Pauline studies toward the end of the second millennium we can trace many changes as scholars learn new things about ancient societies and ask new questions about the texts. One of the most important shifts was recognized and described by Krister Stendahl in his 1963 essay, "The Apostle Paul and the Introspective Conscience of the West."[17] In the essay Stendahl broke with the established interpretations of Paul as a theologian of individual salvation who emphasized justification by faith through grace over against the practice of Jewish law. Scholars began to examine Paul's letters in their own political and social contexts and to emphasize Paul's connection to the world around him rather than just his thought.[18]

Most importantly they recovered Paul's Jewish context.[19] Romans 9–11 shows that Paul was struggling with the implications that could be drawn from his arguments for full acceptance of the Gentiles. He works to make clear that he does not mean that the people whom God had once chosen were now rejected. His arguments with the Jews were intra-Jewish arguments about how to interpret tradition at a time when both Judaism and Christianity were emerging as distinct religions. Paul considered the practices of both Gentile and Jewish Christians to be of penultimate importance in the light of the death and resurrection of Jesus Christ that had brought about the beginning of life in God's new creation (1 Cor 7).[20] In the postscript to Galatians, written in his own hand, Paul declares,

> May I never boast of anything except the cross of our Lord Jesus Christ, by which the world has been crucified to me, and I to the world. For neither circumcision nor uncircumcision is anything; but a new creation is everything! As for those who will follow this rule peace be upon them, and mercy, and upon the Israel of God. (6:14–16)

Once scholars began to look at the letters of Paul as specific to their contexts and not just a series of timeless religious truths, it was possible to entertain many different interpretations of the letters and also to recognize that what might have been their original meaning was distinct from their meaning for Christians today in many different social and political contexts. This opening of perspectives has led to the publication of a number of commentaries and countless articles by male scholars on Galatians in the last fifty years.

To represent this outpouring of Pauline scholarship I will refer to commentaries on Galatians by Hans Dieter Betz (1979), J. Louis Martyn (1997), and Richard B. Hays (2000), with reference to collections of articles by Richard A. Horsley and J. Dominic Crossan (1997, 2004).[21] In particular I will be asking how the three commentaries interpret Paul's rhetorical theology in the Hagar and Sarah allegory. I will then consider the different dimensions that are revealed in the allegory by the work of Horsley and Crossan on Paul as a political theologian.

The overall rhetorical form of the letter is ambiguous and leads to a variety of interpretations in the commentaries. Betz thinks that the letter follows the conventions of ancient judicial rhetoric and fits the framework of an apologetic letter, in which Paul defends himself to the Galatians, who are the jury, against his opponents, who are the accusers.[22] The section containing the allegory is part of the proof presented in his argument and is followed by the exhortation to life in freedom. Martyn thinks rather that the tone is more that of a sermon and announcement of the gospel message. He stresses that this could be an "argumentative sermon" delivered by Paul through one of the local leaders.[23] While acknowledging these other ideas, Hays prefers to think of Galatians as simply a letter, similar in form to his other letters except that it omits the thanksgiving at the beginning and the greetings at the end.[24] Perhaps those parts did not fit into the controversial atmosphere. The lack of women's names, except for Hagar, is conspicuous in Galatians and is probably because the names usually appear in the missing last section of personal greetings.[25]

Paul as a Rhetorical Theologian

In comparing the work of the three commentaries on Paul's allegory, I will consider some of the problems presented by Charles H. Cosgrove in his article entitled "The Law Has Given Sarah No Children." Cosgrove describes Paul's appeal to the story of Hagar and Sarah in Galatians as "enigmatic to interpreters in a number of respects."[26] He points to problems with the position of the allegory in chapter 4, which does not continue the style of Paul's personal parental appeal to the Galatians in 4:12–20. He also says that the form of the allegory is mixed, including a typology of the two mothers in 4:28–31. In addition, the point of the allegory is not clearly made and seems to be a weak form of argument for closing the debate of chapters 3 and 4.[27] Coming in 1987, about ten years after Betz's commentary and ten years before those of Martyn and Hays, Cosgrove's overview at least points to consensus concerning some of the problems with Paul's rhetoric in the allegory.

Position of the Allegory

Regarding the present position of the allegory, Cosgrove considers the possibility that it would fit better with the discussion of Christ as Abraham's true offspring in 3:16–18. Like Betz, the other two commentators recognize that the placement of the allegory could be a problem but conclude that the personal confession is a rhetorical device. It is then followed by another such device in 4:20, where Paul asks his hearers to listen to the law themselves in order to direct attention to his allegorical interpretation. The commentators do not think that the allegory has been misplaced in manuscript copying and concur with Hays that it fits the series of "counter arguments against the rival missionaries" in the proof section of chapters 3–4.[28]

They do, however, disagree about how the series of arguments ends. Cosgrove sees it ending in verse 30 with the second Scripture quote about driving out Hagar. The next section of the letter on pastoral exhortation, about how to live in the freedom of Christ, would then begin with Paul's appeal to the Galatians in verse 31 to understand that they are children "of the free woman."[29] For Betz, the argument ends in verse 31 as Paul calls on the Galatians to think things through for themselves. Paul then begins anew in 5:1 by picking up the freedom theme for the section on pastoral exhortation.[30] However, both Martyn and Hays argue that the allegory section ends with the ringing declaration of 5:1:

> For freedom Christ has set us free. Stand firm, therefore, and do not submit again to a yoke of slavery.

They see this as the climax and message of the letter and not the beginning of the new section. As the textual evidence itself does not give definite clues about the ending of the section, they have opted to highlight the strongest statement about freedom from slavery to the law as the ending of the argument.[31]

Form of the Allegory

Cosgrove raises the question of the allegory's form and points out that it does not conform strictly to the use of allegory in Greek literature.[32] The three commentators agree that the allegory contains a typology in which Hagar and Sarah are used as prototypes of the Galatian struggle over how Christians are to receive God's promise.[33] It was unusual for Paul to use allegory, and he does not conform to its use by Greco-Roman and Jewish philosophy of his time. Paul drew his images from the Hellenistic culture around him as well as from Jewish apocalyptic tradition, but he used them to his own purposes and did not follow any one form either in the allegory or in the overall form of his Galatian letter.

Hays points out that the allegory is a counter reading of the tradition that allows Paul to refute his Jewish Christian opponents, who had probably used the same Scripture texts to prove that the Jews were the children of promise and that following their traditions would make it possible for the Gentile Christians to share God's promise.[34] He uses allegory because he can then appeal to a deeper, hidden truth: that the promise of God is fulfilled in the death and resurrection of Christ and is now offered to all believers without the need for them to fulfill the Jewish law. Paul uses both narratives and legal regulations in the Septuagint and Jewish haggadic material as Scripture or Torah.[35]

The form of the allegory itself receives a great deal of attention because the comparison of the two women and their descendants, a key part of Paul's argument, is missing some of the parts. Paul presents two covenants and then makes two columns of polar opposites under each covenant.[36] Genesis tells of only one covenant with Abraham, and Isaac, "the child of the free woman," inherits that covenant or promise of blessing. Paul adds a second covenant that is inherited by Ishmael, "the child of the slave" (4:22–23), and associates it with the giving of the law on Mount Sinai in Exodus 20. Martyn speaks of "covenants" or "missions," reminding us that the two columns in Paul's allegory do not represent Christianity and Judaism, but rather the conflicting views between Paul's Jewish Christian mission to the Gentiles and his opponents' Jewish Christian mission to the Gentiles.[37] Nevertheless, Paul's use of these sacred Jewish traditions to condemn his opponents' teaching would have been offensive to Jewish Christians as well as those in Jewish synagogues. The inclusion of Jew and Gentile together in God's plan for New Creation is addressed further by Paul in Romans 9–11.[38]

As Paul builds his typology of oppositions in verses 24–26, he seems to pay more attention to the Hagar side representing his opponents. Perhaps this is because he gets distracted as he writes and does not finish. It may also be because he wants to leave out the parts that he can assume his hearers understand so that they will supply the missing parts. If his listeners know and agree with the Sarah column of promise, it is likely that Paul chooses to argue more fully about the "hidden truth": that the Hagar column represents the false path to faithfulness in Jesus Christ.[39]

Paul's statement in verse 25 is perhaps the most difficult and twisted verse in the allegory to understand. Betz points out that Nietzsche calls it an "unheard-of philosophical farce in regard to the Old Testament."[40]

> Now Hagar is Mount Sinai in Arabia and corresponds to the present Jerusalem, for she is in slavery with her children.

Equating Hagar with Mount Sinai has led to many textual variants in the existing manuscripts, some of which simplify the twisted geography by leaving out Hagar and just having Sinai in Arabia correspond with present Jerusalem.[41] Paul may have claimed that Hagar is connected to Mt. Sinai because her name is similar to an Arabic word, *hadjar*, for rock or mountain in that area. But it is more likely that Paul puts both Mount Sinai and Jerusalem in the covenant of slavery column because they both represent following the law.[42] Hagar the slave fled to the wilderness of the Arabian peninsula with her son, Ishmael. Their descendants prospered and lived in that area as Ishmaelites. Therefore, the allegory connects the slave woman with Mount Sinai and the law, and if with the law, also with Jerusalem, the center of the practice of Jewish tradition.

The dualistic contrast of "the present Jerusalem" with "the Jerusalem above" in verse 26 refers to Jewish apocalyptic tradition that anticipated the fulfillment of God's blessing to Israel through a new restored Jerusalem.[43] By using this image and reinforcing it with a familiar text of restoration from Isaiah 54:1, Paul is able to put the Jerusalem of the law in the slavery column and the Jerusalem of promise in the freedom column. Paul is drawing images from the Jewish Scriptures as well as other, current Jewish apocalyptic images of an earthly and heavenly Jerusalem. Martyn and Hays particularly stress that "present Jerusalem" refers to the Jewish Christian church in Jerusalem that is being held up as the model of Christian practice by Paul's opponents.[44] The "Jerusalem above" includes all those who have been baptized into a new life of freedom in Christ, living "in but not of" the present reality around them (Gal. 3:23–29; Cor. 5:17–18, 7:29–31).

Point of the Allegory

For Cosgrove the point of the allegory is to form a bridge from the arguments in chapters 3 and 4 to the apostolic imperative of 4:30–51.[45] We have already seen that Paul seems to end his allegory with the quote from Isaiah 54 without a concluding statement. Betz also notes that the ambiguity of the allegory itself seems to make it a weaker way to argue the final point in chapters 3 and 4.[46] But perhaps, as Martyn and Hays agree, Paul's second argument from the Hagar and Sarah tradition is the ending (4:28–5:1). Paul wants to say in no uncertain terms that those who are teaching a gospel of the law are to be thrown out of the church. Once again he appeals to Scripture or the Torah against his opponents' teaching about the law. This time he uses the words of Sarah against Hagar directly against all those in the church who follow the teachings of his opponents, but ends with a strong appeal to stand firm in the freedom of Christ (4:31–5:1).[47]

To clarify the conflicting positions Paul speaks in verse 28 of birth "according to the flesh" and "according to the Spirit." Martyn considers these two concepts basic to Paul's eschatological argument about the already begun, but not yet completed nature of the New Creation (Rom. 8:1–17).[48] Since the death and resurrection of Jesus Christ the new age of grace and freedom has broken into the old age of sin and death. Living in the old age of the present reality is characterized as living in the flesh (sarx). This is not the same as the physical body (soma), which is part of both life in this world of the "flesh" and life in the new world of Christ's "Spirit."

Through baptism the Christian is born into the community of Christ's resurrection and receives the gift of Spirit (pneuma) to live in a way that has overcome the present fallen reality of the flesh. Thus Paul speaks of himself as being again in "the pain of childbirth" as he seeks the new birth of the Galatian church members (4:19). According to Leander Keck, both flesh and Spirit refer to domains of power: one, the power of evil in our lives and world, and the other, the power of God at work in our lives and in our new communities.[49] In our text "flesh" is also used to refer to circumcision as a symbol of those who want to continue following the law of the flesh rather than living in the Spirit, beyond the law.[50]

The demand that Paul's opponents be driven out reinforces the argument of his allegory, but it also becomes a license for later Christian interpreters to use these words against their opponents. In this book Elizabeth Clark's chapter on the church fathers details this development. Chapter 1 also traces the trajectory of this diatribe as it comes to be used as a justification for Christian anti-Jewish interpretation and oppression up to contemporary times. Hays also points out that Martin Luther read Paul's polemic as an attack on the abuses of the Roman Catholic church of his day, arguing that Rome was teaching justification by works through following the law, rather than justification by grace through faith.[51] It is somewhat surprising, then, that Hays considers Paul's diatribe as his rhetorical "ace, his most dramatic argument" using a direct command from Scripture to cast out all who disagree with him on his interpretation of the gospel.[52] It would seem that Paul would not end on a note of angry rejection but would rather make the point of his argument:

> For freedom Christ has set us free. Stand firm, therefore, and do not submit again to a yoke of slavery. (Gal. 5:1)

Paul as a Political Theologian

Regardless of the rhetorical use of this passage, Betz, Martyn, and Hays consider the identity of Paul's opponents and the problem of anti-Judaism to be a central issue in interpreting Galatians. As much as possible they investigate Galatians in its Jewish and Hellenistic context, seeking to understand how Paul, himself a Jew, can use such strong anti-Jewish rhetoric. One could attribute this rhetoric to his conversion and Paul's continuing zeal for religious truth. As we saw earlier, this zeal first led him to persecute the followers of the Way, and then to resist the persecution of his opponents by demanding that they be thrown out (4:29–30; Acts 9:2).

Jews and Empire

By arguing that Paul is engaged in intrachurch disputes, however, the scholars seek to show that this dispute is over what the gospel means for members of the church community or assembly. Paul employs his rhetoric to refute the Jewish Christians or Judaizers who are challenging his authority and the authority of his gospel message. The scholars are listening to the accusations of Paul's opponents through his answers and seem to agree that Paul is concerned that his mission to the Gentiles not be inhibited by those whose mission is to convert them to practices of Judaism, such as circumcision and observance of the Sabbath and of major Jewish festivals, as a guide of conduct for the newly baptized congregations (4:10). They are also listening to the needs of our own time after the Holocaust, when both Jewish and Christian scholars have been working together to show that the early writings of the Second Testament can be understood in the context of intra-Jewish debate.[53] These scholars distinguish between the early writings of Paul and later writings such as Acts that focus on Jewish opposition to the churches, in order to prove that the Christians disputed only with Jews and were loyal to their Roman rulers (i.e., Acts 14:1–7, 19; 21–24).[54]

Scholars who have investigated even further the impact of the Roman Empire on the mission of Paul are Richard A. Horsley, John Dominic Crossan, and Jonathan L. Reed.[55] In *Paul and Empire* and *Paul and Politics*, Horsley and others argue that Paul's major opponent was the Roman Empire and not Judaism, and they advocate for the importance of this perspective in the postcolonial context of our time.[56] Horsley says that Roman political power established by Caesar Augustus was constructed through religious forms in which the emperor was God and father of his people.[57] Imperial cult pervaded urban ethos in cities such as Corinth and Ephesus and was the most widespread religious cult, particularly in Greece and Asia Minor.[58] In this time before the full development of either Judaism or Christianity, Paul was expecting the early completion of the resurrection and the New Age, but meanwhile his mission, according to Horsley, was "building an international alternative society (the assembly) based on local egalitarian communities or assemblies.[59] These *ekklesiai* were modeled after the political assemblies held in each city. The assemblies were to be the beginning of new life in the Spirit and of resistance to the old life in the flesh of Roman political, economic, cultural, and religious power.

The findings of the representative three commentaries discussed in this essay indicate that the writers are more concerned with Paul's rhetoric and the theological understanding of Galatians than with the church assemblies as centers of resistence to the Roman Empire. Hays does point out that, in chapter 4, verse 25, the "present Jerusalem" that is in slavery could also refer to the fact that it is occupied and controlled by the Romans.[60] But the commentators all focus on the immediate opponents in Galatians—the Jewish Christians or the Judaizing Gentile Christians seeking to control the small assemblies in the Roman province of Galatia in Asia Minor.[61]

A major difference of interpretation by those who stress the Roman Empire as Paul's opponent is that they interpret Paul's eschatology through the lens of the religious, political, economic, and cultural structures and ideology of the Greco-Roman world. The image of new creation, drawn from Jewish apocalyptic, is not only a hoped-for restoration of God's people but also Paul's description of the empire of Caesar as the world that is passing away. The new world is breaking in through the new small assemblies of Christ that demonstrate the power of God's Spirit to overcome "the present evil age" of empire, death, and sin through the resurrection of Jesus Christ as Lord (Gal. 1:4).

Gift of Freedom

God in Christ has broken the power of the religious and political world and entrance into the new world of Christ's rule requires accepting God's gracious gift of freedom, rather than earning one's salvation through conformity to old religious traditions, be they Jewish or Greek or Roman.[62] Horsley, Crossan, and Reed concur with Betz, Martyn, and Hays that the theme of freedom lifted up at the end of the Hagar and Sarah allegory is crucial both to Galatians and to Paul's understanding of the opposition between the realm of slavery ruled over by the present evil powers and the realm of freedom ruled over by God (4:31–5:1).

Paul concludes his two arguments about Hagar and Sarah with an appeal to live in the new realm of freedom. Although all Jewish laws and practices like circumcision are now of penultimate importance, following them can lead to subordination to the old world of "slavery" (5:2–6). Of ultimate importance is living now in the beginning time of this new age through faith in Jesus Christ.

Martyn says that Paul uses the noun "freedom" to describe a space or realm "that is the result of God's act in Christ," where such fruits of the Spirit as "love, joy, peace . . ." are practiced (5:22–26). It is opposed to the old realm of the "slave masters—the Law's curse, Sin, the Law itself, the elements of the cosmos . . . the Impulsive Desire of the Flesh (5:13–21)."[63] These realms may describe the spiritual reality of the Christians in community as is urged by the commentators, and by Crossan and Reed as well. But they may also refer to the concrete changes in God's new community that is coming into being through Paul's mission, as Horsley would argue.[64]

It would seem that even the shift toward examination of the social, political reality of the Roman Empire and of imperial rhetoric has not changed the opinion of these male scholars that Paul is "the apostle of all virtue."[65] Thus we find at the end of In Search of Paul Crossan and Reed's assertion that at the beginning of the book they "did not say 'St. Paul' lest that title prejudge the result. But now we know fully and clearly that we have found a saint not only for then, but for now and always."[66] There is little difference here with the conclusion of Hays concerning the Hagar and Sarah allegory that, despite its possible misuse, it is "a brilliantly successful piece of preaching enabling his readers to envision themselves as free children of Abraham and as children of an eschatologically restored Jerusalem caught up in joyous songs of praise to God."[67]

As we shall see in the next section on feminist and womanist interpretations of the Hagar and Sarah allegory, women scholars do not deny Paul's importance, but they turn their interpretive gaze at Paul's powerful rhetoric and how that was received by the many members of the Christian communities who were marginalized in Greco-Roman society.[68] They ask, "Where are the real women and the real slaves?" "What are they hearing in the allegory and typology of their mothers in slavery and freedom?" For instance, Elisabeth Schüssler Fiorenza points out in "Paul and the Politics of Interpretation" that there is little doubt that Paul uses imperial rhetoric and images, but there is doubt that the rhetoric he uses is always liberating for the marginalized groups he addresses.[69] Perhaps, like some of the Galatians, these groups may not have found Paul's imperial rhetoric of confrontation liberating.[70]

DECENTERING PAULINE THEOLOGY

A leading figure in the feminist reexamination of Pauline history and rhetoric has been Elisabeth Schüssler Fiorenza. Since the publication of In Memory of Her in

1983 she has continued to write about Paul and to encourage other women Second Testament scholars from around the world.[71] Although feminist scholarship seems to be marginal in regard to the Eurocentric, male center of biblical studies, it shares with many writers of liberation and postcolonial hermeneutics in "decentering Pauline theology from an unblinking focus on Paul to a broader reconstruction of early Christian communities."[72]

In her book *Rhetoric and Ethic* Schüssler Fiorenza describes her interpretive work to develop "a reconstructive historical model that valorizes difference, plurivocity, and democratic participation."[73] She says that

> [t]he differences and contradictions in the rhetoric of early Christian sources point to sociopolitical conflicts and religiocultural tensions between Hellenistic, Jewish, or early Christian "egalitarian" movements and their dominant patriarchal Greco-Roman, Jewish, and emerging Christian sociopolitical contexts.[74]

According to Cynthia Briggs Kittridge, reading the arguments between the lines "can make audible different voices" who participate in these debates.[75] She describes how Schüssler Fiorenza, Castelli, Antoinette Wire, and other feminist critics have challenged students of Paul to look for the hidden rhetorical arguments beneath those of Paul and his opponents. Kittridge cites three important contributions of these scholars to the study of Paul's letters. First, they read Paul's rhetoric against the grain, looking for the historical situation beneath the surface. Second, they specifically introduce gender, analyzing the role of women participants in the early Christian communities. Finally, they question the authority of Paul's letters to represent all the early Christian churches and their cultural contexts just because it is his letters and a record of his mission that have survived in the Second Testament.[76]

These scholars and others turned the interpretation of Paul's letters around by trying to reconstruct the historical, religious, and cultural context of his congregations. They listen not only for the voices of those who were Paul's opponents but also for the voices of members of the early Christian communities: "the low and despised in the world" who were called by God (1 Cor. 1:28). By placing emphasis on those whose lives are hidden in the text these women are going a step further than Martyn, who writes his commentary with emphasis on the reactions of Paul's listeners without employing gender analysis to listen for the women's voices.[77]

Paul's allegory of Hagar and Sarah has drawn particular attention not only because of Paul's politics of othering, in which he frames all who disagree with him as outsiders, but also because of his twisted use of the story of Hagar and Sarah.[78] In this last section in our examination of the twists and turns of Paul's allegory we turn to three readings against the grain. The first, by Sheila Briggs, focuses on the sharp contrasts in Paul's metaphors drawn from the institution of slavery and the sexual use of women slaves.[79] The second reading, by Brigitte Kahl, focuses on Paul's twisted gender images.[80] The final reading, by Susan

Elliott, turns to parallels between Paul's discussion of circumcision and the worship of the Anatolian Mother of the Gods in the Roman province of Galatia.[81]

Slavery and Gender

As we saw in the discussion of Pauline anti-imperial rhetoric, Richard Horsley has examined Paul's construction of a counter-imperial society in the context of the hierarchical Roman systems of socioeconomic, patronage power relations; the empire-wide practice of imperial cult and emperor worship, especially in urban centers; and the imperial rhetoric of peace and unity.[82] But Horsley fails to investigate the brutal military force institutionalized in the slave system of captured populations in his research on the political and religious imperial social structures.[83]

Sheila Briggs has worked to make these power structures of slavery more visible. She says that slavery was "not just one aspect of Greco-Roman society; the Roman Empire was a slave society."[84] Slavery was a process of domination that pervaded all the political, economic aspects of the society, and it signified the meaning of power and powerlessness in the society. The slave was considered "dead" in the society, without any existence of her or his own apart from the owner; without honor; and legally without parents, city, or homeland. "The body of the slave, including its sexual and reproductive capacities, belonged to the owner."[85]

According to Briggs, Paul uses slavery as both a metaphor of power and a metaphor of evasion. Paul's theological interpretation of the crucifixion and resurrection of Christ makes use of the *rhetoric of slavery* as power. In Philippians 2:5–11, for instance, Paul quotes a hymn sung in the congregation to speak of Christ as one who gives up power to become a slave.[86] Like other slaves, his slavery ends in death, and his death by crucifixion employs the ultimate form of brutality, designed to be used against slaves and rebellious peoples. But, unlike slaves of the Roman Empire, Christ is raised up as Lord, until the time comes to hand his power back to God.[87] Christians also are liberated from their slavery to the present age by the death and rising again of baptism into new life as slaves of Christ.[88]

Briggs points out that Paul's *rhetoric of evasion* was similar to that of the Greco-Roman society where slavery and its brutality were everywhere present, but seldom discussed or commented upon. For instance, in Paul's discussion of the relationship between slaves and masters in Philemon, it is not clear what his advice is concerning the return of Onesimus to his master. Paul urges that Onesimus not be punished and leaves open the possibility of his release, as manumission was possible in the Roman slave system.[89] Briggs points out that Paul does not directly condemn the social reality of slavery beyond asking that slaves not be treated harshly. "There is no Pauline or New Testament passage that addresses the vulnerability of slaves to sexual exploitation or physical torture."[90]

We can see the same rhetoric of power and evasion at work in the allegory of Hagar and Sarah. The accepted hierarchy of class and gender in Greco-Roman life seem to be reinforced by Paul's particular twist on the story. Abraham's sexual access to the slave Hagar is unquestioned, as is the idea that Ishmael will be born into slavery. The accepted understanding of the social hierarchy in which the one who is slave is dead to her kindred seems to give permission to Sarah to "[d]rive out the slave and her child (4:30)."

The allegory plays on the threat to Sarah's status as mother when she is unable to bear an heir, as well as on the assumed misbehavior of the slave child, Ishmael, in "persecuting" Isaac (4:26–29). In the ancient patriarchal household, gender and slavery were interconnected because persons were subordinated not just by their gender, but by their class, and formed into interconnected parts of the household. The distinction of sex served the purpose of procreation, and both female slaves and free married women were assigned the role of reproducing the social hierarchy of the household and its place in the larger social order.[91]

In the "relentlessly dualistic and appositional" argument in Paul's allegory, the image of freedom derives its meaning as the opposite of slavery.[92] Hagar's rejection seems to deny Paul's earlier argument for unity by using a baptismal liturgy already familiar to the congregations. It undermines Paul's own understanding that the use of difference to reinforce subordination is no longer valid in the messianic community.[93]

In Galatians 3:28 God's gift of freedom is not just the opposite of slavery, but also a new possibility of life in the community of Christ. Christ's Spirit creates the possibility of new unity in community where people no longer live under dualistic hierarchies with patriarchal division of husband and wife, class division of slave or free, or religious division of Jew or Greek (Gal. 3:28).[94] Paul's theological conviction was that social relationships are of penultimate importance at a time when the old social order was passing away.[95] His actual practice was that of including women as coworkers and leaders. He nurtured his small communities of faith so that they could become alternative families for the participants.[96] Nevertheless, Paul's language of slavery and freedom appears to reinscribe the structures of hierarchy at the same time that he is trying to win his Gentile converts to the gospel of freedom.

In responding to Briggs, Wire raises the question of how members from the community from different social locations would respond to Paul's allegory. For instance, how the women who were slaves, the slave men and women of higher or lower rank, and those who were not in slavery but struggling for subsistence would respond to Paul's version of the Sarah and Hagar story, now that Hagar becomes representative of slavery to the law and to the present evil age.[97] No doubt their response, like ours, will be ambiguous, but our questioning of the stereotypes of women who were slaves and mothers can be another step in decentering Pauline theology by turning to a broader and more detailed reconstruction of early communities of faith.

Gender Trouble

In her article "No Longer Male," Brigitte Kahl calls Galatians 4 the "mother-chapter of Paul," and focuses on issues of gender as they surface in the rhetoric of Paul's Galatian letter rather than on the dichotomy of slavery and freedom.[98] She urges us to continue this examination by focusing on the way that Galatians problematizes masculinity, "the male body as a marker of religious identity and superiority (circumcision), and patrilineal kinship," with "motherhood becoming symbolically dominant."[99]

In another article, titled "Gender Trouble," Kahl sets out to show how Paul's twists and turns (the ambiguity, the use of dualistic arguments, stereotypes of women and his opponents, and more) reflect Paul's struggle with the eschatological transformation of human relationships for those who live "in Christ." For Kahl, Galatians 3:28 and the Hagar and Sarah allegory in chapter 4 are not contradictory because they are both expressions of Paul's messianic argument that hierarchical relationships have no place in the New Creation or in the new communities of Christ. She argues that evidence of this overturning of the social structures of the Greco-Roman society can be found in the ethical section of Galatians 5 and 6 where those in Christ are to be slave to one another, serving each other joyfully. It can also be seen in chapters 3 and 4 with the overturning of dominance of men over women, freeborn over slave, and Jew over Gentile.[100]

Kahl sets out to prove that Paul is using semantic confusion as a sign of New Creation by pointing out the way Paul has twisted both patriarchal traditions and Jewish traditions in proclaiming the gospel of the foreskin against those whose who preach the gospel of circumcision (2:7).[101] As our other scholars have indicated, Christianity as a religion has not yet emerged in the period around 50 CE. Because the small Gentile assemblies may be still connected to the Jewish communities, Kahl prefers to use Paul's terms "in Christ" or "of Christ" to speak of the people in the Galatian community as Jews and Gentiles, rather than as "Jewish and Gentile Christians" (3:28–29).[102] In any case, Paul speaks of two ways of following the gospel and defends his gospel of the foreskin by arguing that the gospel of circumcision is a return to the hierarchical structures of the reality that is passing away.

In Kahl's view Paul does this by a process of displacing the assumed structures of gender and of Jewish tradition. Looking at the gender bending of Paul's Galatian letter, Kahl finds it to be the most "'phallocentric' document of the New Testament."

> Hardly any other New Testament document is so densely populated by male body-language as this letter: the terms foreskin, circumcision/circumcise, and sperm occur 22 times, including the stunning polemical reference to castration in 5:12.[103]

In Paul's gospel of the foreskin the Gentiles in Christ are already children of the promise, apart from the law. The struggle to prevent the return to circumcision as the mark of God's promise is a major theme of Paul's letter. Scholars agree on the importance of circumcision in the letter, but some assume it is because circumcision serves as a circumlocution of a variety of regulations from the Torah, or that the focus on circumcision is derived from the importance of the issue for the Galatian assembly. Kahl, on the other hand, understands the argument over circumcision to be part of Paul's gender-bending emphasis, in which those who formerly received privilege as male Jews through circumcision receive no added benefit from their conformity to the law. In fact, she says that the desire of the Galatian Gentiles to practice circumcision may indicate discomfort among the men with this confusing loss of place.[104]

Kahl calls this confusion of customary gender relationships *decentering the male*. Jewish males are no longer physically descended from their father, Abraham. In Paul's argument all nations can become offspring through "sperm Christ."[105] In 3:15–29 this leads to what Kahl calls a "triple effect." First, all those clothed or baptized in Christ are joined to Abraham's seed. Second, the inheritance of Abraham belongs to the entire messianic community. Third, the customary patriarchal hierarchy in society is undermined in the new age. Thus Paul turns phallocentric rhetoric on its head so that there is no longer "inferiority of son vs. father, but also female vs. male, slave vs. master, second-born vs. firstborn, Gentiles vs. children of Israel."[106]

The same sort of twisting of accepted tradition takes place in the Hagar and Sarah allegory of Galatians 4. Kahl calls this *recentering the female* and points to the striking use of mother and birth terminology.

> In one single chapter we come across the mother of Jesus (4:4), the mothers Hagar and Sarah (4:21–31), the mother Jerusalem (4:26), the barren and forsaken mothers of Isaiah who get many children without a male. . . .[107]

In addition, Paul transgenders himself as a mother in pain of childbrith to bring his Galatian converts to rebirth in Christ (4:19).[108] Kahl renames Paul's angry typology and his confusion of those listed in the column of promise and of slavery by calling Paul's allegory "a motherly exhortation of children who are about to forget who they are (4:20)."[109] For Paul, human fathers do not count any longer, only the divine father, and motherhood, although now nonbiological, is retained (3:26–4:7).

Kahl's focus on the concerns of Paul's male listeners leads her to suggest the possibility that Paul's "semantic confusion" is really part of his struggle to preach a gospel of freedom that can be practiced in communities of faith.[110] In these zones of God's power for new creation, unity in Christ makes it possible to respect difference without using it as a marker of privilege.[111] Although Paul accepts the present structures and differences of the patriarchal household, including the subordination of slaves and women, as a continuing part of the created order that is passing away, Kahl argues that he still believes the old inequalities are being subverted in the New Creation (1 Cor. 7). Much research and discussion is still needed to understand how this struggle to overturn the social structures of domination and still maintain unity and order in the congregations was played out in daily life.[112]

It is sometimes difficult to see how Paul can use such strong language to "other" his opponents and still be seeking to support this alternative vision of the new age breaking in. Like many other scholars, Kahl lifts up Paul's apocalyptic perspective in order to downplay the power of Paul's anti-Jewish rhetoric in the context of the Roman Empire. However, she keeps her focus on the twisted gender language rather than considering other social political factors.[113] Her close attention to the phallocentric rhetoric of Galatians opens a new window for reading Paul from the perspective of early communities of faith.

Anatolian Mother of the Gods

Circumcision plays such a prominent part in the debate of Galatians, it is no surprise to find another feminist doing research on reasons for its prominence. In her article "Choose Your Mother, Choose Your Master: Galatians 4:21–5:1 in the Shadow of the Anatolian Mother of the Gods," Susan M. Elliott shifts the focus to the religious background of Paul's listeners as a way of interpreting the rhetoric of Paul's allegory. Other scholars have looked for clues to Paul's rhetoric in Jewish or Greco-Roman traditions of Paul's listeners. Elliott, however, looks in the religious background of the mixture of peoples who were settled in Central Anatolia. In doing so she joins with Kahl in "recentering Paul" by showing that he is not confused in his allegory. On the contrary, his twisted juxtapositions are intentional references to traditional Anatolian cultic practices that would be self-evident to his listeners.

In her section on the "Unsolved Mysteries in Galatians 4:21–5:1" Elliott follows the problems reviewed by Cosgrove and described in the first section of this chapter.[114] The scholarly questions concerning the position, form, and point of Paul's allegory help again to demonstrate the ambiguity of Paul's "shocking realignment" of biblical history in order to reveal a new and hidden meaning of the story of Hagar and Sarah.[115] Elliott singles out two of the mysteries in the text: How Hagar comes to be associated with Mount Sinai; and how Paul, a Jew, makes the negative link to "enslaved present day Jerusalem."[116] Paul's lack of reference to Sarah and to Mount Zion in the promise column of the allegory, in contrast to the reference to Hagar and Mount Sinai in the slavery column, provides the clue for her research. These omissions may be intentional, and not because Paul is carried away by his own rhetoric or because he assumes that his listeners only need to be convinced about his identification of Hagar with God's covenant and the Torah. For Elliott, Paul's omission of the names of Sarah and the mountain is related to the cultic traditions of his Gentile listeners.[117]

In order to test this hypothesis Elliott describes the culture and religion of central Anatolia or Asia Minor, asserting that the religion of the "Anatolian Mountain Mothers and their castrated *galli*" was so widespread in the cities of that region that it would have been practiced in the cities of South Galatia mentioned by Acts, as well as those of North Galatia, where her cult center was at the great trading center of Pessinus (Acts 13:14; 16:6; 18:23).[118] The distinguishing feature of this widespread religious practice in antiquity was "the overseeing presence of the Mountain Mother of the Gods."[119] She was frequently identified with a mountain that overlooked her temple in a particular city and named as Mother of that mountain. Thus Mount Dindymus overlooked the city of Pessinus, and the Mother's name in that location was "Mother Dindymus."[120] In popular religiosity the Mountain Mother was viewed as an enforcer and a protector of the laws in a particular temple state. In Pessinus the residents were often referred to as slaves of the Mother, and she was served by young men who had dedicated themselves to her through an orgiastic ritual in which they castrated themselves and then wore special female garb.[121]

According to Elliott's research, the worship of the Anatolian Mountain Mother in her different manifestations provides a key to the unsolved mysteries of Paul's allegory. Hagar is identified with a distant mountain (Sinai, in Arabia), and with the temple city (present Jerusalem). Her children are enslaved to "Mother Sinai," the keeper of the law, and her most devoted followers practice something similar to self-castration (circumcision). This cultic background apparently has made the Galatians sympathetic to those arguing that the men should follow Jewish tradition and be circumcised.[122]

Paul's argument is against circumcision and enslavement to Hagar, the old Mountain Mother God who is worshiped in the present Jerusalem, and in favor of the superior God who dwells in the "Jerusalem above" and is worshiped through baptism and receives gifts of the Spirit. This argument can thus be seen to be consistent with the religious background of the Galatian congregations, and it answers the mysteries that Elliott discussed as problems in Galatians 4. Hagar is associated with Mt. Sinai so that she is recognized as the Mountain Mother who is to be rejected. Paul can speak of enslaved Jerusalem not as a denial of his Jewish tradition but as a way of convincing the Galatians to choose a new Mother associated with the gospel of Christ. One clue to Elliott's research, the lack of specific reference to Sarah in the promise column of the allegory, is Paul's way to avoid naming her as the Mountain Mother God. She is identified as the "legitimate wife" who bears children "by baptism and reception of the Spirit" (4:6). The other clue, the lack of a corresponding mountain in Jerusalem above, allows the unnamed Mother to dwell in a city above the mountains and bear children who are free.[123]

Elliott closes her alternative reading of the allegory, based on exploration of the religious background of the listeners, by recentering Paul's allegory in Galatians 3 and 4: "Thus, Paul places this graphic presentation at a pivotal position in the rhetorical structure of the letter where it can have the most impact on his audience."[124] She places an exciting alternative reading before us: one that searches into the margins of cultural history to learn more about the background of Paul's listeners. This provides a different reading of Paul's struggle against circumcision and of the much-discussed question of why Paul would equate the Torah with slavery. She uses the "prevalent Anatolian pattern of Mountain–Goddess–City" to reconstruct how Paul's audience would have understood his allegory.[125]

By removing Paul from the context of his own Jewish roots and his small assemblies from association with Jewish synagogues and placing him in a Gentile context, Elliott has found ways to view his allegory from a new perspective that removes some of his contradictions and helps recenter the importance of Paul's rhetoric. Again, she leaves us with new areas to explore and fascinating research to ponder as we continue to follow the twists and turns of the Hagar and Sarah story.

Other Voices

Feminist and womanist scholars are able to offer different readings of Paul's twisted version of Hagar and Sarah by asking new questions from the margin of established Euro-American, male biblical interpretation. As these newer interpretations continue to appear, some of them decenter the scholarly focus on Pauline theology by searching for a deeper appreciation of life in communities of faith struggling to discover what it means to be reborn. Listening for unheard and marginalized voices in the texts, they also try to make it "come out right" or at least to question whether Paul had things right. Sometimes it seems that they even recognize that Paul might not care if he contradicts himself as he searches for new words to carry the power of the gospel message.

One example is the way Pamela Eisenbaum's image of "Paul as the New Abraham" invites us to reexamine Paul's argument that Abraham was father of Christ and of the Galatian Christian converts (Gal. 3:15–18). Asserting that Paul sees himself as the "New Abraham," she shows the parallels between Paul's call and later mission to the Gentiles and the call of Abraham and his subsequent journey to a new country and a new trust in God.[126]

Another example is the research of Christl M. Maier entitled "Psalm 87 as a Reappraisal of the Zion Tradition and Its Reception in Gal. 4:26." Maier says that the song about Mother Zion in the Greek version of Psalm 87 "expresses a highly unique perspective in Hebrew scripture, of Zion as the mother of many nations." It seems to be the source of Paul's idea that Jerusalem can be called the mother of the Gentiles as well as of the Jews and offers a significant clue to understand better Paul's statement about the "Jerusalem above" in Galatians 4:26.[127] Her research has just begun, but it may help us make new connections to how the images of Sarah as our mother and that of "Jerusalem our Mother" functioned in Jewish tradition and in Paul's allegory. And so the conflicted trajectory of the Hagar and Sarah story continues.

TURNING, TURNING . . .

The nineteenth-century Shaker song "Simple Gifts" reminds us of our journey through the twists and turns of Paul's allegory. The song affirms that it is a gift to be simple and a "gift to come down where you ought to be." The refrain then invites us to turn and turn, "til by turning, turning we come round right."[128] Certainly we hoped that by turning and turning we would be able in some way to undo the impact of Paul's angry letter and the continuing divisions created by his use of the Hagar and Sarah story. We began with a letter in which Paul seems to contradict himself, and then moved to many different and contradictory interpretations of what he is saying and what his listeners are hearing.

At the beginning of a new age Paul has to create a new understanding of Christian life from the many contradictory traditions of his present age. In such a liminal situation many things do not fit and many never fit. The only way that we can make the story "come out right" is to move away from the assumption that everything that Paul says is authoritative for Christianity.[129] We can begin to listen to his struggles in the context of those around him: both those who were powerful opponents and those who are seeking to be heard from the margins. In humility we can say we don't know how to make this story come out right, but we are willing to listen to what the Spirit might be saying as we wrestle with its meaning.[130]

If we fail to do this and try to apply Paul's words directly to our own time we will be caught again in their use as weapons in the battle for authoritative truth waged by many spokespersons for Christianity, Judaism, and Islam. Perhaps in studying the dangerous words of what many women would call a "text of terror," we can discern a call to keep seeking beyond the enmity—enmity begun in the Genesis story of Hagar and Sarah, magnified in Galatians, and set loose as a power for division in the present age.[131]

Notes

1. Elisabeth A. Castelli, "Allegories of Hagar: Reading Galatians 4:21–31 with Postmodern Feminist Eyes," in *The New Literary Criticism and the New Testament: Journal for the Study of the New Testament,* Suppl. Series 109, ed. Elizabeth Struthers Malbon and Edgar V. McKnight (Sheffield: Sheffield Academic Press, 1994), 229–31. *Allegory* is a reading of a hidden meaning in the text. *Midrash* and other forms of interpretation also seek meaning, but do so with an explanation or exposition of the significance of the biblical text (cf. chap. 4).
2. J. Louis Martyn, *Galatians,* vol. 33A, *The Anchor Bible* (New York: Doubleday, 1997), 447.
3. Hans Dieter Betz, *Galatians: A Commentary on Paul's Letter to the Churches in Galatia,* Hermeneia—A Critical and Historical Commentary on the Bible (Philadelphia: Fortress Press, 1979), 239.
4. The words "married woman" in v. 27 can also be translated "woman having a man." Paul is quoting from the Septuagint, or Greek Bible, usually designated by the Roman numerals LXX.
5. Martyn, *Galatians,* 42, 29. In Isa. 51 the "barren one" refers to devastated Jerusalem, and "the one in possession (of a man)" refers to Jerusalem before destruction when she was "married" to God. E-mail correspondence with Christl Maier, July 4, 2005.
6. Elisabeth A. Castelli, "Paul on Women and Gender," in *Women and Christian Origins,* ed. Ross Shephard Kraemer and Mary Rose D'Angelo (New York: Oxford University Press, 1999), 230.
7. R. S. Sugirtharajah, *Asian Biblical Hermeneutics and Postcolonialism* (Maryknoll, NY: Orbis Books, 1998), 16–17.
8. Richard A. Horsley, "Feminist Scholarship and Postcolonial Criticism," in *Walk in the Ways of Wisdom: Essays in Honor of Elisabeth Schüssler Fiorenza,* ed. Shelly

Matthews, Cynthia Briggs Kittridge, and Melanie Johnson-Debaufre (New York: Trinity Press International, 2003), 305–10.

9. Richard A. Horsley, "Submerged Biblical Histories and Imperial Biblical Studies," in *The Postcolonial Bible*, ed. R. S. Sugirtharajah (Sheffield: Sheffield Academic Press, 1998), 162.

10. Castelli, "Paul on Women and Gender," 222.

11. Richard A. Horsley, "Paul's Counter-Imperial Gospel: Introduction," in *Paul and Empire: Religion and Power in Roman Imperial Society*, ed. Richard A. Horsley (Harrisburg, PA: Trinity Press International, 1997), 140.

12. Paula Fredriksen, "The Birth of Christianity and the Origins of Christian Anti-Judaism," in *Jesus, Judaism, and Christian Anti-Judaism: Reading the New Testament after the Holocaust*, ed. Paula Fredriksen and Adele Reinhartz (Louisville, KY: Westminster John Knox Press, 2002), 15–16.

13. Alan F. Segal, *Rebecca's Children: Judaism and Christianity in the Roman World* (Cambridge, MA: Harvard University Press, 1986), 2–3; Luise Schottroff, "'Law-Free Gentile Christianity'—What about the Women? Feminist Analyses and Alternatives," in *A Feminist Companion to Paul*, ed. Amy-Jill Levine with Marianne Blickenstaff (Cleveland: Pilgrim Press, 2004), 190–91.

14. Leander E. Keck, *Paul and His Letters*, Proclamation Commentaries, ed. Gerhard Krodel (Philadelphia: Fortress Press, 1979), 3–4.

15. Wayne A. Meeks, "The Christian Proteus," in *The Writings of St. Paul*, ed. Wayne A. Meeks (New York: W. W. Norton and Co., 1972), 436–38. This is an allusion to a sea god in Homer's *Odyssey* who could assume any form it chose.

16. See also the surveys in chaps. 1 and 4 in this book, as well as a survey of the history of interpretation of the story of Hagar and Sarah in Jewish Sources in R. N. Longenecker, *Galatians*, vol. 41 of *Word Biblical Commentary* (Dallas: Word, 1990), 200–206. Cited in Richard B. Hays, "Galatians: Introduction, Commentary, and Reflections," in *The New Interpreter's Bible*, vol. 11, ed. Leander E. Keck (Nashville: Abingdon Press, 1994), 301 n. 230.

17. Meeks, "The Christian Proteus," 409–11.

18. Cf. E. P. Sanders, *Paul and Palestinian Judaism: A Comparison of Patterns of Religion* (Philadelphia: Fortress Press, 1977).

19. Richard A. Horsley, *Paul and Politics: Ekklesia, Israel, Imperium, Interpretation: Essays in Honor of Krister Stendahl* (Harrisburg, PA: Trinity Press International, 2000), 2.

20. Meeks, "The Christian Proteus," 441–42.

21. Betz, *Galatians*; Martyn, *Galatians*; Hays, "Galatians"; Horsley, *Paul and Empire*; John Dominic Crossan and Jonathan L. Reed, *In Search of Paul: How Jesus' Apostle Opposed Rome's Empire with God's Kingdom* (New York: HarperSanFrancisco, 2004).

22. Betz, *Galatians*, 14–15, 24.

23. Martyn, *Galatians*, 21.

24. Hays, "Galatians," 188.

25. Margaret Y. MacDonald, "Reading Real Women Through the Undisputed Letters of Paul," in Kraemer and D'Angelo, eds., *Women and Christian Origins*, 199–220.

26. Charles H. Cosgrove, "The Law Has Given Sarah No Children," *Novum Testamentum* 29 (1987): 219.

27. Ibid., 219–22.

28. Hays, "Galatians," 249.

29. Cosgrove, "The Law Has Given Sarah No Children," 235.

30. Betz, *Galatians*, 238–39.

31. Martyn, *Galatians*, 446–47; Hays, "Galatians," 306–7. For the view that 4:21–31 is the open appeal in the ethical section that ends at 6:10, see G. Walter Hansen,

Abraham in Galatians: Epistolary and Rhetorical Contents, Journal for the Study of the New Testament Suppl. Series 29 (Sheffield: JSOT Press, 1989), 152–54.

32. Cosgrove, "The Law Has Given Sarah No Children," 219–20.
33. Betz, *Galatians*, 239; Hays, "Galatians," 300.
34. Hays, "Galatians," 300.
35. Betz, *Galatians*, 239–40.
36. Martyn, *Galatians*, 456; Hays, "Galatians," 303; Betz, *Galatians*, 245.
37. Martyn, *Galatians*, 454–57.
38. Hays, "Galatians," 302.
39. Cosgrove, "The Law Has Given Sarah No Children," 226.
40. Frederich Nietzsche, *Morgenrote,* in *Werke* (Darmstadt: Wissenschaftliche Buchgesellschaft, 1963), 1.1068, quoted by Hans Joachim Schoeps, *Jewish Christianity: Factional Disputes in the Early Church,* trans. John E. Steely (Nashville: Abingdon Press, 1972), 235. Quoted in Betz, *Galatians*, 244.
41. Betz, *Galatians*, 246.
42. Ibid., 245; Martyn, *Galatians*, 438; Hays, "Galatians," 303.
43. Martyn, *Galatians*, 457.
44. Ibid., 457–66; Hays, "Galatians," 303; Betz, *Galatians*, 246 (see above n. 4).
45. Cosgrove, "The Law Has Given Sarah No Children," 235.
46. Betz, *Galatians*, 239–40.
47. See above, n. 29.
48. Martyn, *Galatians*, 252.
49. Keck, 105–8. See also Dale B. Martin, *The Corinthian Body* (New Haven, CT: Yale University Press, 1995), 168–74.
50. Martyn, *Galatians*, 442.
51. Hays, "Galatians," 194.
52. Ibid., 306.
53. Martyn, *Galatians*, 35–38; Horsley, "Introduction: Krister Stendahl's Challenge to Pauline Studies," *Paul and Politics*, 9–10. The commentators cite the Jewish scholar, Daniel Boyarin, most frequently; cf. Alan Segal, *Paul the Convert: The Apostolate and Apostasy of Saul the Pharisee* (New Haven, CT: Yale University Press, 1990); and Daniel Boyarin, *A Radical Jew: Paul and the Politics of Identity* (Berkeley: University of California Press, 1994).
54. Hays, "Galatians," 194.
55. Horsley, ed., *Paul and Empire*; Horsley, ed., *Paul and Politics*; John Dominic Crossan and Jonathan L. Reed, *In Search of Paul: How Jesus's Apostle Opposed Rome's Empire with God's Kingdom* (New York: HarperSanFrancisco, 2004).
56. Horsley, "Introduction," *Paul and Empire*, 6.
57. Ibid., 20–23.
58. Ibid., 20.
59. Ibid., 8.
60. Hays, "Galatians," 303.
61. Ibid., 191–92.
62. Martyn, *Galatians*, 71.
63. Ibid., 446.
64. Horsley, "Paul's Counter-Imperial Gospel: Introduction," 141.
65. Antoinette Clark Wire, "RESPONSE: The Politics of the Assembly in Corinth," in Horsley, *Paul and Politics,* 127.
66. Crossan and Reed, *In Search of Paul*, 413.
67. Hays, "Galatians," 309.
68. Antoinette Clark Wire, *The Corinthian Women Prophets: A Reconstruction Through Paul's Rhetoric* (Minneapolis: Fortress Press, 1990).

69. Elisabeth Schüssler Fiorenza, "Paul and the Politics of Interpretation," *Paul and Politics,* 45–47.

70. Martyn, *Galatians,* 26; 222–28. As Martyn notes, the Galatians seem to have rejected Paul's appeal as we hear no more about them except that they seem to have refused to join their brothers and sisters in Macedonia and Achaia (Greece) in contributing to the collection that Paul intends to take for the church in Jerusalem (Gal. 2:9–10; Rom. 15:26–27; 2 Cor. 8:2; 9:2, 4).

71. Elisabeth Schüssler Fiorenza, *In Memory of Her: A Feminist Theological Reconstruction of Christian Origins* (New York: Crossroad, 1983). Cf. three different books honoring Elisabeth Schüssler Fiorenza's sixty-fifth birthday: Shelly Matthews, Cynthia Briggs Kittredge, and Melanie Johnson-Debaufre, eds., *Walk in the Ways of Wisdom* (cited above, n. 8); Fernando F. Segovia, ed., *Toward a New Heaven and a New Earth* (Maryknoll, NY: Orbis Books, 2003); Jane Schaberg, Alice Bach, and Esther Fuchs, eds., *On the Cutting Edge.*

72. Cynthia Briggs Kittridge, "Rethinking Authorship in the Letters of Paul: Elisabeth Schüssler Fiorenza's Model of Pauline Theology," in *Walk in the Ways of Wisdom,* 318. Cf. international writers in Daniel Patte, ed., *Global Bible Commentary* (Nashville: Abingdon, 2004); Elisabeth A. Castelli, "Heteroglossia, Hermeneutics, and History: A Review Essay of Recent Feminist Studies of Early Christianity," *Journal of Feminist Studies in Religion* 10, no. 2 (Fall 1994): 73–98; "Paul on Women and Gender" (cited above, n. 6), 221–35.

73. Elisabeth Schüssler Fiorenza, *Rhetoric and Ethic: The Politics of Biblical Studies* (Minneapolis: Fortress Press, 1999), 145.

74. Ibid.

75. Cynthia Briggs Kittredge, "Corinthian Women Prophets and Paul's Argumentation in 1 Corinthians," in Horsley, *Paul and Politics,* 103.

76. Kittredge, "Corinthian Women Prophets," 103–4.

77. Martyn, *Galatians,* 41–42.

78. Schüssler Fiorenza, *Rhetoric and Ethic,* 180–82.

79. Sheila Briggs, "Hagar: Hagar in the New Testament" and "Sarah 1/Sarai: Sarah in the New Testament," in *Women in Scripture: A Dictionary of Named and Unnamed Women in the Hebrew Bible, the Apocryphal/Deuterocanonical Books, and the New Testament,* ed. Carol Meyers, Toni Craven, and Ross S. Kraemer (New York: Houghton Mifflin Co., 2000), 88, 151–52; "Galatians," in *Searching the Scriptures: A Feminist Commentary,* ed. Elisabeth Schüssler Fiorenza (New York: Crossroad, 1994), 2:219–36; "Slavery and Gender," in Schoberg et al., *On the Cutting Edge,* 171–92; "Paul on Bondage and Freedom in Imperial Roman Society," in Horsley, *Paul and Politics,* 110–23.

80. Brigitte Kahl, "Gender Trouble in Galatia? Paul and the Rethinking of Difference," in *Is There a Future for Feminist Theology?* ed. Deborah F. Sawyer and Diane M. Collier (Sheffield: Sheffield Academic Press, 1999), 58–73; "No Longer Male: Masculinity Struggles behind Galatians 3:28," *Journal for the Study of the New Testament* (September 2000): 37–49.

81. Susan M. Elliott, "Choose Your Mother, Choose your Master: Galatians 4:21–5:1 in the Shadow of the Anatolian Mother of the Gods," *Journal of Biblical Literature* 118, no. 4 (Winter 1999): 661–83.

82. Horsley, "Introduction," 3–5.

83. Wire, "RESPONSE," 128.

84. Briggs, "Paul on Bondage," 110.

85. Ibid., 118.

86. Briggs concurs with most contemporary scholars that this was an earlier hymn not composed by Paul, but others have begun to argue that Paul composed the

hymn. Cf. Adele Yarbro Collins, "The Psalms and the Origins of Christology," in *Psalms in Community: Jewish and Christian Textual, Liturgical, and Artistic Traditions*, ed. Harold W. Attridge and Margot E. Fassler, Society of Biblical Literature Symposium Series 25 (Atlanta: Society of Biblical Literature, 2003), 113–23.

87. Ibid., 120. The theme itself is not new as it is present in Greco-Roman literature and through the ages. A highly born child is mistakenly raised as a slave until the true identity is discovered and the child or adult is joyously elevated.

88. Ibid., 117–18. Cf. Sheila Briggs, "Can an Enslaved God Liberate? Hermeneutical Reflections on Philippians 2:6–11," *Semeia* 47 (1989): 137–53; Luise Schotroff, *Lydia's Impatient Sisters: A Feminist Social History of Early Christianity* (Louisville, KY: Westminster John Knox Press, 1995), 43–46, 124–31.

89. Cf. James Albert Harrill, *The Manumission of Slaves in Early Christianity* (Tübingen: J. S. B. Mohr, 1995).

90. Briggs, "Paul on Bondage," 117.

91. Briggs, "Slavery and Gender," 178–79.

92. Castelli, "Paul on Women and Gender," 230 (cited above, n. 6).

93. Schüssler Fiorenza, *Rhetoric and Ethic*, 155.

94. Luise Schottroff, *Let the Oppressed Go Free: Feminist Perspectives on the New Testament* (Louisville, KY: Westminster John Knox Press, 1991), 46.

95. Briggs, "Slavery and Gender," 186.

96. Cf. John H. Elliott, "The Jesus Movement Was Not Egalitarian but Family-Oriented," *Biblical Interpretation* 11, no. 2 (2003): 173–210.

97. Wire, "RESPONSE," 129.

98. Kahl, "No Longer Male," 43.

99. Briggs, "Slavery and Gender," 184.

100. Kahl, "Gender Trouble," 67–68.

101. Ibid., 58.

102. Ibid., 62.

103. Ibid., 58; Kahl, "No Longer Male," 40.

104. Kahl, "No Longer Male," 49.

105. Ibid., 41. The Greek word *sperma* may be translated "sperm" or "seed."

106. Ibid., 41–42.

107. Ibid., 42.

108. Ibid., 43.

109. Ibid., 43; Kahl, "Gender Trouble," 68.

110. Kahl, "No Longer Male," 46.

111. Kahl, "Gender Trouble," 66–68.

112. Cf. Wire, *The Corinthian Women Prophets*; Schottroff, *Lydia's Impatient Sisters*.

113. Khal, "Gender Trouble," 71. Paul was writing before Roman forces destroyed the temple in 70 CE and Jerusalem in 135 CE.

114. Elliott, "Choose Your Mother," 664 (cited above, n. 81). Cf. Susan M. Elliott, "The Rhetorical Strategy of Paul's Letter to the Galatians in Its Anatolian Cultic Context: Circumcision and the Castration of the Galli of the Mother of the Gods" (PhD. diss., Loyola University, Chicago, 1997); "Paul and His Gentile Audiences: Mystery Cults, Anatolian Popular Religiosity, and Paul's Claim of Divine Authority in Galatians," *Listening* 31 (1996): 117–36.

115. Elliott, "Choose Your Mother," 666; Cosgrove, "The Law Has Given" (cited above, n. 26, and in the section on "Straightening up the Mess").

116. Elliott, "Choose Your Mother," 668.

117. Ibid., 671 (see other views cited in n. 40).

118. Ibid., 671–73.

119. Cf. Adele Yarbro Collins, "Pergamon in Early Christian Literature," in *Pergamon: Citadel of the Gods,* Harvard Theological Studies 46 (Harrisburg, PA: Trinity Press International, 1998), 163–84.

120. Ibid., 672–73.

121. Ibid., 675.

122. Ibid., 676–78.

123. Ibid., 681–82.

124. Ibid., 683.

125. Ibid., 682.

126. Pamela Eisenbaum, "Paul as the New Abraham," in Horsley, *Paul and Politics,* 130–45. For additional discussion of Abraham in Galatians, cf. G. Walter Hansen, *Abraham in Galatians* (cited above, n. 31).

127. Christl M. Maier, "Psalm 87 as a Reappraisal of the Zion Tradition and Its Reception in Galatians 4:26," paper delivered at the IOSOT Conference, Leiden, August 4, 2004, and the Society of Biblical Literature, San Antonio, November 21, 2004.

128. Joseph Brackett Jr., "Simple Gifts," *The Gift to Be Simple: Shaker Rituals and Songs,* 1848. http://www2.gol.com/users/quakers/simple gifts.htm.

129. Horsley, "Introduction," 5; Wire, "RESPONSE," 127–28.

130. Schottroff, *Lydia's Impatient Sisters,* 45. See also chap. 8 in this book.

131. Many thanks to the biblical scholars who shared their insights and supportive assistance in the writing of this chapter on Galatians: Adela Yarbro Collins, Mary Rose D'Angelo, Hisako Kinukawa, Christl Maier, Diana Swancutt.

PART TWO
HAGAR AND SARAH IN JEWISH, CHRISTIAN, AND MUSLIM TRADITIONS

Chapter 4

Conflict and Coexistence in Jewish Interpretation

Adele Reinhartz and
Miriam-Simma Walfish

In the biblical version of their story, Hagar and Sarah vie for position in the household of Abraham and in the eyes of God. As a freeborn, Israelite matriarch, Sarah is clearly superior to Hagar, her maidservant and Abraham's Egyptian concubine. But in conceiving Abraham's son Ishmael, Hagar, though still inferior in ethnicity and in social and marital status, surpasses Sarah on the most important factor of all: fertility. Sarah's superiority is restored when God intervenes on Sarah's behalf so that Sarah conceives and then bears Abraham's son Isaac.

The ups and downs of this relationship are propelled by the actions of the two women themselves. When she conceives, Hagar taunts Sarah, pointedly reminding her mistress of her own infertility. Sarah in turn deals harshly with Hagar, who runs away, only to return when God commands her to do so. This return is merely temporary; after Isaac is born, Sarah banishes both Hagar and her son Ishmael. Yet Sarah's expulsion of her rival, intended to ensure Isaac's succession, and perhaps also to seal her position within her own household, ultimately backfires. If Hagar is now banished from Abraham's estate, she has also escaped from Sarah's heavy hand. And whereas Sarah does not live to see Isaac grow to adulthood, marry, and have children, Hagar not only survives but also finds her son Ishmael a wife. The narrator thus deftly assures the fulfillment of God's covenant with Abraham, which has promised numerous offspring, while at the same time restoring Hagar to freedom, honoring her personhood and looking ahead to the broader context of Israelite history.

For Jewish commentators through the ages, the biblical story of Hagar and Sarah forces a choice between two central principles: reverence for their Jewish ancestors, through whom God creates the nation of Israel,[1] and concern for the powerless, which is enshrined in biblical and subsequent Jewish law.[2] Whose side to be on, that of the revered matriarch whose son signified God's fulfillment of the covenantal promises to Abraham and resulted in the eventual appearance of the Jewish people on the stage of history? Or that of the beleaguered maidservant who suffered at that matriarch's hands, though her pregnancy had been engineered by the matriarch herself?

As they struggled with this issue, Jewish interpreters from the postbiblical period to our own time rewrote the story of Hagar and Sarah to reflect their own sensibilities as well as the norms and values of their own time and place. In this chapter, we will trace the ways in which the story was told and retold through the postbiblical, rabbinic, medieval, and modern/postmodern periods. In doing so, we shall see a complex, shifting, often uneasy relationship between Hagar and Sarah that over time and with liberal doses of patience and imagination evolves into a story of mutual respect, coexistence, and hope.

POSTBIBLICAL SOURCES

The postbiblical period, from the second century BCE through the second century CE, has left us with a significant number of Jewish texts that retell biblical stories, including that of Hagar and Sarah.[3] For example, the book of Jubilees, stemming from Palestine[4] in the mid-second century BCE, provides an account of what God ostensibly revealed to Moses during his forty days on Mount Sinai. It follows the basic outline of Genesis and the first several chapters of Exodus, but both adds and compresses, as well as interprets, the biblical narrative. Jubilees lingers only briefly on the stories of Hagar and Sarah. Jubilees 14:21–24 summarizes Genesis 16 but, significantly, omits Hagar's arrogance towards Sarai, as well as Sarai's behavior towards Hagar and Hagar's attempted escape. These omissions eliminate the problems inherent in the biblical account, and avoid the difficult moral dilemmas it invokes.[5] Jubilees 17 summarizes Genesis 21 but does not add any details to or comment upon the story of Hagar and Sarah.[6] Even sketchier is the account in the *Biblical Antiquities* of Pseudo-Philo, a work that likely dates from first-century CE Palestine, which mentions only that, due to Sarai's infertility, Abram took Hagar, "his maid," who then bore him Ishmael.[7] No other details are forthcoming, not even Sarah's ownership of Hagar or the banishment of mother and child.[8]

A more extensive account is provided by Josephus Flavius, the first-century Jewish historian who is the source of much of our knowledge of Jewish life, society, and history in Judea under Roman domination in the first century of the common era. His series of treatises, entitled *Jewish Antiquities*, begins with a retelling of biblical history. Here is his account of Genesis 16:

> God bade him [Abram] be assured that, as in all else, he had been led out of Mesopotamia for his welfare, so children would come to him; and by God's command Sarra brought to his bed one of her handmaidens, an Egyptian named Agar, that he might have children by her. Becoming pregnant, this servant had the insolence to abuse Sarra, assuming queenly airs as though the dominion were to pass to her unborn son. Abraham having thereupon consigned her to Sarra for chastisement, she, unable to endure her humiliations, resolved to fly and entreated God to take pity on her. But as she went on her way through the wilderness an angel of God met her and bade her return to her master and mistress, assuring her that she would attain a happier lot through self-control, for her present plight was but due to her arrogance and presumption towards her mistress; and that if she disobeyed God and pursued her way she would perish, but if she returned home she would become the mother of a son hereafter to reign over that country. Obedient to this behest she returned to her master and mistress, was forgiven, and not long after gave birth to Is(h)mael, a name which may be rendered "Heard of God," because God had hearkened to her petition. (*Ant.* 1.187–90)[9]

This section clearly takes the "side" of Sarai, but it does not portray Hagar as evil, merely as immature, ignorant, and misguided. Josephus returns to Hagar in his paraphrase of Genesis 21:

> Sarra at the first, when Ishmael was born of her servant Hagar, cherished him with an affection no less than if he had been her own son, seeing that he was being trained as heir to the chieftaincy; but when she herself gave birth to Isaac, she held it wrong that her boy should be brought up with Ishmael, who was the elder child and might do him an injury after their father was dead. She therefore urged Abraham to send him and his mother away to settle elsewhere. He, however, at first refused to consent to Sarra's scheme, thinking nothing could be more brutal than to send off an infant child with a woman destitute of the necessaries of life. But afterwards, seeing that Sarra's behests were sanctioned also by God, he yielded and, committing Ishmael to his mother, the child being not yet of age to go alone, bade her take a skin full of water and a loaf and be gone, with necessity to serve as her guide . . . An angel of god . . . told her of a spring hard by and bade her look to the nurture of the young child, for great blessings awaited her through the preservation of Ishmael. These promises gave her new courage, and, meeting some shepherds, she through their care escaped her miseries. (*Ant* 1.215–19)[10]

This account adds three important details to the biblical story. First, Sarah genuinely loved Ishmael, at least until Isaac was born. Second, Sarah's concern was primarily for the safety of her son Isaac, not the security of his inheritance. Third, Hagar and Ishmael survived their banishment to the desert at least in part due to the help of shepherds. Josephus here maintains and even enhances the positive evaluation of Abraham and Sarah, even as it does not denigrate Hagar, but he glosses over the moral issues that are inherent in the biblical account.

Among postbiblical authors it is Philo of Alexandria who pays the most attention to Hagar. Philo (approximately 50 BCE to 30 CE) was a Jewish philosopher
whose goal was the reconciliation of Jewish Scripture with Greek philosophy,
especially Stoicism and Neoplatonism.[11] He achieved this reconciliation primarily by interpreting the Bible as an elaborate allegory for the soul's journey to wisdom. Philo does not attach great importance to Hagar as an individual or as a
character in a biblical story, nor does he show much concern for the moral issues
raised by Genesis 16 and 21. Rather, he treats Hagar solely as an element in his
thorough allegorical interpretation of Genesis. For Philo, "Hagar" means
"sojourning," and refers specifically to the academic subjects with which the soul
must "sojourn" temporarily on its way to wisdom and truth (*Allegorical Interpretation* 3.244; *On the Cherubim* 3–8).[12] When the seeker attains those truths, an
achievement that is symbolized in Philo's allegorical system by the birth of Isaac,
"then will be cast forth those preliminary studies which bear the name of Hagar,
and cast forth too will be their son the sophist named Ishmael."[13]

But this is not to say that Hagar, that is, these preliminary studies, are unim-
portant. Indeed, Philo devotes an entire treatise to the subject of *Mating with the
Preliminary Studies*. The preliminary studies that "virtue" employs are "no minor
kind of introduction, but grammar, geometry, astronomy, rhetoric, music, and
all the other branches of intellectual study. These are symbolized by Hagar, the
handmaid of Sarah" (*Cong.* 11).[14] He explains further that Sarah, whose allegorical meaning is "virtue,"

> bears . . . the same relation to Hagar, education, as the mistress to the ser-
> vant maid, or the lawful wife to the concubine, and so naturally the mind
> which aspires to study and to gain knowledge, the mind we call Abraham,
> will have Sarah, virtue, for his wife, and Hagar, the whole range of school
> culture for his concubine . . . he, then, who gains wisdom by instruction,
> will not reject Hagar, for the acquisition of these preliminary subjects is
> quite necessary. (*Cong.* 23–24)[15]

He concludes his treatise with a line addressed directly to his reader:

> When, then, you hear of Hagar as afflicted or evil-entreated by Sarah, do
> not suppose that you have here one of the usual accompaniments of women's
> jealousy. It is not women that are spoken of here; it is minds—on the one
> hand, the mind which exercises itself in the preliminary learning, on the
> other, the mind which strives to win the palm of virtue and ceases not till it
> is won. (*Cong.* 180)[16]

If his postbiblical peers simply ignore the difficult elements of the story, Philo
allegorizes the story to the point where the surface meaning of the text is almost
completely undone. In failing to address the moral dimensions of the text, all of
these authors fail to call Sarah's behavior into question and hence implicitly validate her position of superiority. Our information is too sparse to permit specu-
lation as to whether or how the situation of Roman domination may have led

these authors to emphasize Sarah's superiority over against the injustices done to Hagar.

RABBINIC SOURCES

Rabbinic literature, by contrast, is much less evasive. Rabbinic interpreters generally comment on specific verses or even parts of verses; they do not engage in a continuous narrative retelling of the Bible but their comments are often compiled in the order of the biblical verses to which they pertain. This genre of literature exists in the gray area between pure commentary and original creative composition. Comments are often prompted by linguistic, theological, narrative or homiletical peculiarities, problems, or issues that emerge from the biblical text.[17] This type of commentary is referred to as "midrash," a Hebrew term deriving from the root "d-r-sh." This root literally means "to seek out" or "to inquire after," but in the context of biblical interpretation the term refers more specifically to the act of studying and interpreting the biblical text. As a genre of literature, midrash was prevalent in the rabbinic period, dating from the third through the tenth centuries CE. Individual comments, as well as collections of such comments, are called "midrashim." The rabbis to whom midrashic comments are attributed are often called "the Sages"; scholars disagree on the extent to which these attributions are historically correct.[18]

Rabbinic midrashic texts are often grouped into two categories. Midrash halakhah deals with the legal portions of the Bible, whereas midrash haggadah deals with the nonlegal sections of the biblical text. Discussions of Hagar and Sarah occur primarily in texts that belong to the category of midrash haggadah.[19] Many midrashic interpretations play on Hebrew homonyms, an aspect that often gets lost in translation. This playfulness suggests that midrashim were originally meant to be heard rather than read. Another important feature of midrash haggadah is polysemy—the belief that the text is subject to multiple interpretations and therefore cannot be reduced to one single "correct" meaning.[20]

Not surprisingly, rabbinic midrash tends to resolve the moral issues at stake in the biblical story of Hagar and Sarah in favor of the Israelite matriarch, but as we shall see, they are by no means blind to the moral dilemmas nor uniform in their assessment of the situation. We shall look briefly at rabbinic midrashim under four headings: status, fertility, revelation, and finally, Sarah's treatment of Hagar.

Status

The rabbis were well aware of the factors that from the Israelite point of view marked Sarah as superior to Hagar. One midrashic thread links Hagar's Egyptian identity to her status as Sarah's slave. The most developed example of this thread is found in *Genesis Rabbah*, a midrashic collection stemming from the area now known as Israel/Palestine, in the second half of the fifth century CE.[21]

> R. Simeon b. Yohai said: Hagar was Pharaoh's daughter. When Pharaoh saw what was done on Sarah's behalf in his own house, he took his daughter and gave her to Sarah, saying, Better let my daughter be a handmaid in this house than a mistress in another house. (*Gen. Rab.* 45:1)[22]

According to R. Simeon b. Yohai, Hagar is no ordinary slave woman, sold into slavery because of her lowly status. Rather, Hagar is the daughter of Pharaoh who could have had any prince as her husband. Yet her father gives her as a slave to the house of Abraham, in recognition of God's powerful, and dire, intervention on Sarah's behalf during the time that Sarah was in the Pharaoh's household (cf. Gen. 12:14–19).

Other midrashim suggest that Hagar's Egyptian origins mark her as an unreformed idolater. She may have worshiped the God of Israel while she was a member of Abraham's household, but Hagar reverted to her idolatrous state as soon as she was outside Abraham's sphere of influence. *Pirqe d'Rabbi Eliezer*, an eighth- or ninth-century compilation,[23] states that when Abraham banished Hagar and Ishmael the water did not run out until they reached the desert, as until that point they were still under the positive influence of Abraham's monotheism. When they reached the desert, however, "[s]he started wandering after the idol worship of her father's home and immediately the water ran out" (*Pirqe R. El.*, "Horeb," 29).

Less restrained in its negative assessment of Hagar's Egyptian origins is a midrash found in *Aggadat Bereshit*, a tenth-century collection of homilies on Genesis. Here the Sages draw a rather unflattering comparison between Hagar and a blob of donkey fat that has accidentally fallen into rose oil:[24]

> Even though its smell became pleasant from the rose oil, it ended up stinking as it had before. . . . The fat of a donkey is Hagar the Egyptian, as it says of the Egyptians (Ezek. 23:20) "whose members were like those of asses. . . ." Hagar cleaved to Abraham and gave birth to Ishmael . . . but in the end she returned to her stench as it is written, "And his mother took for him a woman from the land of Egypt" (Gen. 21:21). And this is why [the Bible] says that Abraham gave birth to Isaac whereas it says that Hagar gave birth to Ishmael.[25]

The quotation from Ezekiel connects idolatry to sexual promiscuity. Ezekiel 23:20 describes the lusting of Israel after the Egyptians: "She lusted for concubinage with them, whose members were like those of asses and whose organs were like those of stallions" (Ezek. 23:20). In drawing on this biblical passage, *Aggadat Bereshit* claims that Hagar is fertile because she comes from a sexually promiscuous people, not because she has found divine favor.

Not all the midrashim, however, view Hagar's Egyptian origins as an impediment to monotheism. *Yalkut Shimoni*, a compilation of midrashim composed in the twelth to thirteenth century from fifty earlier works,[26] lists Hagar first among nine righteous converts[27] including such important figures as Zipporah, Moses' wife, and Shifra and Puah, the Egyptian midwives who saved the Jewish boys from being drowned in the Nile.[28]

The Sages were attuned not only to Hagar's Egyptian origins but also to her status as a slave. So, for example, *Genesis Rabbah* 45:7 asserts that Hagar receives revelation solely to inform her that she is a slave:

> *And the angel of the Lord found her . . . and he said: Hagar, Sarah's handmaid* (Gen 16:8):[29] So runs the proverb: 'If one man tells you that you have ass's ears, do not believe him; if two tell it to you, order a halter.' Thus, Abraham said: Behold, thy maid is in thy hand (Gen 16:6); the angel said: Hagar, Sarai's *handmaid . . .* hence. *And she said, I flee from the face of my mistress Sarai.*[30]

The analogy invokes the image of a donkey, this time as a reflection not upon Hagar's ethnicity or sexuality, but her servitude. Like the donkey, Hagar the slave is a work animal. If Hagar believed that sharing her mistress's husband also meant sharing Sarah's social status, she was deluding herself. The angel confirms the contrary, by echoing Abraham's designation of Hagar as Sarah's handmaid.

Pirqe Rabbi Eliezer categorically denies the possibility that any events can change the inherently superior status of Sarah. In this text, God says to Abraham:

> Did you not know that Sarah was arranged for you from the time her mother conceived her and she is both your partner and a woman of your covenant. Sarah is not called your servant, rather your wife, and Hagar is not called your wife, rather your servant. (*Pirqe R. El.*, "Horeb," 29)

But just as Hagar's Egyptian origins did not irredeemably exclude her from the ranks of the righteous, neither did her lowly status as a slave. This point is illustrated by the following comment from midrash *Tanhuma Yelammedenu*, a group of homiletic midrashim on the Pentateuch from fifth-century Palestine.[31]

> May our rabbi teach us why a slave is counted among the seven that read from the Torah. [Answer]: Just as Eliezer, the servant of Abraham, because he was righteous, was compared to his master (Gen. 24:30), and the sons of the slave women [Bilha and Zilpa, the concubines of Jacob] were counted among the tribes,[32] so too God caused suffering to Abraham and Sarah and did not give them sons for the sake of Hagar who was a righteous woman, so that she would go in to Abraham, and he would have a son from her. (*Otsar HaMidrashim* [*OM*] 222:9–10).

Fertility and Divine Favor

On the whole, rabbinic literature does not fundamentally challenge Sarah's ethnic, marital, and social superiority to Hagar. But for the Sages, as for the biblical narrator, fertility destabilizes the fixed hierarchy between Hagar and Sarah. The high value placed on fertility as a marker of status is evident throughout *Genesis Rabbah*, chapter 45.

This chapter, like the majority of the chapters in *Genesis Rabbah*, begins with a proem, that is, a homily that takes a verse from the "Writings" portion of the Scriptures as the starting point for its discussion of a verse from the Torah or Pentateuch.[33] The proem that introduces *Genesis Rabbah* 45 builds its homily around Proverbs 31:10: "Who can find a worthy woman whose price (*mikhrah*) is beyond rubies?" The midrash asks: "What does 'mikhrah' mean? R. Abba b. Kahana said: 'Her pregnancy, as you read, *Thine origins (mekhorot) and thy nativity*'" (Ezek. 16:3). The Jerusalem Talmud explains that "righteous women, as in the case of Sarah, find pregnancy more difficult of attainment than rubies."[34] But underlying the midrash is also the notion that fertility is the trait that raises a woman's value—or status—"beyond rubies."[35]

Fertility is also important theologically. The central component of God's covenantal promise to Abraham is that he will be the patriarch of a great nation: "'Look towards heaven and count the stars, if you are able to count them.' Then [God] said to [Abraham], 'So shall your descendants be'" (Gen. 15:5). In order for God's promises to be fulfilled, Abraham must have at least one child, yet Sarah, like two of the three matriarchs who came after her, experienced extended periods of infertility before God finally intervened. This procreative delay creates a narrative crisis that is particularly disturbing in the story of Sarah and Abraham, the founders of the Israelite nation, as it is here that the question of continuity is most urgent.

In biblical narrative, it is God who controls female fertility. The biblical Sarai notes that it is God who has prevented her from giving birth (Gen. 16:2); in Genesis 18:10, one of the angels who comes to visit Abraham promises, on God's behalf, "I will surely return to you in due season, and your wife Sarah shall have a son." The promise is fulfilled in Genesis 21:1: "God remembered Sarah as God said; God did for Sarah what God had spoken." Most striking, however, is the fact that Hagar, Sarah's Egyptian handmaid, both gives birth and receives divine revelation before Sarah does.

If fertility is so closely connected to the divine will, how is it that Hagar—an Egyptian slave woman—conceives before Sarah—an Israelite and designated matriarch of the Jewish people? Rabbinic literature records two contrary responses to this question. One is to accept the presumed connection between fertility and divine favor; the other is to reject this link. The former response views Sarah's eventual conception of Isaac as a sign that she did indeed find favor in the eyes of the divine. This response is evident in midrashim that comment on the miraculous nature of Isaac's conception and birth. One example can be found in *Pesikta d'Rav Kahana*, a fifth-century homiletic midrash structured around the special readings for the festivals.[36] It reads,

> R. Berakhyah in the name of R. Levi said: You find that when our mother Sarah gave birth to Isaac the nations of the world said, "Impossible! Sarah did not give birth to Isaac, rather Hagar the maidservant of Sarah gave birth to him." What did God do? God dried up the teats of the women in the other nations and the matrons among them came and kissed the dust at

Sarah's feet and said, "Do a good deed and breast feed our children." And Abraham said to Sarah: Sarah, this is not the time for modesty, sanctify the name of God by sitting in the market and breastfeeding their children. Thus it is written, "Sarah breastfed *children* [*banim*]" (Gen 21:7). It was not written "*ben*" (sg.) rather "*banim*" (pl.), not one child [*ben*], but many children [*banim*].[37]

The non-Jewish nations' misconception that Hagar gave birth to Isaac is an ironic echo of Sarah's hope that she will have a son through her maidservant. In order to rectify the misunderstanding, God causes a drastic miracle. Here, God's relationship with Sarah is not manifest through prayer and response, but rather through a miraculous birth.

In other midrashim, Sarah herself expresses the fear that her infertility may be a sign of divine disfavor. For example, in their comments on the verse "May the wrong done to me be upon you" (Gen. 16:5), the rabbis of *Genesis Rabbah* 45:5 portray Sarah as blaming Abraham for the fact that God has overlooked her desire for a child. According to this midrash, the situation responsible for Sarah's infertility "may be compared to two people who went to borrow seed from the king."

> One of them asked, "Lend me seed," and he ordered, "Give it to him." Said his companion to him, "I have a grievance against you. Had you asked, 'Lend *us* seed,' he would have given me just as he gave you; now however that you said, 'Lend *me* seed,' he has given you but not me." Similarly, hadst thou said, "Behold, to us Thou hast given no seed," then as He gave thee so had he given me. Now however that thou didst say, "Behold, to *me* Thou hast given no seed (Gen. 15:3), he gave to thee but not to me."[38]

Here Sarah insists that had her husband asked God for a son using the plural pronoun "we" rather than the singular pronoun "I," it would have been she and not Hagar who would have conceived and given birth. This midrash implies that women, whether Israelite or not, could connect with God only through the mediation of their husbands, and not through their own prayers.

Elsewhere, however, Sarah's fertility is seen as the ultimate proof of divine favor. In addition, Sarah's ability to breastfeed a multitude of children, described above in *Pesikta d'Rav Kavana*, demonstrates a radical shift in her status. A parallel to this midrash, found in the Babylonian Talmud *Bava Metzia* 87a,[39] describes her breasts as two fountains that flowed with enough milk to feed whoever came. God has transformed Sarah from a dry, barren, old woman to a goddess-like fertile mother.

Other midrashim reverse the presumed connection between fertility and the divine. For them, it is Sarah's very infertility that signifies her positive relationship to God. Commenting on the verse "and he went into Hagar and she conceived," *Genesis Rabbah* 45:4 explains:

> R. Levi b. Hayta said: [Hagar] became pregnant through the first intimacy. R. Eleazar said: A woman never conceives by the first intimacy. An objection is raised: surely it is written *Thus were both the daughters of Lot with*

child by their father (Gen. 19:36)? . . . . R. Hanina b. Pazzi observed: Thorns are neither weeded nor sown, yet of their accord they grow and spring up, whereas how much pain and toil is required before wheat can be made to grow![40]

From the biblical perspective, the daughters of Lot, who got their father drunk, slept with him, and conceived his children (Gen. 19), exemplify fertility gone awry. The Sages use the example of these sisters to denigrate Hagar's own fecundity. Just as the offspring of Lot's daughters were the result of corruption, so too there is something suspect about Hagar's quick and easy conception. Hagar, like Lot's daughters, is compared to unruly weeds that impede rather than promote legitimate propagation. This metaphor not only casts aspersions on Hagar's divine connection but also delegitimizes Ishmael as the offspring of Abraham.

The continuation of this midrash provides two positive reasons for the infertility of Sarah and the other Israelite matriarchs. The first is "Because the Holy One . . . yearns for their prayers and supplications. . . ." The second, more pragmatic reason is explicated by R. Huna, R. Idi, and R. Abin in R. Meir's name:

> So that their husbands might derive pleasure from them, for when a woman is with child she is disfigured and lacks grace. Thus the whole ninety years that Sarah did not bear she was like a bride in her canopy. Ladies used to come to inquire how she was, and she would say to them, "Go and ask about the welfare of this poor woman [Hagar]." Hagar would tell them: "My mistress Sarai is not inwardly what she is outwardly: she appears to be a righteous woman, but she is not. For had she been a righteous woman, see how many have passed without her conceiving, whereas I conceived in one night!" Said Sarah, "Shall I pay heed to this woman and argue with her! No; I will argue the matter with her master!"[41]

Sarah's infertility is a divinely initiated communication; by referring to the biblical stories regarding the mothers' prayers for children, the midrash maintains that infertility, and not fertility, is in fact a sign of divine connection. And when Hagar attempts to convince the visiting matrons that fertility reflects one's righteousness and connection to God, the rabbis claim that Hagar's accusation is so far off the mark that Sarah refuses even to discuss it with her. By undermining the assumption that fertility signifies divine favor, the Sages are able to maintain Sarah's superiority despite her infertility.

Revelation and Divine Favor

But it is not only, or even primarily, her fertility that implies the biblical Hagar's link with the God of Israel. Rather, it is Hagar's encounters with angels in the desert that stress God's sympathy for Hagar and her plight (Gen. 16:7–13; 21:17–20). Indeed, the rabbis must contend seriously with the contrast between Hagar and Sarah in this regard: whereas Hagar met God's angels—and communicated with God directly, Sarah does so only once (Gen. 18:10), and even then it is Abraham who is the main audience for this revelation.[42]

The rabbinic responses to Hagar's angelic encounters vary widely. *Genesis Rabbah* 45:7 intensifies the biblical account by suggesting that Hagar sees not one angel but many:

> How many angels visited her? R. Hama b. R. Hanina said: Five, each time "speech" is mentioned it refers to an angel. The rabbis said: Four, this being the number of times "angel" occurs. R. Hiyya observed: Come and see how great is the difference between the earlier generations and the later ones! What did Manoah say to his wife? *We shall surely die, because we have seen God* (Judges 13:22); yet Hagar, a bondmaid, sees five angels and is not afraid of them! . . . R. Yitzhak said: *"She seeth the ways of her household"* (Proverbs 31:27). Abraham's household were seers, so she [Hagar] was accustomed to them.[43]

This midrash struggles with the question of why Hagar merited such abundant revelation. It diminishes the uniqueness of her experience by attributing her ability to see angels to her place in Abraham's household. Although Hagar is a mere servant in Abraham's household, she is accustomed to seeing angels and therefore she is not particularly bothered when she meets one (or five), while Manoah, despite his more illustrious lineage, believes that he will die because he has seen one.

In *Genesis Rabbah* 45:10, however, the Sages are less disparaging; they allow for the possibility that Hagar may have been able to see angels that were invisible to Sarah.

> I was favoured [to see an angel] not only when with my mistress, but even now that I am alone. R. Samuel said: This may be compared to a noble lady whom the king ordered to walk before him. She did so leaning on her maid and pressing her face against her. Thus her maid saw [the king], while she did not see him.[44]

This midrash emphasizes Hagar's ability to see angels by suggesting that even when the two women were together, there were times when Hagar was able to see divine beings and Sarah was not.

Sarah's Treatment of Hagar

The question of Sarah's divine favor is important not only for its own sake but also as a basis for the moral evaluation of her behavior towards Hagar. Some Sages tried to account for the fact that it was Sarah and not Abraham, the head of the household, who acted against Hagar. In *Genesis Rabbah* 45:6, Abraham draws on biblical verses to impress upon Sarah that he cannot act on her behalf in this matter:

> I am constrained to do her neither good nor harm. It is written, *Thou shalt not deal with her as a slave, because thou hast humbled her* (Deut 21:14): After we have vexed her, can we now enslave her again? I am constrained to do her neither good nor harm. It is written, *And Sarah dealt harshly with her,*

> *and she fled from her face* (Gen 16:6), while it is written, *To sell her unto a*
> *foreign people he shall have no power, seeing he hath dealt deceitfully with her*
> (Ex 21:8): after we have made her a mistress, shall we make her a bondmaid
> again? I am constrained to do her neither good nor harm; hence it is writ-
> ten, *and Sarah dealt harshly with her, and she fled from her face.*[45]

This passage betrays a hint of ambivalence with regard to Sarah's treatment of
Hagar. In the midrash, Abraham bases his refusal to intervene upon verses from
Deuteronomy and Exodus that describe the treatment of female war captives and
Hebrew slaves. Deuteronomy forbids the enslavement of the captive taken for
marriage (21:10–17); Exodus prohibits the selling of the Hebrew maidservant to
foreign men (Exod. 21:7–11). These biblical instructions provide a striking coun-
terpoint to our story. It would seem that Abraham has acquired Hagar in a man-
ner prohibited by biblical law.[46] A wrong has already been done to Hagar;
Abraham is unwilling to add to that wrong by punishing her on Sarah's behalf.
For this reason, it is Sarah, not Abraham, who deals harshly with Sarah.

The Sages explicate the text in order to understand it better in all its dimensions, to articulate their own values, and to impress these values upon their audiences. Given their self-understanding as descendants of the covenantal people
springing from the union of Abraham and Sarah, it is not surprising that many
uphold Sarah's superior status and try to explain both her infertility and her behavior towards Hagar in a positive light. In this context, it is perhaps the dissenting
voices—those that are willing to criticize Sarah and that view Hagar as an
autonomous and worthy person in her own right—that are most significant. While
their voices are not in the majority, neither have they been erased or suppressed.

MEDIEVAL JEWISH COMMENTARIES

Rabbinic midrash was succeeded in the Middle Ages by a new mode of biblical
exegesis called *peshat*.[47] In contrast to rabbinic midrash, *peshat* did not posit a
multitude of possible readings for each biblical verse but rather limited the possibilities to a small and finite number. Not for the medieval commentators was
the midrashic tendency to lift words, phrases, or verses out of their immediate
contexts in the biblical text. Nevertheless, midrashic interpretations had a measure of authority and were often quoted, if selectively. This was the practice of
Rabbi Shlomo Yitzchaki (more commonly known as Rashi; 1040–1105 CE in
Northern France), one of the earliest, and unquestionably the most famous, of
the *pashtanim* (practitioners of the *peshat* method of exegesis).

In contrast to the Sages, most medieval Jewish commentators do not dwell on
the relationship between Hagar and Sarah. Rashi quotes *Genesis Rabbah* at length
in his comments to Genesis 16 and 21, and adds virtually no original ideas. Ibn
Ezra, the Spanish grammarian (1089–1164), discusses various grammatical
points but offers no insights into the characters or their actions. There are four
commentators, however, who discuss the story in greater depth. These are Rabbi

David Kimchi (also known as Radak), Rabbi Levi ben Gershom (known as Ralbag), Nahmanides (known as Ramban), and Don Isaac Abarbanel. These commentators address the issue of morality in the context of Sarah and Abraham's marital relationship, and come to rather different conclusions as to the extent of Sarah's moral accountability for her behavior towards Hagar.

Rabbi David Kimchi (Radak), who lived in medieval Provencal (ca. 1160–1235), strongly condemns Sarah's treatment of Hagar:

> She did too much to her and she worked her ruthlessly, and it is possible that she hit her and cursed her until she could not endure it and she fled from before her. Sarah displayed in this neither the quality of morality and nor the quality of piety. Not morality because even though Abraham gave up his honor for her and said to her, *"Do what is right in your eyes,"* she [Sarah] should have restrained herself for his honor and should not have tortured her [Hagar]. And not piety and compassion, for a person should not do whatever is in their power to those who are subject to their authority. . . . And what Sarah did was not pleasing to God, as the angel said to Hagar: God heard your suffering, and he repaid her suffering with a blessing. And Abraham did not stop Sarah from torturing her—even though it was wrong in his eyes—for the sake of domestic harmony. This whole story was written in the Torah to teach people good qualities and to distance them from bad qualities.[48]

Radak's commentary holds Sarah to a high moral standard and blames her for failing to live up to these standards. In torturing Hagar, Sarah violates Abraham's honor; it reflects poorly on Abraham if his concubine is beaten by his own wife. More important, Sarah's actions violate the requirements of piety. Hagar, after all, is a human being even if she is a slave and therefore inferior in status. In Radak's view, Sarah's superiority should have been demonstrated not by cruelty and violence but by benevolence. Radak concludes his comments by affirming that the intention of the Torah is not to present idealized characters but to urge its readers towards self-improvement.

Rabbi Levi ben Gershom (Ralbag; France, 1288–1344) also views the text as a manual of moral behavior for its readers. In contrast to Radak, however, he is not willing to view the matriarchs and patriarchs as fallible. Ralbag recounts the story as follows:

> Behold Abram cohabited *with Hagar, and she conceived,* and her mistress was lessened in her eyes because of this, until she could not endure [the slavery]. (5) And Sarah did not want to torture her in order to remove Hagar's bad trait without the permission of Abram, and to this end she told him the way Hagar behaved towards her. And she got angry at Abram because he did not reprove Hagar, [and did not tell her] that she should not behave towards her mistress in this way. (6) And *Abram said to Sarai* that she should do to her maidservant as she sees fit, so that she would remove the lesser quality. Sarai tortured her to reprove her and Hagar fled. (7–8) And one of the prophets of that generation found her *at the well,* for she was fleeing, and he already knew that she was fleeing from Sarai her mistress. That prophet told her to

return to her mistress and submit under her hand, and receive reproof from her, because Sarah's intent was for Hagar's own good, not to extract revenge from her.[49]

Ralbag, like Radak before him, comments on Hagar's inability to endure, but for a different reason. According to Radak, Hagar could not endure the harsh treatment of her mistress; her flight is therefore understandable and should be viewed with sympathy. For Ralbag, however, Hagar's inability to endure is evidence of her lower status as slave. In his view, the biblical statement that Sarah was lessened in the eyes of Hagar (Gen. 16:4) indicates that Hagar began to question the heretofore stable hierarchy of mistress and slave. Sarah's harsh treatment of Hagar was intended to remove this weakness from Hagar's character, for Hagar's own good, of course.[50]

Nahmanides (Ramban; Spain, 1194–1271) was trained in the philological approach to the biblical text, but did not hesitate to use midrash and other rabbinic literature and analyze it critically. One aspect that makes Ramban's commentary unique is his use of typology. He views the actions of the matriarchs and patriarchs as prefiguring events that will happen to future generations.[51] Ramban arrives at a similar conclusion to Radak about the moral valence of Sarah's treatment of Hagar, but because his view of the biblical text is different, his response to her actions varies accordingly. He writes:

> Our mother sinned with this act of torture, as did Abraham by letting her do so. "And God heard her suffering" and gave her a son who would be a wild man to torture the seed of Abraham and Sarah with all sorts of mistreatment.[52]

In Ramban's view, the deeds of the ancestors foreshadow the fate of their progeny. Although he criticizes Sarah, and even blames her for the future enslavement of her children in Egypt, the homeland of Hagar, he affirms the ultimate superiority of Sarah and thus of her offspring to Hagar and her descendants:

> He [the angel] commanded her to return and accept Sarah's authority. This alludes to the fact that she would not be freed of Sarah, and that the children of Sarah would rule over her children forever.[53]

Don Isaac Abarbanel (1437–1508; Spain, Italy) disagrees vociferously with Ramban's moral assessment of Sarah's behavior. He quotes Ramban's interpretation and then responds to it:[54]

> But this [Ramban's interpretation] is wrong, because the author of the Ethics [Aristotle] already wrote that correcting someone who has been imprinted with a lesser quality requires bending that person and forcing her to the opposite extreme. This is similar to the practice of those who try to straighten a bent stick by bending them in the opposite direction, so that when it springs up again it will stand straight. So too Sarah, when

she saw Hagar behaving with arrogance and overweening pride, she tortured her and enslaved her more rigorously than normal. And all this [she did] towards a positive end, in order to return her to the mean. And she [Hagar], like one who rejects lessons, ran away from her by way of the desert.[55]

Like Ralbag before him, then, Abarbanel argues that Sarah did not act out of jealousy but out of a desire to improve Hagar's character by removing the negative traits of arrogance and pride.

Medieval commentators express their individual opinions regarding Sarah's behavior in the context of their overall perspective on the appropriate role of the Bible with regard to its audience. In all cases they view the Bible as instructive, though whether it fulfills this goal by elevating or by critiquing its protagonists is a matter of debate.

MODERN ANALYSES AND CREATIVE REINTERPRETATIONS

If the majority of medieval commentators are content to ignore Hagar and Sarah, their modern counterparts—including feminist writers and commentators—breathe new life into these matriarchs. In doing so, they allow us to view their relationship from different perspectives, often by revising the biblical story itself. Like their predecessors in the postbiblical, medieval, and rabbinic periods, contemporary writers address the issues of status and morality, but they also add a pressing political dimension. As Naomi Graetz notes, "Sarai and Hagar's discord have [sic] reverberated until the present day"[56] through the conflict between the peoples—Palestinians and Israelis—who trace their spiritual and even biological lineage back to the sons of Hagar and Sarah.

Many of these modern treatments adopt the norms and methods of modern biblical criticism and scholarship. That is, they place the events of Genesis 16 and 21 in their literary, social, and historical contexts, within the Bible as a literary composition, within Israelite history and law, and within the broader sphere of the ancient Near East, in particular its codes of law. Other contemporary reflections on the story can be classified as creative midrash. While they take the biblical story as their starting point, and often draw on traditional rabbinic and medieval commentaries, modern midrashists will rewrite the story to reflect or address contemporary concerns, or else imagine in some details the emotions and thoughts of the story's actors in ways that go well beyond either Bible or midrash. In doing so, they are also able to bring their readers into a dynamic engagement with the story and to encourage them (us) to consider the story's potential meanings for our own lives and times. We shall briefly survey the field by looking at comments pertaining to status and morality on the one hand and the pertinence of our story to history and politics on the other.

Status

As in earlier eras, modern writers on the biblical Hagar and Sarah comment extensively on issues pertaining to status. Tikva Frymer-Kensky's study of Hagar, for example, draws on the law codes of the surrounding peoples to explicate the legal background to the story: "The Hammurabi laws acknowledge the possibility that the pregnant slave woman might claim equality with her mistress, and they allow the mistress to treat her as an ordinary slave (Law 146)."[57] While Frymer-Kensky is not condoning the behavior of Sarah and Abraham in the biblical story, she finds that it is in accord with other ancient Near Eastern law codes. Elsewhere, however, the narrative deviates, not from Near Eastern law but from biblical law itself. She points out that in light of biblical law, it is odd that God requires Hagar to return. "Why should an angel [or God] respect property rights over the freedom of persons," particularly in the light of biblical law, which requires that runaway slaves should not be returned to their masters (Deut. 23:16)?[58] Frymer-Kensky's comments remind us that the status issues in Genesis 16 and 21 need to be understood in the broader context of the ancient Near East, not solely in terms of the biblical narrative and legal contexts.

Another writer who addresses status in terms of historical issues is Savina Teubal. In *Hagar the Egyptian*, Teubal argues that, contrary to the impression created by the biblical narrative, there was parity, not disparity, in the relative social status of Hagar and Sarah. According to Teubal's analysis, Hagar is neither slave nor concubine but the matriarch of a nation whom Teubal calls "Hagarites." In her view, both Hagar and Sarah were women struggling for religious and social rights in the context of an environment in which they enjoyed some measure of divinely sanctioned authority. As for the discrepancy between her reconstruction of the social context and the biblical account, Teubal blames the androcentrism of the latter. She argues that the men who constituted the military elite of ancient Israel suppressed Hagar's real story in favor of "the image of the archetypal hero": "If, during the early monarchy's recompilation of the biblical material, the powerful tribe of the Hagarites was known to acknowledge the matriarch Hagar as their common ancestoress [sic], a problem would have been posed for the androcentric writers who were attempting to highlight the patriarch: Descent was to be changed to the male line."[59] While creative, this analysis is so speculative as to be unconvincing from a historical point of view. Nevertheless it takes seriously a basic tenet of feminist interpretation, namely, the androcentrism of the biblical narrative.

Whereas Frymer-Kensky and, to some extent, Teubal, adopt the norms and approaches of the modern study of the Bible, Ellen Frankel's commentary takes the form, and allows itself the freedom, of traditional midrash. She sets up her commentary, *The Five Books of Miriam*, as a traditional Jewish commentary in which the biblical text is surrounded by the comments of the Sages, in this case including Sarah the Ancient One and Hagar. In Frankel's commentary, it is Hagar herself who ponders the instability of status in her relationship with Sarah: "When I conceived Abraham's child, my status was irrevocably changed. I became the mother of my master's firstborn son. I fulfilled God's promise to grant seed to Abraham. And in so doing, I became Sarah's rival."[60]

Other writers approach the question of status through a creative and imaginative retelling of the story. Rosellen Brown, for example, simply reverses the plot as she rewrites the story. In her able hands, the biblical prophecy that Ishmael will be a "wild ass of a man" (Gen. 16:12) is transformed into a kinder, gentler prediction: "He shall be a gentle deer of a man." Her version of the story ends with the two brothers living peacefully and in harmony with each other.[61]

Vanessa Ochs tells the story of banishment from Hagar's point of view. She explores Hagar's feelings as mother who watches helplessly as her child is in dire distress, then receives divine revelation in a dream, understands its meaning, and musters the strength to carry on, day by day. Ochs brings these insights into reflections on her own parallel experience during the illness of a daughter and offers suggestions for how Hagar's story, via Ochs's reading, may be of help as we face similar situations.[62] In a similar vein, Naomi Rosenblatt offers a detailed set of reflections on the story and its implications for families and gender relations, especially in blended families in which there will be an inherent conflict of interest between stepmother and stepchildren.[63]

Norma Rosen has Sarah dream of Hagar as she seeks advice for how to deal with Abraham's near-sacrifice of Isaac (Gen. 22). In facing the possibility that her own child will die—at the hands of his father—Sarah appeals to Hagar's maternal experience with regard to the near-death of her own child. "When death stalked your son in the desert, didn't you utter some prayer, some special supplication, that brought God's mercy down? You, whose son survived, can't you teach me words that give such blessing?" Hagar, who is now enthroned as an Egyptian queen, advises Sarah to submit, as she had once done, to the divine will: "If you are worthy, reap reward and rescue. Otherwise, your son's as good as dead." Hagar's advice is delivered with understandable coolness; she offers neither comfort nor blessings, and when Sarah embraces her knees, Hagar pushes her away.[64] Frankel has Hagar acknowledge that "both of us suffered in making this bargain—I because I remained a slave even after I bore Abraham a son; Sarah because her adopted son, Ishmael, always remained my son, the child of an Egyptian, a stranger to her."[65] For Rosen and Frankel, Hagar does not ever truly forgive Sarah for her behavior. Alicia Ostriker's Hagar is also not wholehearted in her willingness to match Sarah's contrition with her own forgiveness. Ostriker's Sarah tells Hagar, "We should be allies/we are both exiles, all women are exiles/I tell her/She smiles slyly. . . ."[66]

Karen Prager provides a warmer ending to a similar rewritten story. In Prager's creative midrash, Sarah prays to God out of remorse for how she had behaved towards Hagar: "God, I have wronged another women with what I demanded. How can I deserve Your benevolence?" God tells her to speak to Hagar. Sarah cries to Hagar and explains her bad behavior as residual anger from the time that she was Pharaoh's plaything (Gen. 12; cf. *Gen. Rab.* 45:1). Hagar offers Sarah a way to make amends: "Let Ishmael and Isaac grow up as brothers. Each shall have two mothers and one father. You alone shall be my family. Together we will teach our children about the God we have found. Your child shall have his inheritance. Ishmael will know his homeland through our stories, and will return to Egypt to build a nation."[67] Prager's Hagar, in contrast to Rosen's, is ready to forgive Sarah for the well-being of their children.

A similar solution is offered in Brown's retelling, in which Hagar tells Sarah, "Let him do no thing that is grievous in thy sight. Thou also shall be as a mother to this child." Sarah, in turn, lays down the law to Abraham, who favored Isaac over Ishmael: "There shall be no peace in our house if thou dividest thy love as a loaf of bread in unequal portions. Forasmuch as God hath opened our wombs together to thee, neither son shalt thou put above the other."[68] As Frankel's Sarah notes, Sarah and Hagar have more in common than they themselves realized. "Shekhinah [God's female manifestation] understood that I was the pragmatist and Abraham the dreamer. Hagar too was a realist."[69]

Morality

The biblical narrator does not pass explicit moral judgment against either of the characters although, as we have seen, the story itself implicitly treats Sarah more harshly than it does Hagar. Like some of the Sages of the midrash, some of the contemporary commentators engage in apologetics. For example, Tamar Frankiel excuses Sarah's behavior, and in fact elevates it, on the grounds that women often have greater insight than men. According to Frankiel, Sarah "foresaw that the presence of Hagar's son would be dangerous to the future of the family, so he and his mother had to be separated from Isaac."[70]

Many others try to understand Sarah's behavior in a sympathetic way and to justify it without necessarily trying to excuse it. According to Tikva Frymer-Kensky, neither Sarai, who proposes Hagar, nor Abram, who agrees, mentions obtaining the consent of the slave girl. To contemporary readers, such consent seems necessary for the arrangement to be moral. But, as Frymer-Kensky notes, none of the ancient texts sees any ethical problem with this arrangement. Ancient societies accepted slavery as a regular part of social life. Using another person's body as a surrogate for one's own is part of the fabric of slavery.[71]

In Frankel's Torah commentary, Hagar asks for pity as "a powerless Egyptian slave, a shadow to Wife Number One, a surrogate womb." Sarah, in turn, explains that her actions were motivated by a larger divine plan, as a foreshadowing of the experience of slavery. But she acknowledges, "It cost me everything—from that moment on, I disappear from my own story. I am not heard from again in the Bible."[72] Mother Rachel explains: "Clearly, it's not easy for Sarah to share her marriage bed, especially with her own slave."[73] Here, Sarah's problematic behavior is explained on two grounds: jealousy and the exigencies of history, and the cost is acknowledged.

Like Frankel's "Mother Rachel," Norma Rosen tries to re-create the feelings of the biblical characters. When she realizes that Abraham is preparing to take Isaac away from her (Gen. 22), Rosen's Sarah laments, "He had been more attentive when he sent Hagar from the house with Ishmael. He had been more reluctant to expel *them*. He had caressed *that* mother, kissed *that* child."[74] Naomi Rosenblatt also focuses on Sarah's jealousy and attributes Sarah's violent behavior to her emotional state: "She hadn't meant to chase Hagar away from their camp. She only wanted to teach her her place, remind her who was the wife and who the servant. . . . She went too far by beating her, and deeply regretted it. But Hagar had provoked her with her insolence, and Sarai had been careful only to strike her on the hands and feet, so as not to harm the child."[75] This explanation verges on apologetics. In fact there is no hint in the text that Sarah exercised any restraint. On the other hand, the absence of interiority on the part of the characters does allow for the possibility that Sarah did not go as far as she could have. Along the same lines, Marsha Pravda Mirkin states that "Sarah became the oppressor as well as the oppressed, too caught up in her own sorrow to reach out to her servant with that woman-to-woman empathy that could transcend their ethnic and class differences."[76]

History

Many commentators look at the story in terms of the broad sweep of Israelite history. For Tikva Frymer-Kensky, Hagar serves as a model for later Israelite history. As an Egyptian slave, she foreshadows the period of Israel's own slavery in Egypt, and God's intervention on behalf of Hagar and Ishmael similarly foreshadows his later intervention in rescuing Israel from Egypt. It is somewhat ironic that the Egyptian slave woman becomes the archetype of or model for Israelite history, but the parallels are clear. In Frymer-Kensky's words, "[t]he pattern of Hagar and Abram and of later Israel shows that the way to God's reward is through the margins of society and the depths of degradation. Only then, it seems, does God redeem."[77]

Like the medieval commentator Ramban, Ellen Frankel sees Hagar as the beginning of a recurring pattern in Israelite history. She has the "historian," Serah bat Asher, comment that

> Hagar's first exile is temporary. But after the birth of Isaac, Sarah orders Hagar and her son banished for good. And so begins the fateful swing of history's pendulum: Abraham banishes Ishmael; two generations later, the Ishmaelites sell Abraham's great-grandson Joseph into Egyptian slavery. Sarah banishes Hagar the Egyptian; later, Egypt enslaves Sarah's descendants for four hundred years.[78]

Frankel thereby brings Hagar into the main sweep of Israelite and Jewish history in which slavery and the exodus are the formative events of Jewish identity and the prime evidence of God's intervention in history on behalf of God's people.

Politics

Perhaps the major difference between the approach of contemporary writers to that taken by their predecessors throughout the history of Jewish literature is the political dimension. One such approach is visible in the Jewish response to the use of the Hagar and Sarah story in womanist biblical interpretation. Ruth Behar notes that "African American readers have lovingly claimed Hagar as their own, made her a foremother, taken pride in her struggle, formed spiritual churches in her name, and led the way in creative appropriations of her story," especially when slaves were forced to bear children by their masters because wives were barren.[79] She concludes: "We were slaves in Egypt, yes, but let us not forget that we also enslaved. Let us not forget that slavery was carried by human beings, by the very human beings whose names we invoke in our Jewish prayers, but it was inhuman. . . . Reading the story of Sarah and Hagar, we can begin to risk compassion for ourselves and for others."[80] A very different response is recorded by Pamela Tamarkin Reis, who describes her pain and discomfort at a scholarly meeting in which she listened to a womanist reading of the Hagar and Sarah story that identified the oppressors of black slaves as Jews. "This speaker's vilification of Sarah went beyond the fringes of biblical exegesis into the outskirts of anti-Semitism. She spoke of what she considered the racism of the ancient Hebrews, of their preoccupation with financial matters, of their insistence on their chosenness, and compared these traits with those of contemporary people."[81]

More often, however, the Hagar and Sarah story is seen both as a precursor of and an analogy to the Israeli-Palestinian conflict. Ruth Behar urges us to "lay Sarah and Hagar to rest, side by side, in the same blood-ravaged land."[82] Lynn Gottlieb is perhaps the most eloquent voice on this theme:

> Sarah and Hagar are the first matriarchs of the Jewish and Muslim peoples. . . . It is a tragedy that religion and ideology have transformed this story into a conflict of faiths and peoples. The ultimate irony is the consequent suffering of the hundreds of thousands of women and children who have died as a result of religious and national wars fought in the name of this text. Let us give honor to the origins of our people by reframing the story. Let us stand together against the abuse of children and women in the name of religion. Women, let us extricate our peoples from the patriarchal borders that make it impossible to see one another as sisters sharing a common bond.[83]

Gottlieb's poem *Achti* was intended to encourage "Jews and Palestinians to acknowledge our common humanity and end the violence between our peoples." Here Sarah begs Hagar, her sister, for forgiveness, in a cadence reminiscent of the solemn prayers of atonement that characterize the High Holy Day liturgy: "Forgive me, Achti/For the sin of neglect/For the sin of abuse/For the sin of arrogance/Forgive me, Achti,/For the sin of not knowing your name."[84]

The story has also been introduced in contemporary creative liturgy. Genesis 21 is already part of the annual New Year (Rosh Hashanah) liturgy, as the Torah reading chanted on the first day of this two-day festival. But in recent years, some households have incorporated a blessing that there be peace between the sons of Sarah and Hagar into their recitation of the grace after meals.[85]

CONCLUSION

Hagar and Sarah have traveled long and far, together and apart. They begin their journey in Genesis 16 and 21 as rivals, jostling for position in the eyes of their husband, in the eyes of God, in the eyes of the narrator, and in the eyes of their readers. As their story is told and retold from the postbiblical period to our own day, their roles are sometimes entrenched, sometimes questioned, sometimes reversed, according to the personal views of their successive story-tellers and the ways in which these storytellers themselves understood their situation as Jews. While each age shows a greater or lesser amount of diversity in the roles assigned to Hagar and Sarah and in the moral evaluation of their behavior, it is palpably in the last thirty years that commentators have felt freest to exercise their creativity, and to rewrite and rework these stories thoroughly enough to make them speak to and resonate with contemporary female experience, in the light of personal relationships and/or in the light of the political considerations raised by the Israel/Palestine conflict. The reconciliation of Hagar and Sarah in many of these stories eloquently articulates the hopes and prayers for peace. May it also be a foreshadowing of peace, grounded in profound respect for humankind and the commonality of human experience, shared by women and men across cultural, religious, and political boundaries that both define us and yet unite us.

Notes

1. See Gen. 12:2: "I will make of you a great nation, and I will bless you, and make your name great, so that you will be a blessing."
2. See, for example, Deut. 15, which discusses the treatment of the poor and disadvantaged.
3. For an introduction to the literature of this period, see Bruce N. Fisk, *Do You Not Remember? Scripture, Story and Exegesis in the Rewritten Bible of Pseudo-Philo*, Journal for the Study of the Pseudepigrapha Suppl. Series 37 (Sheffield: Sheffield Academic Press, 2001).
4. The term "Palestine" is not intended as a reference to the modern-day territories in the Middle East that are now or may at some point come under the control of the Palestinian people in the context of a political settlement of the current conflict. Rather, this is the usual usage in the field for the Middle East areas where Jews were the ethnic majority in the postbiblical period.
5. James H. Charlesworth, *The Old Testament Pseudepigrapha*, 1st ed., 2 vols. (Garden City, NY: Doubleday, 1985), 2:85.
6. Ibid., 2:89–90.
7. This text was attributed incorrectly to Philo of Alexandria, as the Latin text circulated along with the Latin translations of Philo's works, hence the attribution of authorship to "Pseudo-Philo."
8. Charlesworth, *Old Testament Pseudepigrapha*, 2:313.

9. Flavius Josephus et al., *Jewish Antiquities*, vol. 4, Loeb Classical Library (Cambridge, MA: Harvard University Press, 1998), 93–95.

10. Ibid., 107–9. For a detailed study of Josephus's works as rewritten Bible, see Louis H. Feldman, *Studies in Josephus' Rewritten Bible*, Journal for the Study of Judaism Suppl. 58 (Leiden: New York: Brill, 1998).

11. For a useful introduction to Philo, see Samuel Sandmel, *Philo of Alexandria: An Introduction* (New York: Oxford University Press, 1979). See also Maren R. Niehoff, "Mother and Maiden, Sister and Spouse: Sarah in Philonic Midrash," *Harvard Theological Review* 97, no. 4 (October 2004): 413–44.

12. Philo of Alexandria, vol. 1, *Philo: With an English Translation*, trans. F. H. Colson and George Herbert Whitaker (Cambridge, MA: Harvard University Press, 1929), 467.

13. Ibid., vol. 2, 11–13.

14. Ibid., vol. 4, 463.

15. Ibid., vol. 4, 467–71.

16. Ibid., vol. 4, 551. For a detailed study of this subject, see Alan Mendelson, *Secular Education in Philo of Alexandria*, Monographs of the Hebrew Union College, no. 7 (Cincinnati: Hebrew Union College Press, 1982).

17. David Stern, "Midrash and Midrashic Interpretation," *The Jewish Study Bible* (New York: Oxford University Press, 2004), 1872.

18. For discussion about historicity and other central issues pertaining to the academic study of rabbinic literature, see Richard Lee Kalmin, *Sages, Stories, Authors, and Editors in Rabbinic Babylonia*, Brown Judaic Studies, no. 300 (Atlanta: Scholars Press, 1994).

19. In this paper are included aggadic works both from the rabbinic and postrabbinic periods. These latter works (such as *Pirqe Rabbi Eliezer* and *Aggadat Bereshit*) do not fall strictly under the category of midrash, but are rather more fluid retellings of biblical narrative or homiletical discourses.

20. For an excellent introduction to midrash see Stern, "Midrash and Midrashic Interpretation," 1863–1875. See also Michael A. Fishbane, *The Midrashic Imagination: Jewish Exegesis, Thought, and History* (Albany: State University of New York Press, 1993); Irving Jacobs, *The Midrashic Process: Tradition and Interpretation in Rabbinic Judaism* (New York: Cambridge University Press, 1995). For dating and other technical information see H. L. Strack and Günter Stemberger, *Introduction to the Talmud and Midrash,* ed. and trans. Markus Bockmuel (Minneapolis: Fortress Press, 1991).

21. For more information see Strack and Stemberger, *Introduction*, 276–83.

22. H. Freedman and Maurice Simon, *The Midrash Rabbah Genesis*, new compact ed., vol. 1 (London: Soncino, 1977), 380.

23. For an English translation see Gerald Friedlander, *Pirke d'Rabbi Eliezer* (New York: Sepher-Hermon Press, 1981).

24. For more information see Strack and Stemberger, *Introduction*, 311. For an English translation see Lieve M. Teugels, *Aggadat Bereshit* (Leiden; Boston: Brill, 2001).

25. Menahem Cohen, ed., *Mikraot Gedolot HaKeter* (Ramat Gan, Israel: Bar Ilan Press, 1997), 159.

26. Ibid., 351–52.

27. The word *ger* used here can mean either stranger or convert, but in rabbinic literature the latter meaning is predominant.

28. The full text of the midrash reads, "There are righteous *giyorot* (converts): Hagar, Osnat, Zipporah, Shifra, Puah, the daughter of Pharaoh, Rahab, Ruth and Yael the wife of Heber the Kenite" (*Yalkut Shimoni, Remez* 9).

29. In these quotations, biblical citations are italicized.

30. Freedman and Simon, *The Midrash Rabbah Genesis*, 385.
31. Strack and Stemberger, *Introduction*, 4–6. Since this literature is not one unified work, it is difficult to date each individual midrash. See Mark Bregman, *Tanhuma-Yelammedenu Literature: Studies in the Evolution of the Versions* (Piscataway, NJ: Gorgias Press, 2003).
32. Cf. Gen. 30:6 and 30:11 for the names of the sons of Bilha and Zilpa. Cf. Exod. 1:1–4 for a listing of the sons of Jacob that went to Egypt.
33. The Hebrew Scriptures are divided into three sections: Torah (Pentateuch), the Prophets, and the Writings. The last-named category includes the books of Psalms, Proverbs, Job, Song of Songs, Ruth, Lamentations, Ecclesiastes, Esther, Daniel, Ezra, Nehemiah, and 1 and 2 Chronicles.
34. Freedman and Simon, *Midrash Rabbah*, 379; see also n. 22, loc cit.
35. This is an equivocal comment, for it implies the commodification of a woman's value insofar as it can be compared to that of rubies. Another, less objectionable interpretation would be that fertility is of greater value to a woman's status than the possession of rubies would be for her status.
36. Strack and Stemberger, *Introduction*, 291–96. For an English translation see William G. (Gershon Zev) Braude and Israel J. Kapstein. *Pesikta de-Rav Kahana*, 2nd ed. (Philadelphia: Jewish Publication Society, 2002).
37. Variations on this midrash occur in the Babylonian Talmud (BM 87a) and in *Genesis Rabbah* 53.9.
38. Freedman and Simon, *Midrash Rabbah*, 383.
39. Redacted in the sixth century, the Babylonian Talmud is a work structured not around the biblical text but rather around the text of the Mishna, an earlier legal code. It includes both discussions that are halakhic in nature as well as those aggadic in nature.
40. Freedman and Simon, *Midrash Rabbah*, 381.
41. Ibid., 381–82.
42. There Sarah speaks to Abraham and denies her laughter. The response "No but you laughed" could either be read as a response from God (as *Genesis Rabbah* 45:9 wants to read it) or as a response from Abraham to Sarah's denial.
43. Freedman and Simon, *Midrash Rabbah*, 385.
44. Ibid., 388.
45. Ibid., 384.
46. Variations on the argument between Abraham and Sarah can be found in *Tosefta Sotah* 5:12 and *Midrash Mishlei* 26:24.
47. For an overview of medieval exegesis see Barry Walfish, "Medieval Jewish Interpretation," *The Jewish Study Bible* (New York: Oxford University Press, 2004), 1876–1900.
48. Except for the passages from *Genesis Rabbah*, which are taken from Freedman and Simon, *The Midrash Rabbah*, vol. 1, all other translations are those of Miriam-Simma Walfish.
49. Cohen, *Mikraot Gedolot HaKeter*, 159.
50. At the end of his commentary on the episode, Ralbag mentions that the being whom Hagar met in the desert was not an angel but a prophet. This revision to the biblical story may simply be his attempt to deny Hagar her divine encounter. It is possible, however, that this interpretation does not express a negative attitude towards Hagar so much as Ralbag's own rationalist discomfort with the very notion of angels.
51. Walfish, "Medieval Jewish Interpretation," 1892.
52. Cf. Barry D. Walfish, "An Introduction to Medieval Jewish Biblical Interpretation," in *With Reverence for the Word: Medieval Scriptural Exegesis in Judaism,*

Christianity, and Islam, in ed. Jane Dammen McAuliffe, Barry Walfish, and Joseph Ward Goering (New York: Oxford University Press, 2003).

53. Cohen, *Mikraot Gedolot HaKeter,* 159.
54. Abarbanel's commentary is not verse by verse. Rather, he takes a larger passage, asks a number of questions regarding it, and proceeds to answer them.
55. Cohen, *Mikraot Gedolot HaKeter,* 159.
56. Naomi Graetz, *Unlocking the Garden: A Feminist Jewish Look at the Bible, Midrash and God,* 1st Gorgias Press ed. (Piscataway, NJ: Gorgias Press, 2005), 91.
57. Tikva Frymer-Kensky, "Hagar," in *Women in Scripture: A Dictionary of Named and Unnamed Women in the Hebrew Bible, the Apocryphal/Deuterocanonical Books, and the New Testament,* ed. Carol L. Meyers, Toni Craven, and Ross Shepard Kraemer (Grand Rapids: Wm. B. Eerdmans Publishing Co., 2001), 86.
58. Frymer-Kensky, *Reading the Women of the Bible* (New York: Schocken Books, 2002), 230.
59. Savina J. Teubal, *Hagar the Egyptian: The Lost Tradition of the Matriarchs,* 1st ed. (San Francisco: Harper & Row, 1990); and *Sarah the Priestess: The First Matriarch of Genesis* (Athens, OH: Swallow Press, 1984).
60. Ellen Frankel, *The Five Books of Miriam: A Woman's Commentary on the Torah* (New York: G. P. Putnam's, 1996), 18.
61. Rosellen Brown, "Hagar and Sarah, Sarah and Hagar," in *Beginning Anew: A Woman's Companion to the High Holy Days,* ed. Gail Twersky Reimer and Judith A. Kates (New York: Simon & Schuster, 1997), 33.
62. Vanessa L. Ochs, *Sarah Laughed: Modern Lessons from the Wisdom & Stories of Biblical Women,* 1st ed. (New York: McGraw-Hill, 2005).
63. Naomi H. Rosenblatt and Joshua Horwitz, *Wrestling with Angels: What the First Family of Genesis Teaches Us about Our Spiritual Identity, Sexuality, and Personal Relationships* (New York: Delacorte Press, 1995), 190.
64. Norma Rosen, *Biblical Women Unbound: Counter-Tales* (Philadelphia: Jewish Publication Society, 1996), 48.
65. Frankel, *The Five Books of Miriam,* 17.
66. Alicia Ostriker, *The Nakedness of the Fathers: Biblical Visions and Revisions* (New Brunswick, NJ: Rutgers University Press, 1994), 68.
67. Karen Prager, "God's Covenant with Sarah," in *Biblical Women in the Midrash: A Sourcebook,* ed. Naomi M. Hyman (Northvale, NJ: Jason Aronson, 1998), 25.
68. Brown, "Hagar and Sarah, Sarah and Hagar," 33–34.
69. Frankel, *The Five Books of Miriam,* 19.
70. Tamar Frankiel, *The Voice of Sarah: Feminine Spirituality and Traditional Judaism,* 1st ed. (San Francisco: HarperSanFrancisco, 1990), 7.
71. Frymer-Kensky, *Reading the Women of the Bible,* 227.
72. Frankel, *The Five Books of Miriam,* 18.
73. Ibid., 19.
74. Rosen, *Biblical Women Unbound,* 46.
75. Rosenblatt and Horwitz, *Wrestling with Angels,* 141.
76. Marsha Pravder Mirkin, "Hearken to Her Voice: Empathy as Teshuvah," in *Beginning Anew: A Woman's Companion to the High Holy Days,* ed. Gail Twersky Reimer and Judith A. Kates (New York: Simon & Schuster, 1997), 65.
77. Frymer-Kensky, *Reading the Women of the Bible,* 232–33.
78. Frankel, *The Five Books of Miriam,* 19.
79. Ruth Behar, "Sarah and Hagar: The Heelprints Upon Their Faces," in Reimer and Kates, *Beginning Anew,* 40.
80. Mirkin, "Hearken to Her Voice: Empathy as Teshuvah," in Reimer and Kates, *Beginning Anew,* 42.

81. Pamela Tamarkin Reis, *Reading the Lines: A Fresh Look at the Hebrew Bible* (Peabody, MA: Hendrickson, 2002), 56.
82. Behar, "Sarah and Hagar," 43.
83. Lynn Gottlieb, *She Who Dwells Within: A Feminist Vision of a Renewed Judaism*, 1st ed. (San Francisco: HarperSanFrancisco, 1995), 88–90.
84. Ibid., 89–90.
85. Often these are in unpublished but nonetheless broadly circulating copies of the Grace After Meals. One such is called *Anim Zemirot*, copyright Leah J. Solomon, 1999. Another is the book created by Barry Walfish et al., for the occasion of the wedding of Miriam-Simma Walfish and Michael Rosenberg.

Chapter 5

Interpretive Fate amid the Church Fathers

Elizabeth A. Clark

This chapter details the interpretive fate of Hagar and Sarah in patristic exegesis, that is, in writings by the church fathers from the second through the sixth centuries. None of their interpretations, to be sure, is informed by the perspectives of postcolonial, feminist, or critical race theory, perspectives that have so engaged the attention of commentators in our own era. As Phyllis Trible notes, Hagar has become a symbol with whom oppressed and rejected woman can identify. She is "the faithful maid exploited, the black woman used by the male and abused by the female of the ruling class, the surrogate mother, the resident alien without legal recourse, the pregnant young woman alone, the expelled wife, the homeless woman, the welfare mother."[1] But the church fathers did not view Hagar in any of these sympathetic ways. Indeed, their deployments of the narratives in Genesis about Abraham, Sarah, and Hagar may appear callous to contemporary readers. This study will show the theological, ecclesiastical, and other purposes for which the church fathers used these biblical characters to "think with," that is, to help them reflect on issues of religious concern in their own era.[2] It will illustrate the major exegetical themes attending these narratives in numerous works by early Christian writers and then conclude with a more extended discussion of Augustine's manipulation of the themes to achieve his particular interpretive ends.

HAGAR AND SARAH IN EARLY CHRISTIAN WRITERS

To begin, let us recall how Paul in Galatians 4 mobilized the Genesis story to argue against the Galatian "Judaizers," for his allegorical reading had a long after-life in the Christian exegetical tradition. Paul contrasted the servile status of the Old Covenant, symbolized by Hagar, with the "free" condition of the New Covenant, represented by Sarah. Repeating God's admonition to "cast out the slave and her son" (Gal. 4:30, citing Gen. 21:10), he assured his readers/hearers that "we" (i.e., Christians) are children of the "free woman," Sarah (Gal. 4:31), and so "free" from servitude to the Old Covenant (Gal. 4:31). This figurative reading of Sarah and Hagar became central to the interpretations of postbiblical Christian writers, both because it encouraged "spiritual" readings of the Hebrew Bible in general and because it removed Hagar and Sarah from their particular-ized, local context in ancient Israelite history, thereby enabling their use as sym-bols in a larger Christian discourse. *Which* larger Christian discourse, as we shall see, was largely of the church fathers' own creative devising.

Anti-Jewish Polemic of the Early Christian Era

Given the centrality of the Hagar and Sarah story in Paul's challenge to the Gala-tian "Judaizers," modern readers might expect that the story would figure promi-nently in early Christian anti-Jewish polemic. It is thus surprising to discover how rarely these verses are cited in Christian literature of the second and third cen-turies, even in such notably anti-Jewish writings as the *Epistle of Barnabas* and Justin Martyr's *Dialogue with Trypho*. Indeed, one of the ploys used by Celsus, a second-century pagan who wrote a trenchant attack on Christianity, is to repre-sent a Jewish spokesman asking Christians, "What induced you to abandon the law of your fathers?" The proper Christian reply, according to his later Christian respondent Origen (d. 254 CE), is to claim on the basis of Galatians 4 that Chris-tians have *not* abandoned the law of their fathers, for they constantly refer to Old Testament persons and the significance of the Law.[3] Rather than casting off the Old Testament, says Origen, Christians have invested it with its "true" spiritual meaning.

From the middle of the third century, however, instances of the anti-Jewish use of Galatians 4:21–31 multiply. In his *Three Books of Testimonies Against the Jews* (a work providing biblical passages with which to counter alleged Jewish arguments against Christianity), Cyprian, bishop of Carthage in North Africa (d. 258 CE), cites Galatians 4 to claim that the formerly barren church has birthed more chil-dren from among the Gentiles than the synagogue had formerly been able to pro-duce. Isaac, the son of Sarah (and children of other Hebrew women who were long barren), are all cited as "types of Christ."[4] The rapidly growing church built with Gentiles is contrasted with the now "infertile" status of "the synagogue." Cyprian here links the allegory in Galatians with Paul's theme in Romans, namely, that in ancient times when God called the Israelites to be his people, the Gentiles were disobedient. Now, however, the Gentiles have been favored while the Jews display their disobedience. Paul hopes that the "wild olive shoot" of the Gentiles will be grafted onto the "tree" of God's covenant with the Jews, so that both Jew and Gentile will be "saved" in the new covenant (Rom. 11). Cyprian in his exegesis merges ecclesiology with anti-Jewish sentiment. Judaism stagnates while Christianity remains increasingly productive of new adherents.

Later church fathers argue that there is no room for the synagogue in the New Covenant. "Hagar" and "Sarah" become codes for "synagogue" and "church," respectively, with the implication that the former has been abandoned, not incorporated into the latter.[5] Thus Ambrose, bishop of Milan in the late fourth century (d. 397 CE), explains why Matthew's genealogy of Jesus (Matt. 1) does not mention the wives of the patriarchs but rather includes the names of such women as Tamar and Ruth: because Matthew chose to focus on women who either were not part of the Jewish covenant or who left "the bonds of the Law" in order to enter the church, thereby exemplifying Paul's message in Galatians 4 regarding "synagogue" and "church."[6] The Latin-writing church father and renowned biblical scholar Jerome (d. 420 CE) also warms to this theme. He holds that the formerly barren one who has produced abundant children (i.e., Sarah) is a prophecy of the rapid growth of the church. Referring to narratives concerning massive conversions in Acts (2:41, 4:4), he marvels at the numbers who converted in just one day.[7]

Other examples of the use of this biblical passage in anti-Jewish polemic come from the city of Antioch in the late fourth century. That Galatians 4 contains a citation of Isaiah 54:1, "Rejoice, O barren one that dost not bear; break forth and shout, thou who art not in travail; for the desolate hath more children than she who hath a husband," signals to John Chrysostom, priest at Antioch (386–397 CE) and later bishop of Constantinople (398–407 CE), that the growth of the Gentile church now far surpasses "the synagogue." Indeed the church stretches to Greeks and barbarians, across lands and seas, to the whole habitable world.[8] Moreover, Chrysostom, disturbed that Antiochene Christians were participating in Jewish festivals, mobilizes Galatians 4:25 against "Judaizing Christians." He mocks Christians who tolerate their fellow devotees' participation in Jewish rites and practices. "What do you have to do with the 'free Jerusalem,' the 'heavenly Jerusalem'? You chose the earthly; be a slave just like she is."[9]

Patristic Polemic against Gnostics

The Fathers use Paul's treatment of Hagar and Sarah in somewhat surprising contexts, one of which surfaces in debates about Gnosticism.[10] Writing in the late second century, Irenaeus, bishop of Lyons (d. 202?), cites the phrase "the Jerusalem above who is free" (Gal. 4:26) in his attempted refutation of Gnosticism. He refers to one version of a gnostic myth in which the world and its woes originated when a female divine power deviated from her established place in the *pleroma*, the fullness of the divine powers. By contrast, Irenaeus notes that this "Jerusalem above" does not signal an erratic aeon or some power (he supplies "Prunikos," a name taken to mean "the whore") that has abandoned the *pleroma*.[11] Here an appeal to Galatians is employed to bolster Catholic tradition against gnostic adversaries.

But the gnostic "opposition," so to speak, could also enlist these verses. The (gnostic) Naasenes are represented as appealing to "Jerusalem above" in their exhortation that true gnostics—unlike more "carnal" humans—should flee from the "earthly intercourse" of "Egypt." They should fly away to that "Jerusalem above, the mother of the living."[12] This exegesis hints at the ascetic purposes to which the Hagar and Sarah story would be put in later times.

Justification of Allegory

The chief "work" to which second- and third-century church fathers put Galatians 4 was to justify their use of allegory. This text showed that Paul, the prince of the apostles, himself "allegorized."[13] So when pagan detractors of Christianity, such as Celsus, taunted Christians that their resort to allegory stemmed from their embarrassment at the crudeness of many biblical stories, Origen in *Against Celsus* replied—citing Galatians 4—that since Scripture *itself* contains allegories, allegory was a divinely sanctioned mode of reading.[14] Indeed, Origen championed allegory as a necessary tool for Christians readers or hearers. Without it, they would be left with foolish, "impossible," and even scandalous biblical narratives that failed to edify.[15] Galatians 4 teaches Christians the important lesson that stories of marriages and intercourse with maidservants in the Hebrew Bible *need* to be allegorized. Scripture, Origen claims, does not wish us to imitate the literal and "carnal" acts reported of Sarah, Abraham, and Hagar but to understand their spiritual significance. Scripture uses real events of history to manifest more important truths.[16] In this argument allegory serves as a means to "save" the Old Testament for Christians.

Writing at the turn to the third century, the North African church father Tertullian (d. ca. 225 CE) mocks resistance to orthodox Christians' employment of figurative interpretation offered by the alleged second-century "heretic" Marcion (d. ca. 154 CE). Marcion had scandalized mainstream Christians by rejecting the authority of the Old Testament, excising parts of the New Testament that placed Jesus in overly close relation to the Hebrew forefathers and "Jewish" practice, and appropriating a "de-Judaized" Paul as his religious hero. Rebutting Marcion's arguments, Tertullian notes that "the very apostle whom our heretics adopt" (namely, Paul) constructs allegories in such passages as Galatians 4—a discrepancy that his Marcionite opponents have failed to note.[17] If Paul himself used allegory, Tertullian reasons, Marcion has no grounds for complaint against mainstream Christians' use of figurative interpretation. Allegorical exegesis was essential to the church fathers' retention of the Old Testament as God's revelation; without it, the Fathers would have deemed too many Old Testament stories "unedifying."

Debates over Marriage and Asceticism

God's promise to Abraham that his descendants would number as "the stars in the heaven" (Gen. 15:5) portended for patristic exegetes the multiplication of Christians.[18] If, as Paul argued in Romans 4, those who "had faith" were to be reckoned as the children of Abraham, Christians of the church fathers' own era should be identified with Abraham's descendants, the inheritors of God's promise. But the implication that these numerous descendants meant "real" children begotten of sexual intercourse, the Fathers roundly rejected as revealing a "carnality" no longer appropriate to Christians. Accordingly, the stories pertaining to Hagar and Sarah entered into patristic debates over marriage and ascetic renunciation.

Once the battle for the retention of the Hebrew Scriptures as a Christian book had been won in the second century, Christians of later times were compelled to read *all* parts of the Bible as meaningful and edifying. In particular, the Genesis accounts of the patriarchs must be construed to support the values of later, more ascetically minded Christians. The startling ingenuity of the church fathers' interpretations of these tales of patriarchal sexual practice as lessons in chastity yet again illustrates the wondrous powers of "interpretation."

As early as the turn to the third century, Tertullian summons the story of Abraham to argue (amazingly) for "monogamy," by which he means only one marriage throughout a lifetime. No second marriage was to be countenanced, even if a spouse died. When Tertullian's opponents—those who believed that remarriage after the death of a spouse is biblically sanctioned—point to the example of Abraham who, in addition to his relations with Hagar, took Cetura (Keturah) as a wife after Sarah's death (Gen. 25:1), Tertullian engages in a clever bit of exegesis. At what point, he muses, did "Abraham believe God" and have his belief "reckoned to him as righteousness" (Gen. 15:6)? Tertullian answers that it was while Abraham still lived in "monogamy" with Sarah, before the law of circumcision was given. Abraham's descent into "digamy" through his relations with Hagar are here aligned with his reception of physical circumcision, a much-maligned feature of Jewish law among the church fathers. If you wish to follow the "digamist" Abraham, so Tertullian taunts his opponents, then you must also follow him in circumcision. But if you reject circumcision, then you are bound to "monogamy," indeed to one marriage in a lifetime. Since Christians are "children of Isaac" (Gal. 4:28, 31), they, like him, should remain "monogamous" to the end of life.[19] Tertullian's argument was considered so wittily trenchant that it was later borrowed, without acknowledgment, by Jerome (d. 420 CE) and by the anonymous, perhaps Pelagian, early fifth-century author of a treatise *On Chastity*.[20]

Writing in the mid–third century, Origen as well ingeniously argues a case for single marriage from the example of the patriarchs. He acknowledges that although both Abraham and Jacob had sexual relations and produced children with women other than their first wives, each was buried in a tomb with his first wife alone, his wife "by nature" (Gen. 25.10, 49.31). Only of a first wife, Origen argues, can one say "bone of my bones, flesh of my flesh" (Gen. 2:23). Origen, however, slides over the detail that the wife with whom Jacob is buried is *not* she who was the bearer of the promise descending to Christ (namely, Rachel), but rather Leah. So strong was Origen's desire to argue for monogamy that his ascetic concerns here trumped Christological considerations.[21]

Allegory was a useful ally in the campaign to asceticize the stories of Abraham, Sarah, and Hagar. Origen is here the master allegorizer—although, as we shall see, on other occasions he can interpret these tales more prosaically as examples of proper marital order and wifely subservience. In his allegorizing and asceticizing mode, Origen reckons that since Abraham was 137 years old when he married Cetura (Keturah),[22] their marriage could not have been undertaken out of passion. Origen rather finds in it a mystical and sacred meaning through a clue provided in Wisdom of Solomon 8:9: "Take wisdom as thy wife." If we heed this useful admonition, Origen counsels, we can "marry" even into old age, as Abraham did, for there is no end of wisdom. Reflecting on such passages as Deuteronomy 25:9 (the curse on the man who refuses to impregnate his dead brother's wife and raise children for him), Leviticus 21:20 (the law excluding men with crushed testicles from assuming the priesthood), and Isaiah 56:3 (the plaint of the eunuch who says he is a "dry tree"), Origen argues that it is because the unmarried man and the eunuch have not "married wisdom"—*not* because they have not physically reproduced—that the Old Testament puts a curse on them.[23] Rather, the curse condemns only those who have not *spiritually* reproduced. If the Bible were thought to condemn those who had not physically reproduced, Origen reasons, then the virgins of the church would stand condemned—which is manifestly *not* the case, since the state of virginity is more blessed than that of marriage.[24] In a second example, commenting on the story of the two wives of Samuel's father (1 Sam. 1:1–2) Origen notes that since "wives" here denote "virtues," one can have as many as one desires. The plural marriages depicted in the Old Testament should be taken figuratively to stand for "multiplicity of virtues."[25]

A strong asceticizing note is also introduced into the stories of Abraham, Sarah, and Hagar by Clement of Alexandria (d. ca. 215 CE), writing at the turn to the third century. The "asexuality" of his portrayal of Sarah and Abraham would be rehearsed by other writers in the centuries that followed. Clement focuses, with approval, on the passage in which Abraham explains that Sarah really *is* his sister, or at least his half-sister, in order to justify his handing over of Sarah to Abimelech, king of Gerar (Gen. 20:1–2). For Clement, this story strikes an edifying note for Christians of his own time: that Sarah is Abraham's "sister" suggests that Christian wives should live as "sisters" (i.e., asexually) with their husbands in a marriage that imitates in this respect Abraham's and Sarah's. Moreover, the report that Sarah "laughed" when the (angelic) visitors at the oaks of Mamre told her that she would bear a son within the year (Gen. 18:9–14) should not, Clement argues, be taken as a sign of her disbelief, but rather of her shame at sexual intercourse.[26] Thus Tertullian, Origen, and Clement all manage to turn the Genesis narrative into counsels of chaste marriage—with "chastity" variously understood.

Asceticizing interpretations of the Abraham, Sarah, and Hagar stories in the fourth and fifth century likewise range from arguments that the stories reveal the trio's sexual "restraint" to those which advance a more rigorous sexual renunciation. Ambrose of Milan interprets the fact that the aged Sarah brought forth a child as a sign calculated to convince future generations that even a virgin (i.e., Mary) can give birth.[27] Further, that Sarah bore Isaac as a child "of the promise" when she was old and barren signaled to later writers that he served as a "type of Christ."[28] Likewise, the several Old Testament examples of sterile women giving birth should be taken as "types" of Jesus' conception,[29] confirming Christians' faith in his virgin birth.[30] But Ambrose also attends to the story of Abraham's passing off Sarah to Pharaoh (Gen. 12:11–20), which he thinks provides a moralizing tale in which "reason conquers passion." That Abraham allowed his "duty to God" to prevail over his fears for Sarah's chastity and for his own safety bespeaks behavior that Christians might well emulate.[31] The fact that God punished Pharaoh and preserved Sarah, Ambrose argues, proves how much God loves and guards chastity.[32] Throughout his moralizing expositions, Ambrose represents the patriarchs as ascetic exemplars who leave homeland and family to devote themselves to chaste living.[33]

In addition to the Fathers' promoting radically ascetic interpretations of the patriarchal narratives through allegory, they also accomplished the same end through a distancing of Old Testament mores from those appropriate for Christians. Authors such as Jerome and the anonymous (Pelagian?) author of the treatise On Chastity advanced a chronologically oriented critique that stressed the outdatedness and inferiority of patriarchal mores. Jerome, writing at the end of the fourth century, emphasizes the "difference in times" between the marital arrangements of the Old Testament and the promotion of celibacy in the Christian dispensation. Although he (grudgingly) acknowledges that Abraham "pleased God" while a married man, he argues that those days lie in the past. Now, virgins "please God" with their perpetual virginity. Abraham "served the Law in his era; so let us 'upon whom the end of the ages has come' (1 Cor. 10:11) serve the Gospel" in the way fitting to the New Dispensation.[34] In Jerome's view, second marriage after a spouse's death (such as Abraham undertook) should be tolerated only in the case of "incontinent persons." This concession for remarriage, Jerome muses, must have been that to which Paul alludes when he confessed that he "became a Jew to the Jews" (1 Cor. 9:20).[35] Although Jacob had two wives while he was "in bondage" in Mesopotamia, Jerome adds, one of them (conveniently) died once he moved close to Bethlehem, the birthplace of the herald of virginity. "The intimacies of Mesopotamia died in the land of the Gospel," he intones.[36] Jerome even advances the claim—citing no evidence—that early Christian converts from Judaism had to be wooed away from the "polygamy" that characterized their earlier faith in order to embrace the new Christian regime.[37]

The marriages of the patriarchs appear in one more important guise in Jerome's writings. In a literary dispute with a late-fourth-century opponent named Helvidius (who believed that although Mary was a virgin when she conceived Jesus, she and Joseph bore children through sexual intercourse after Jesus' birth), Jerome represents Helvidius as plaintively asking, "Are virgins better than Abraham, Isaac, and Jacob, who were married men?"[38] Although Jerome does not here answer Helvidius's question directly, his discussions elsewhere suggest that his answer is resoundingly "yes." Jerome's interpretation of the thirty-fold, sixty-fold, and one hundred-fold harvests in the parable of the Sower, for example, with the married reckoned as the "thirty" and virgins as the "one hundred," leaves no doubt as to his assessment of the relative merits of each.[39]

Writing in the early fifth century, the anonymous author of the presumably Pelagian treatise *On Chastity* likewise faced opponents (whether real or imaginary) who argued that since Abraham "pleased God" even though he had a wife, it was not necessary for Christians to adopt celibacy in order similarly to "please."[40] The anonymous author retorts sharply: it was not because Abraham was *married* that he pleased God; he was already married (Gen. 12) before his "belief was reckoned to him as righteousness" (Gen. 15:6). Rather, Abraham "pleased God" through his obedience, as manifest in his leaving home, homeland, and family (Gen. 12), receiving the "wound" of circumcision (Gen. 17), renouncing his son (albeit one begotten of a handmaid [Gen. 21]), and willingly sacrificing Isaac (Gen. 22), thus showing a spiritual disregard for earthly affairs, including children. This overwhelming display of obedience to God indicates to the author of *On Chastity* that if Abraham had heard Paul's advice—namely, that "it is well for a person to remain as he is" (1 Cor. 7:26) and that "it is good for a man not to touch a woman" (1 Cor. 7:1)—he would "joyfully have obeyed." Abraham would easily have made light of a son he had not yet begotten, the author argues, since he did not hesitate to slay the one he had reared.[41]

Patristic Defense of Marriage

Such ascetically inclined interpretations of the Abraham story prompted the fear that too rabid an embrace of asceticism might render the exegete liable to charges of "heresy" on the grounds that he was denigrating God's good creation, including the creation of humankind in two sexes and the provision for marriage and reproduction. Thus Ambrose of Milan, whose several treatises on the topic of virginity testify to his enthusiasm for that state, nonetheless enlists the stories of Sarah to display his praise for marriage. Declaring himself to be "pro-marriage," Ambrose points to the examples of the patriarchs' wives as evidence of the blessedness of wedlock. Only wicked men speak against marriage, he avers; perhaps they should not have received the benefit of being born![42] Likewise, Ambrose argues that when Jesus proclaimed, "Woe to those who are with child and give suck in those days" (Luke 21:23), he was not implying that conception was a "crime"; otherwise, how would God have blessed Sarah (cf. Gen. 18:10)?[43]

Championing the goodness of marriage on the basis of Sarah and Abraham's union—Hagar is usually omitted from these accounts—easily advanced to championing a conservative marital order. As early as 1 Peter 3:5–6, Sarah's obedience to Abraham and her calling him "lord" (Gen. 18:12)[44] were noted as enjoining Christian women to similar subservience. In Origen's view, Sarah stands as a prime example of appropriate wifely behavior. Despite his preference for celibate living, when Origen offers advice and instruction for "real life" marriage, he promotes marital hierarchy. Two passages, based on his characteristically close attention to individual words and phrases of Scripture, are enlisted to support his interpretation. The first is Genesis 18:10, in which Sarah is said to stand "behind" Abraham in listening to the visitors at the oaks of Mamre. Origen argues on the basis of this verse that Sarah should serve as an example to married women of his time, who should "follow" their husbands' lead to the way of the Lord. Since "man" signifies "reason" while "woman" connotes "flesh," it is proper that flesh should follow reason, not vice versa.[45] The second passage is Gen. 21:12, in which God instructs Abraham, "Whatever Sarah says to you, do as she tells you." This advice, if taken literally, alarms Origen, since Genesis 3:16 puts women in subjection to their husbands, a matron's proper role. Origen escapes his dilemma by an etymological ruse. The name "Sarah" means "virtue," he claims. Abraham's lending of Sarah to Abimelech (Gen. 20) then becomes explicable, for "virtue" can be shared. When a couple reaches perfection, Origen argues, the wife becomes a "sister" (cf. Prov. 7:4, "Say to wisdom, 'You are my sister'"), and, as such, "we may unite her with others who wish her."[46] Thus does Origen circumvent the implication that Sarah exercised authority over Abraham.

John Chrysostom likewise mines these and other patriarchal stories to bring home messages of proper marital behavior to his congregations in Antioch and Constantinople. A lofty marital relation based on love and self-sacrifice—such as that of Sarah and Abraham—is a theme to which Chrysostom warms. He praises Sarah for her untiring energy. Although of the "weak sex," she moves with Abraham on little notice and without complaint, making no difficulties for her husband.[47] So firm is the concord between Abraham and Sarah that she does not protest when he hands her over to other men. Like a good wife, she takes her husband's advice, even to the point of endangering her honor and being insulted by "barbarians," in order to save him.[48] When she discovers that she cannot bear children, she urges Abraham to take Hagar. "What righteousness! What ineffable behavior!" Chrysostom exclaims.[49] He especially praises Sarah's willingness to serve. Despite her great age, she does not disdain to fill the role of a servant. Unlike the wives of Chrysostom's day, Sarah prepares food and makes bread for the visitors at Mamre with her own hands.[50] And throughout, Chrysostom marvels, she remains beautiful![51]

Abraham too exhibits proper husbandly virtues. In fact, he displays *all* the virtues, Chrysostom testifies.[52] He is not jealous when the Egyptians desire Sarah; Abraham's equanimity is a "wonderful" trait.[53] Loving his wife before all else, he sends away his "bed partner," Hagar, so as not to grieve Sarah.[54] Both he and Sarah were exempt from passion. They wanted offspring only so as not to die childless. Abraham's relation with Hagar was not undertaken from passion or with a view to pleasure. Nor did he blame his wife for her lack of fertility, knowing that fecundity is a gift from God.[55] And when Sarah became angry at Hagar's conception, Abraham displayed forbearance for her female weakness and pardoned her: "What virtue and tolerance!" Chrysostom again exclaims. Abraham's tenderness toward his wife, he writes, is exemplary, a model for Christian men to follow.[56] Christian marriages in the present might well emulate Sarah and Abraham's. As is evident from Chrysostom's discussion, Hagar is present in the stories only to be cast off.

One last theme that surfaces briefly in Chrysostom's exposition but that, as we shall see, plays a major role in Augustine's exegesis pertains to his interpretation of "persecution" in Galatians 4:29. There Paul claims that at the time of the Genesis narratives "he who was born according to the flesh [Ishmael] persecuted him who was born according to the Spirit [Isaac]." Chrysostom pictures Christians asking, "How are we to be 'free' (as Gal. 4:23 suggests) if the Jews seize and scourge the believers?" He responds that the bondman may have "the reward of tyranny" for a while, but then will be cast out with his mother [Hagar] to become an exile and a wanderer.[57] That Jewish "oppression" of Christians will not last, Chrysostom is certain. Moreover, the Jews will receive their deserved punishment. Here the theme of who is a "persecutor" and who is the "persecuted" comes vividly to the fore.[58]

AUGUSTINE'S USE OF THE HAGAR, SARAH STORY

With Augustine (354–430 CE), priest and then bishop of Hippo Regius in North Africa, the themes surveyed above reappear and are given new meanings that suit his different historical and ecclesiastical situation. He uses the stories of Abraham, Sarah, and Hagar to combat Jews and "heretics," to defend marriage against the onslaughts of ascetic interpreters, to champion the church's dominance over "the synagogue," and, most startlingly, to justify Catholic "discipline" (i.e., strong-arm measures) against dissident Christian sects in North Africa. The "heretics" against which Augustine railed were Manicheans, devotees of a dualistic religion, Persian in origin, that denigrated procreation. Manicheans had made inroads in fourth-century North Africa, and Augustine wrote several treatises to counter their interpretations.

Against Jews and Manicheans

Augustine avails himself of Paul's allegory of Sarah and Hagar to dispute the Jews' claim to descent from Sarah; they should rather be classified as descendants of Hagar the bondwoman.[59] Christians, not Jews, are the seed of Abraham, the inheritors of the promise through Isaac.[60] Elsewhere, in his treatise *An Answer to the Jews*, Augustine only once, and that obliquely, calls on Galatians 4 to explain that Jews mistakenly imagine that "Sion" is the earthly city of Jerusalem, the city that Paul proclaims to be "in slavery." Augustine corrects this misimpression, appealing to Galatians 4:25–26: "Sion" refers to the "Jerusalem above that is free," symbolized by Sarah, the city to which *Christians* belong.[61] It is of interest that the treatise in which we might most expect Augustine to appeal to Galatians 4 gives the allegory of Sarah and Hagar short attention.

Augustine emphasized the stories of Sarah, Abraham, and Hagar more fully when he dealt with adversaries other than the Jews. Manichean opponents, for example, called upon Augustine to justify the Christian retention of the Old Testament as a holy book and to defend its less edifying aspects, which Manicheans had noted in minute detail.[62] Among these were stories of the patriarchs and their dubious (from a later ascetic viewpoint) behavior with women. On more than one occasion, Augustine was stirred to defend the patriarchs' behavior against such criticism. Since he believed that there were no meaningless or useless passages in Scripture,[63] tales of the patriarchs' sexual exploits needed to be rendered "edifying."

It is important to remember that Augustine himself had been a Manichean "auditor"—the lower of two tiers in the sect—for nine years.[64] In the *Confessions*, he reports that he had eagerly awaited the arrival of Faustus the Manichean in his town to explicate various puzzling points of doctrine for him. Although in that work he expressed disappointment at Faustus's limited literary and scientific education that rendered him unable to answer those questions,[65] it seems evident to the modern scholar that Faustus had a thorough knowledge of Scripture. In the Manichean Faustus, Augustine met his match as an interpreter. Although Augustine deemed Faustus's approach "malicious"[66] and faulted his "poor reading" of the Scriptural narratives,[67] his charge appears to mean that Faustus did not read Scripture, as did Augustine, so as to "save the text." Often Faustus chose a blatantly literal interpretation of a text simply to bring out its disquieting elements.[68]

Augustine's treatise *Against Faustus the Manichean*, composed in 397–398, is one of the most massive and fascinating of his polemical works. It was in Faustus's interest, as a scorner of the Hebrew Bible but admirer of at least some portions of the New Testament, to detach Old Testament narratives from New Testament meanings.[69] For example, the Old Testament curse on those who fail to "raise up seed for Israel" (Deut. 25:5–10), Faustus argues, stands contrary to the chastity the New Testament recommends, and hence the curse should be rejected.[70] Faustus, confessing himself as a true follower of Christ, writes that *he*—unlike many Catholic Christians—has obeyed Jesus' stringent injunction to leave wife, children, home, and riches.[71]

Deprecating the sanctity of the Old Testament, Faustus singles out the patriarchal narratives, especially those pertaining to Abraham, Sarah, and Hagar, for attack. He argues that Abraham "defiled himself with a concubine," impelled by "an irrational craving for children."[72] Abraham's appropriation of Hagar indicates that he lacked faith in God's promise, his faithlessness exacerbating his sexual sin.[73] Abraham's handing over of Sarah to Pharaoh and Abimelech indicates that he was guilty of avarice.[74] Nor does Sarah escape condemnation: she connived with Abraham in his sexual defilement with Hagar.[75] Thus Faustus scornfully declines the invitation of Matthew 8:11 to sit at table with the patriarchs in the kingdom of heaven. In his judgment, they should rather, on the basis of their behavior, have been consigned to "the dungeons below."[76]

It was Augustine's task, in response, to defend these biblical narratives against charges of moral unworthiness. Whereas Faustus (a good poststructuralist, *avant la lettre*) looked for the disjunctions, gaps, and disparities in biblical texts, Augustine's "idealist" project was to harmonize and smooth over the seeming discrepancies as well as the dubious morals. Responding to Faustus's attacks, Augustine argues that Faustus should attend better to "chronology." He should follow the order of the text more closely—and Augustine will show him how. At the beginning of the Abraham narrative (Gen. 12:2; 13:16), Augustine notes, God promises Abraham many descendants but does not yet reveal how they are to be produced; in chapter 15, Abraham still imagines that his servant will be his heir. Only now does God reveal to Abraham that he will beget his *own* son but does not further specify who will be the mother of the child. Thus, with Hagar's appearance in chapter 16, Abraham still remains ignorant of the future mother's identity. Not until chapter 18 does God promise Sarah that *she* will bear the child whose descendants will number as the stars in the heavens.[77] A closer reading of the Abraham narratives, Augustine implies, would have kept Faustus from making unfounded allegations against the patriarch's morals. Abraham's ignorance was entirely excusable.

Likewise, if Faustus had investigated the linguistic and marital customs of the age, Augustine argues, he might not have deemed it shocking that Abraham called Sarah his "sister."[78] Moreover, Augustine stresses that Abraham did not act out of lust but simply from the understandable concern that the human race continue.[79] No wife who loves her husband—as Sarah did Abraham—would encourage him in an extramarital affair if he were motivated by "animal passion." Sarah also acted only from the pious motive of wishing to increase the Israelite race.[80] In addition, Augustine reminds his readers, Abraham acted "out of obedience to conjugal authority" (i.e., at Sarah's request) in taking Hagar—a principle that Paul recommends in 1 Corinthians 7:4.[81]

Augustine's debate with the Manichean Secundinus, although more briefly recorded, repeats several of the same themes. Secundinus had included among the biblical passages ripe for mockery those of Abraham's repeated willingness to pass off Sarah for the sexual use of other men and of Sarah's "donation" of Hagar for Abraham's procreative use.[82] Augustine replies that Abraham acted with "human prudence" in allowing Pharaoh and Abimelech to have Sarah, leaving it to God to rescue her modesty. In a novel theological twist, Augustine argues that Abraham would have been "tempting God" if he had not done what was in his own power to save their lives. Besides, Augustine scornfully adds, alluding to the Manichean creation myth in which the Power of Light is dismembered and dispersed upon his defeat by the Power of Darkness, the Manichean god willingly allowed *his* members to be dishonored.[83]

Antiprocreative Manicheans such as Secundinus mocked in particular the Genesis 16 story of Sarah and Hagar, but what they really faulted, in Augustine's view, was Sarah's fecundity as described in chapter 21, not her sterility. In producing a child (birth, for Manicheans, is thought further to entrap the dispersed particles of Light in the darkness of matter), the Manicheans think that Sarah occasions "a dreadful calamity for God." Rather, Augustine counters, her sterility should be seen as "prophetic." Although he does not here elaborate, he appears to imply that her infertility points ahead "prophetically" to the virginal conception of Jesus.[84]

That Augustine developed his exegesis of the Abraham, Sarah, and Hagar stories in connection with more general principles of scriptural interpretation is revealed in a treatise whose first sections he completed shortly before his reply to Faustus, namely, *On Christian Doctrine*. There Augustine lays down the principle that Christians should take as "figurative" anything in Scripture "which cannot in a literal sense be attributed either to an upright character or to a pure faith."[85] Pointing to the example of Hagar and Sarah, Augustine argues that "in old times" it was not objectionable to have several wives; in cases such as this, figurative (i.e., nonliteral) exegesis helps save the text and renders it edifying. Otherwise, readers might imagine that the behaviors attributed to the trio were sinful.[86] Besides, men at that time could have many wives without lust; now, Augustine regrets, men with only one wife do not avoid lust.[87] A charitable reading of the text suggests to Augustine that we can interpret literally those acts that merit praise by the standards of its time—even though our standards are different.[88] These general directives regarding biblical interpretation in *On Christian Doctrine* accord well with Augustine's approach in the anti-Manichean treatises.

Debates on the Status of Marriage

A few years after Augustine composed *Against Faustus*, he learned—somewhat belatedly—of a debate between Jovinian and Jerome regarding the status of marriage. Jovinian, a Christian monk in the early 390s, became alarmed at what he construed as the assault on marriage embedded in Jerome's lavish praise of virginity. In a treatise directed against Jerome's view, Jovinian argued that once Christians have passed through the baptismal laver, virgins should not be considered "better" than married Christians if their merits are equal in other respects.[89] Jovinian's claim attempts both to deflate the pride of ascetic renunciants and to emphasize the equalizing force of baptism, which wipes clean the sinner's slate and renders all the newly baptized on a par. Attacking Jerome's excessive exaltation of sexual renunciation, Jovinian compiled a list of biblical passages to argue that God had blessed marriage at the world's beginning, and that Jesus repeated this blessing (cf. Matt. 19:5).[90] Abraham and Sarah stand as one of Jovinian's cases in point. Abraham had three women (not quite up to Jacob's four, Jovinian notes) and yet received God's blessing, as shown by the begetting of a special son by merit of his faith. Likewise, Sarah in old age had "exchanged the curse of sterility for the blessing of childbearing."[91] Anyone who forbids or discourages marriage in the name of a "higher" Christianity is playing into the hands of the Manicheans, in Jovinian's view.[92]

Jerome responded with outrage to Jovinian's treatise: how dare a Christian imagine that the state of marriage was equal to that of Christian virginity! Jerome's *Against Jovinian* was considered, even by his friends, to constitute such a slander on marriage that they attempted to remove copies from circulation in Rome.[93] Jerome's primary argument against making the patriarchs exemplars of moral behavior appealed to "the difference in times": Christians are called to fulfill God's quite different command under the gospel.[94] Abraham's three wives, however, proved too much for Jerome's attempted restraint. If Christians wish to follow Abraham in his marital habits, he scornfully writes, let them follow him in circumcision as well! No half acceptance and half rejection of Abraham![95] Although Abraham served God through marriage, we "upon whom the end of the ages has come" (1 Cor. 10:11) should serve him in virginity.[96]

Close to a decade after Jovinian and Jerome had exchanged their literary blows, Augustine, rather belatedly, entered the fray. Augustine saw his task as upholding the Christian preference for asceticism while simultaneously stressing the goodness of marriage. Jovinian had perhaps not accorded sufficient weight to the superiority of virginity, but Jerome had most certainly not credited marriage as an honorable Christian calling.[97]

Probably in 401, Augustine wrote two companion pieces, *On Holy Virginity* and *On the Good of Marriage*. In both, his main concern is to defend Christian marriage. The conjugal life of Old Testament people was "prophetic," he states at the beginning of *On Holy Virginity*.[98] Throughout the treatise, he argues that those who have devoted themselves to Christian virginity should not become proud.[99] In *On the Good of Marriage*, Augustine warms further to his theme and explicates many biblical passages pertaining to marriage. Among them, Abraham stands as case in point. Although Manicheans denigrate Abraham's production of children,[100] Augustine notes, others (presumably Jovinian's allies) taunt Catholic virgins and widows with the query "Do you think that you are better than Abraham?" Augustine prepares an elaborate answer for the troubled celibate to whom this question was allegedly addressed. In it he stresses the point that the Christian celibate is *not* better than Abraham, although celibacy in principle is superior even to chaste marriage. The "difference in times" allowed Abraham a different behavior that was blessed by God. Unmarried women who are taunted with the question "Are you better than Sarah?" should respond similarly.[101] Probably recalling Faustus's declination to sit at table with the patriarchs in the kingdom, Augustine concludes his treatise with the assurance that Christians with various virtues will recline with Abraham, Isaac, and Jacob in the kingdom (Matt. 8:11). The latter, Augustine reminds readers, were married and became parents "not for the sake of this world but for the sake of Christ."[102]

In later treatises and letters, Augustine continued to deploy the married and reproducing patriarchs and their women to uphold the goodness of marriage. In *On the Good of Widowhood*, written around 414, Augustine returns to the theme, defending the patriarchs' abundant reproduction with the justification that they were obeying God's command. He adduces several arguments. First, men who did not at that time "raise up seed for Israel" were cursed (Deut. 25:5–10). Moreover, the patriarchs' wives were holy women who would have entirely renounced sexual intercourse if there were any other way to produce children. Last, answering the question of why only males (not females) had multiple spouses in these stories, Augustine argues that men can beget many children if they have more than one woman, whereas women cannot give birth to a greater number of children even if they have sexual relations with several men. So polygamy was a "natural" arrangement, given the desire to increase the world's population. Besides, Augustine concludes, the patriarchs should be viewed as "types" of Christianity's advent.[103]

In book 16 of *The City of God*, Augustine also deals at some length with Abraham, Sarah, and Hagar. There, as part of his explication of Old Testament history, he returns to his earlier justification of the patriarchs' behavior. Repeating some of his arguments from *Against Faustus*, Augustine notes that Abraham did not lie in calling Sarah his sister; he was following Old Testament custom. Moreover, he entrusted Sarah's chastity to God, and, as a man, took what precautions he could. Had he done otherwise, he would have been "testing God."[104] As for Abraham's appropriation of Hagar, he should not be deemed guilty; he had his mind only on procreation, not on lust. Moreover, he was obeying his wife. Augustine asks readers to remember Paul's claim that the wife has authority over the husband's body (1 Cor. 7:4). Besides, we can infer that Abraham had not become attached to Hagar, because he let Sarah do with her as she wanted. Apparently Augustine believes that this reasoning helps to exonerate Abraham, not to damn him further. Abraham, in Augustine's assessment, stands as a "true man" insofar as he "treated no woman intemperately."[105] As for his taking Cetura (Keturah) as a wife, he was not motivated by "incontinence." Augustine suggests that the women of Abraham stand for different types: Hagar belongs to the Old Covenant; Sarah, to the New; and Cetura and her sons perhaps represent "carnal people" who mistakenly imagine that they belong to the New Covenant. This passage may have been included in Scripture, Augustine muses, to refute heretics who condemn second marriage.[106] In any event, Augustine rates Abraham's faith as superior to Isaac's, despite the fact that Abraham had two wives and a concubine, whereas Isaac is represented as married to one wife alone. This example shows, in Augustine's view, that the married man who has faith is superior to the continent man who is faithless.[107]

Anti-Donatist Writings

A last and startling use to which Augustine puts the story of Abraham, Sarah, and Hagar appears in his anti-Donatist letters and treatises. Donatism was a form of North African Christianity that came to prominence shortly after the close of the Roman persecutions of Christians in the early fourth century. Its adherents alleged that Catholic Christians had been unfaithful during the persecutions. In consequence, bishops and priests who had been ordained by the "traitors" were not true holders of ecclesiastical office, and the sacraments they gave were invalid.

Donatists claimed that they represented the pure Christian church of North Africa descended from earlier centuries of which Cyprian of Carthage stood as a hero. Modern scholars estimate that throughout some parts of fourth-century North Africa, Donatists may have outnumbered Catholics, especially in the Numidian hinterlands.[108]

The controversy between Donatists and Catholics still raged when Augustine returned to North Africa from Italy in the late 380s and a few years thereafter assumed the priesthood and then the bishopric of Hippo Regius. At first Augustine thought that the Donatists could be won over by persuasion and scriptural argument. With the passage of time and the failure of these techniques to convince, however, he moved to stronger measures, justifying the use of imperial force—or "discipline," as Augustine preferred to call these strong-arm tactics—against Donatists, whom he now saw as "heretics," not just as misguided Christians.[109] One scriptural justification for rationalizing such behavior on the part of Catholic leaders he found in the story of Hagar and Sarah.

In his defense of the state's (and the Catholic Church's) use of coercive measures against the Donatists, Augustine rejected the Donatist protest against the Catholics' use of force as well as their claim to be "martyrs." The story of Sarah and Hagar gave Augustine justification for the Catholic and imperial position. Sarah rightfully "persecuted" Hagar, who behaved as a "haughty handmaid" and deserved correction. Not everyone who "suffers" is a martyr, Augustine argues, but only those who are persecuted for righteousness' sake, as Jesus proclaimed in the Beatitudes (Matt. 5:10). In the case of Sarah and Hagar, it was Sarah who was a righteous persecutor, and Hagar who, as unrighteous, deserved punishment.[110] As Galatians 4 intimates, Sarah represents the true church of God, and, as such, she is commissioned to enforce proper discipline against the recalcitrant. If we scrutinize the story, Augustine argues, we find that it was rather Hagar who persecuted Sarah by her haughtiness, and for that reason Sarah justifiably disciplined her. Christians should learn the difference, he concludes, between righteous and unrighteous persecution. The church's persecution, moreover, is always undertaken in the spirit of love, not of anger, and with the desire to correct, to recall the wandering from error.[111]

In other writings, Augustine notes that Sarah's treatment of her bondwoman was not called "persecution" by Paul in Galatians 4. God may use authorities to punish heretics, schismatics, and rejectors of Christ in ways that may seem repressive. Christian authorities must be able to "render account of their rule" to God. How would they do this if they allowed such wickedness to flourish? Besides, Augustine claims, the very point of Hagar's leaving Sarah was so that she could return—and Donatists should heed this moral and return to the Catholic Church.[112] Arguing against the Donatists' protest that they should not be "forced" into the Catholic Church, Augustine claims that God punished Sarah's handmaid through the authority given her by God, and hence she acted correctly. Sarah, he notes, had not hated Hagar earlier; she had kindly allowed her the opportunity to become a mother. It was only when Hagar exhibited her "pride" that Sarah acted as she did, and this for Hagar's "own good."[113] Thus is Christian coercion of "wayward" Christians justified by an appeal to the story of Sarah and Hagar.

CONCLUSION

Exegeses of the stories of Hagar, Sarah, and Abraham by the church fathers were born of needs, as they perceived them, of their own day: to argue for Christianity's superiority to Judaism and other religious movements and for Christianity's "inheritance" of and right to interpret the Hebrew Scriptures as edifying both for Christian ascetics and for the married. Above all, the Old Testament must be seen as a "worthy" book whose narratives could enlighten more ascetically minded Christians of late antiquity.

That the Fathers' interpretations seem less than "enlightened" to many readers in the present is obvious. There is considerable silence surrounding the figure of Hagar in their discussions. (By contrast, Islam found an honored place for her, as the next essay demonstrates.) And when the Fathers do refer to Hagar, it is as a symbol of erring Jews who did not accept Jesus as Savior, or as a figure guilty of "unchristian" sexual behavior. Nowhere does she seem to be a character for whom sympathy might be shown, a character who all too well recalls the plight of homeless, destitute, abandoned, and mistreated women. Although Sarah fares better as representative of the "New Covenant" of Christianity, she too signals an era of sexual values that the church fathers are eager to leave behind. Throughout, the Fathers' main concern is to defend the honor and reputation of Abraham, the forefather of the Messiah, often at the expense of the women with whom he shares the story. That Sarah and Hagar are "used" by the Fathers to illustrate other points of Christian theology shows, above all else, that however little concern they had for these female characters in their own right, they, like women elsewhere, were "good" for men "to think with." That remains their interpretive fate.

Notes

1. Phyllis Trible, "Hagar: The Desolation of Rejection," in *Texts of Terror: Literary-Feminist Readings of Biblical Narratives* (Philadelphia: Fortress Press, 1984), 28.
2. For anthropologist Claude Lévi-Strauss's use of the phrase "good to think with," see his *The Elementary Forms of Kinship* (rev. ed.; Boston, 1969 [1949, 1967]), 496. Lévi-Strauss was criticized for his seemingly insensitive comment that in primitive economies based on notions of exchange, women, like pigs, are good to "think with." For his explication of the phrase, see his *Structural Anthropology* (New York: Basic Books, 1963; French original, 1958), 61; here, he emphasizes that although women are "exchanged," they "speak" and cannot be reduced to the "status of symbols or tokens"; that is, they are more than just items to be exchanged, even in primitive societies.
3. Origen, *Against Celsus* 2.3.
4. Cyprian, *Three Books of Testimonies Against the Jews* 1.20. Cyprian also includes Joseph (born of the long-barren Rachel) and Samuel (born of the long-barren Hannah) as "types of Christ."

5. Ambrose of Milan, *Exposition on Luke* 3.17–18; John Chrysostom, *Commentary on Galatians* (4:27–28).

6. Ambrose, *Exposition on Luke* 3.21, 28–30.

7. Jerome, *Commentary on Galatians* (on 4:27).

8. Chrysostom, *Commentary on Galatians* (on 4:27).

9. Chrysostom, *Homily 1 Against Judaizing Christians* 4.

10. "Gnosticism" (based on the Greek word for "knowledge") was the "umbrella term" traditionally used to refer to writings and sects of second- and third-century religious enthusiasts, some of whom (at least) were Christians; they were attacked, scholars now think somewhat unfairly, by the mainstream church fathers for fostering a dualistic religion of salvation that welcomed only the spiritual elite.

11. Irenaeus, *Against Heresies* 5.35.2. On "Prunikos," see Anne Pasquier, "Prouneikos. A Colorful Expression to Designate Wisdom in Gnostic Texts," in *Images of the Feminine in Gnosticism*, ed. Karen L. King (Philadelphia: Fortress Press, 1988), 47–66. The *pleroma* refers to the fullness of the divine powers that comprise the gnostic Godhead.

12. Hippolytus, *Refutation of All Heresies* 5.2.

13. The importance of this justification for later Christian allegory should not be minimized: see comments in Elizabeth A. Clark, *Reading Renunciation: Asceticism and Scripture in Early Christianity* (Princeton: Princeton University Press, 1999), 70–78 passim.

14. Celsus and Origen, in Origen, *Against Celsus* 4.48–49.

15. Origen, *On First Principles* 4.2.5, 4.2.8–9; for cases in the patriarchal narratives in which Origen claims that the Holy Spirit must surely mean something deeper, see *Homily 7 Genesis* 1; *Homily 10 Genesis* 2.

16. Origen, *Against Celsus* 4.44. Similarly, the anonymous Pelagian author of the treatise *On Chastity* argues that some statements in the Bible are to be taken figuratively, as the use of the story of Abraham's wife and concubine in Galatians 4 proves (*On Chastity* 15.2).

17. Tertullian, *Against Marcion* 3.5. Marcion and his followers allegedly accepted Paul's writings as the basis of their own Scripture, with the corresponding excision of other, more "Jewish-oriented" verses and books of the New Testament. According to Tertullian, the meaning of the Galatians 4 passage is that both old and new dispensations are from God: *Against Marcion* 5.4. And in the late fourth century, Jerome also notes how Marcion and other detractors of the Old Testament resist mainstream Christian practice of appropriating Old Testament passages through allegorical interpretation (Jerome, *Commentary on Galatians* [on 4:25–26]).

18. Origen, *Homily 5 Leviticus* 2, 3.

19. Tertullian, *On Monogamy* 6.

20. Jerome, *Against Jovinian* 1.19 (If you want to follow Abraham in his three wives, then get circumcised!); Anonymous, *On Chastity* 15.4.

21. Origen, *Commentary on I Corinthians* (on 7:8–12) (*Journal of Theological Studies* 9 [1908]: 504).

22. Origen must reckon this number from the reports that Sarah was ten years younger than Abraham (Gen. 17:17) and that she lived 127 years (Gen. 23:1).

23. Cf. Deut. 7:14; 25:5–10.

24. Origen, *Homily 11 Genesis* 1.

25. Ibid., 2.

26. Clement of Alexandria, *Miscellanies* 6.12. According to Maximus of Tyre, writing several centuries later, Sarah "laughed" because through God's grace, her sterility overcome, she would bear a son in joy; we (i.e., Maximus's congregation) should

rather "laugh" because our sins have been taken away (*Sermon* 21, *On Hospitality 2*), For Jerome, the fact that Abraham also "laughed" (Gen. 17:17) shows that even holy men can sin—an anti-Pelagian note (*Dialogue against the Pelagians* 3.12).

27. Ambrose, *On Isaac* 1.1.
28. Cyprian, *Three Books of Testimonies Against the Jews* (=*Treatise 12*) 1.20.
29. Jerome, *Letter 22*.21.
30. Chrysostom, *Homily 49 Genesis* 2; *Against Publicizing the Errors of the Brethren* 6–7.
31. Ambrose, *On Duties* 1.14.107–8.
32. Ambrose, *Letter 6* (=57) to Syagrius (actually, Ambrose here cites the story of Sarah and Abimelech in Gen. 20, not the earlier story of Sarah and Pharaoh in Gen. 12).
33. Ambrose, *On the Belief in the Resurrection* 2.95–99. Ambrose alludes to Gen. 12:1.
34. Jerome, *Against Jovinian* 2.4; also see Jerome, *Against Helvidius* 22 for a discussion of the "difference in times" between the Old Dispensation and the New.
35. Jerome, *Against Jovinian* 1.15. Paul allows, but counsels against, the remarriage of widows in 1 Cor. 7:39–40.
36. Ibid.
37. Jerome, *Letter 69*.5.
38. Helvidius, in Jerome, *Against Helvidius* 20.
39. Jerome, *Letter 22*.15; 48(49).3; 66.2; 123.9.
40. (Anonymous), *On Chastity* 15.1.
41. Ibid., 15.3.
42. Ambrose, *Concerning Virgins* 1.7.34.
43. Ambrose, *Exposition on Luke* 10.22 (*on Luke* 21:23).
44. In the Septuagint version of Genesis, Sarah refers to Abraham as *kyrios*; in the Vulgate version, as *dominus*. English translations tend to soften the meaning to "husband."
45. Origen, *Homily 4 Genesis* 4.
46. Origen. *Homily 6 Genesis* 1.
47. Chrysostom, *Homily 32 Genesis* 3.
48. Ibid., 5–6; also idem., *Homily 45 Genesis* 2.
49. Chrysostom, *Homily 38 Genesis* 1.
50. Chrysostom, *Homily 41 Genesis* 4; cf. *Homily 30 Romans*; *Homily 14 I Timothy*.
51. Chrysostom, *Homily 32 Genesis* 4.
52. Chrysostom, *Homily 35 I Corinthians* 10.
53. Chrysostom, *Homily 32 Genesis* 4–5.
54. Chrysostom, *Homily 20 Ephesians* (on Eph. 5:33).
55. Chrysostom, *Homily 38 Genesis* 2; cf. *On Virginity* 15.1; *Commentary on Galatians* (on 4:21–31); that children come about by the word of God, not simply by sexual relations, is a favorite theme of Chrysostom.
56. Chrysostom, *Homily 38 Genesis* 4–5.
57. Chrysostom, *Commentary on Galatians* (on 4:28).
58. Jerome, too, discussing Galatians 4:28, reminds readers of the "madness" of the Jews, who killed Jesus and the prophets, and persecuted the apostles; history teaches of the great persecutions that Jews have stirred up against Christians (*Commentary on Galatians* [on 4:28]).
59. Augustine, *Letter 196*.3.12–13.
60. Ibid., 4.14.
61. Augustine, *In Answer to the Jews* 5(6).
62. For an overview of Manicheanism, see Samuel N. C. Lieu, *Manichaenism in the Later Roman Empire and Medieval China* (Tübingen: J. C. B. Mohr [P. Siebeck], 1992).

63. Augustine, *Against Faustus* 22.96.
64. Augustine, *Confessions* 3.11.20; 4.1.1; *Against the Epistle Called Fundamental* 10; *On the Morals of the Manicheans* 68 (19).
65. Augustine, *Confessions* 5.3.3; 5.6.10–11; 5.7.13.
66. Augustine, *Against Faustus* 22.23.
67. Ibid., 22.32.
68. Ibid., 15.6.
69. Faustus in Augustine, *Against Faustus* 6.1.
70. Ibid., 14.1.
71. Ibid., 5.1.
72. Ibid., 22.5.
73. Ibid., 22.30.
74. Ibid., 22.33. In answering questions of a certain Dulcitius regarding the difference between the way God dealt with Pharaoh and with Abimelech in these narratives, Augustine refers his questioner to this section of *Against Faustus* (*On Eight Questions of Dulcitius* 7.4).
75. Faustus in Augustine, *Against Faustus* 22.31.
76. Augustine, *Against Faustus* 33.1.
77. Ibid., 22.32.
78. Ibid., 22.35.
79. Ibid., 22.30.
80. Ibid., 22.31.
81. Ibid., 22.31–32.
82. Secundinus, *Epistle to Augustine* 3, in Augustine, *Against Secundinus*.
83. Augustine, *Against Secundinus* 23. Augustine may here hint at something even more shocking: according to the Manichean creation myth, in the battle extending over several rounds between Light and Darkness, the power of Light made images of beautiful naked male and female forms, so that the archons of Darkness would either ejaculate or abort upon viewing these beauties, thus releasing some of the particles of Light they had trapped within themselves after Light's initial defeat. For a summary of the Manichean creation myth and its implications for sexual ethics, see Elizabeth A. Clark, "Vitiated Seeds and Holy Vessels: Augustine's Manichean Past," in *Images of the Feminine in Gnosticism*, Karen King, ed. (Philadelphia: Fortress Press, 1988), 391–400; also in Clark, *Ascetic Piety and Faith Women's: Essays on Late Ancient Christianity* (Lewiston/Queenston: Edwin Mellen Press, 1986), 315–24.
84. Augustine, *Against Secundinus* 22.
85. Augustine, *On Christian Doctrine* 3.10.14.
86. Ibid., 3.12.20, 3.14.22.
87. Ibid., 3.18.27.
88. Ibid., 3.22.32.
89. Jovinian, in Jerome, *Against Jovinian* 1.3. Jovinian's treatise is not extant.
90. Jovinian, in Jerome, *Against Jovinian* 1.5.
91. Ibid.
92. Ibid.
93. Jerome, *Letter* 48(49).2. For the opposition to Jerome, see David Hunter, "Resistance to the Virginal Ideal in Late Fourth-Century Rome: The Case of Jovinian," *Theological Studies* 48 (1987): 45–64.
94. Jerome, *Against Jovinian* 1.24; cf. 1.30, 1.37.
95. Ibid., 1.19.
96. Ibid., 2.24.
97. Augustine, *Retractions* 2.48 (=22).1 shows that Augustine's main concern in these debates was with combating Jerome's position.

98. Augustine, *On Holy Virginity* 1.1.
99. Ibid., 31.31; 32.32; 38.39.
100. Augustine, *On the Good of Marriage* 21.26.
101. Ibid., 22,27.
102. Ibid., 26.35.
103. Augustine, *On the Good of Widowhood* 7.10. Elsewhere, Augustine justifies patriarchal polygamy with the explanation that it is more consonant with "the order of nature" for men to rule over several women than vice versa (*On Marriage and Concupiscence* 1.9.10). Cf. *Sermon* 51.25, in which Augustine also argues that the patriarchs were simply obeying their wives, not committing adultery, in taking the maidservants as sexual partners [28]). And in *Against Lying* (10.23), Augustine defends Abraham against charges of lying when he claimed that Sarah was his "sister"; Augustine admits that Abraham concealed something of the truth, but he did not say anything false.
104. Augustine, *City of God* 16.19.
105. Ibid., 16.25.
106. Ibid., 16.34.
107. Ibid., 16.36.
108. For an extended analysis of Donatism, see W. H. C. Frend, *The Donatist Church: A Movement of Protest in Roman North Africa* (Oxford: Clarendon Press, 1952).
109. See the following articles of Peter Brown collected in his *Religion and Society in the Age of Saint Augustine* (New York: Harper and Row, 1972): "Religious Dissent in the Later Roman Empire: The Case of North Africa," "St. Augustine's Attitude to Religious Coercion," and "Religious Coercion in the Later Roman Empire: The Case of North Africa," 237–59, 260–78, 301–31.
110. Augustine, *Letter* 185=*On the Correction of the Donatists* 2.9.
111. Ibid., 2.11.
112. Augustine, *Tractate 11 on John* 13.3–15.2.
113. Augustine, *Letter* 93.6. The theme of Hagar's "pride" that needed correction is also stressed by Augustine in *Homily 10 on I John* 10.

Chapter 6

Islamic Hagar and Her Family

Riffat Hassan

The deepest truths and insights that lie at the heart of each major religious tradition are represented by myths and symbols that are able to inform, form, and transform the inner and outer lives of millions of human beings through the ages. By commemorating such myths and symbols we celebrate the pivotal role they have played in our individual and communal lives in the past. At the same time we reflect on ways in which they may be relevant to our lives in the present and the future. In this essay I would like to honor one of my foremothers, Hagar (*Hajira* in Arabic), whose role in Islam's "Abrahamic" narrative is not known to many outsiders. The narrative in which she appears contains five characters: two wives, their common husband, and two sons. They are Hagar and Sarah, Abraham, Ishmael, and Isaac. Their story in the Islamic tradition is of central significance as narrated in the Qur'an and in the hadith (oral traditions of the Prophet Muhammad).[1]

Hagar and Sarah are important not only by virtue of their role in the story of the Prophet Abraham, but also because of what they represent as women in the Jewish-Christian-Muslim patriarchal culture. Before reflecting on the latter aspect of their story, I will look at the "normative" Islamic view of Hagar and Sarah that emerges from a reading of the most authoritative sources of the Islamic tradition. Among these sources the most important is the Qur'an, which Muslims believe is the Word of God, revealed through the Archangel Gabriel to the Prophet Muhammad, who lived in Arabia in the seventh century. Next in authority to the Qur'an in Sunni Islam are the two hadith collections *Sahih al-Bukhari* and *Sahih Muslim*. They are believed to contain the most authentic traditions ascribed to the Prophet Muhammad.

SARAH IN THE TRADITIONS

The Qur'an does not mention either Hagar or Sarah by name. There is, however, one reference to Sarah (Surah 51: *Adh-Dhariyat*) in the story of Abraham's "honored guests." The relevant passage reads as follows:

> When those (heavenly messengers) came unto him and bade him peace, he answered, "(And upon you be) peace!" (saying to himself,) "They are strangers." Then he turned quietly to his household, and brought forth a fat (roasted) calf, and placed it before them, saying, "Will ye not eat?" (And when he saw that the guests would not eat) he became apprehensive of them; (but) they said, "Fear not"—and gave him the glad tidings of (the birth of) a son who would be endowed with deep knowledge. Thereupon his wife approached (the guests) with a loud cry, and struck her face (in astonishment) and exclaimed: "A barren old woman (like me)!" They answered: "Thus has thy Sustainer decreed; and, verily, He alone is truly wise, all-knowing!" (verses 25–30)[2]

In addition to this reference to the Qur'an, Sarah figures significantly in two stories narrated by Bukhari and Muslim. In them Hagar is also mentioned. Bukhari's narrative states:

> Narrated by Abu Hurairah: The Prophet said, the Prophet Abraham emigrated with Sarah and entered a village where there was a king or a tyrant. (The king) was told that Abraham had entered (the village) accompanied by a woman who was one of the most charming women. So, the king sent for Abraham and asked, "O Abraham! Who is the lady accompanying you?" Abraham replied, "She is my sister (i.e., in religion). Then Abraham returned to her and said, "Do not contradict my statement, for I have informed them that you are my sister. By Allah, there are no true believers on this land except you and I." Then Abraham sent her to the king. When the king got to her, she got up and performed ablution, prayed and said, "O Allah! If I have believed in You and Your Apostle, and have saved my private parts from everybody except my husband, then please do not let this pagan overpower me." On that the king fell in a mood of agitation and started moving his legs. Seeing the condition of the king, Sarah said, "O Allah! If he should die, people will say that I have killed him." The king regained his power, and proceeded toward her but she got up again and performed ablutions prayed and said, "O Allah! If I have believed in You and Your Apostle and have kept my private parts safe from all except my husband then please do not let this pagan overpower me." The king again fell in a mood of agitation and started moving his legs. On seeing that state of the king, Sarah said, "O Allah! If he

should die, the people will say that I have killed him." The king got either two or three attacks, and after recovering from the last attack he said, "By Allah! You have sent a satan to me. Take her to Abraham," and gave her Ajar. (Hagar). So she came back to Abraham and said, "Allah humiliated the pagan and gave us a slave-girl for service."[3]

A different version of the story is given by Muslim:

> Abu Hurairah reported Allah's Messenger (may peace be upon him) as saying: "Prophet Ibrahim (peace be upon him) never told a lie but only thrice: two times for the sake of Allah (for example, his words): 'I am sick,' and his words: 'But it was the big one amongst them which had done that' and because of Sarah (his wife). He had come in a land inhabited by haughty and cruel men along with Sarah. She was very good-looking amongst the people, so he said to her: 'If these were to know that you are my wife they would snatch you away from me, so if they ask you tell them that you are my sister and, in fact, you are my sister in Islam, and I do not know of any other Muslim in this land besides I and you.' And when they entered that land the tyrants came to see her and said to him (the king): 'There comes to your land a woman, when you alone deserve to possess,' so he (the king) sent someone (towards her) and she was brought and Ibrahim (peace be upon him) stood in prayer, and when she visited him (the tyrant king came) he could not help but stretch his hand towards her and his hand was tied up. He said: 'Supplicate Allah so that He may release my hand and I will do no harm to you.' She did that and the man repeated (the same highhandedness) and his hand was again tied up more tightly than on the first occasion and he said to her like that and she again did that (supplicated), but he repeated (the same highhandedness) and his hands were tied up more tightly than on the previous occasion. He then again said: 'Supplicate your Lord so that He may set my hand free; by Allah I shall do no harm to you.' She did and his hand was freed. Then he called the person who had brought her and said to him: 'You have brought to me the satan and you have not brought to me a human being, so turn them out from my land,' and he gave Hajira as a gift to her. She returned (along with Hajira) and when Ibrahim (peace be upon him) saw her, he said: 'How have you returned?' she said, 'With full safety (have I returned). Allah held the rein of that debauch and he gave me a maid-servant.'" Abu Hurairah said: "O sons of the rain of the sky, she is your mother."[4]

In both versions of the story given above, Sarah is able to protect her chastity by means of her personal piety and faith in the face of a tyrannical king and a society that placed little value on the lives of strangers, particularly women. While Abraham felt compelled to abandon her when confronted by the superior might of those who wished to take his wife/sister from him, Sarah did not allow herself to become a sacrificial victim. She prayed for divine intervention, confident that her faithfulness to God and to her husband rendered her worthy of being saved from the adulterous designs of the king who held her captive. That God responded to her prayers in both binding and releasing the hand of the aggressor showed that there was a direct relationship between Sarah and her Creator-Sustainer. Placed in a situation of great jeopardy, she returns not only without being molested, but also with a gift, that of Hagar, who, in turn, was to become the pioneer of a new civilization.

HAGAR IN THE TRADITIONS

The story of Hagar, not mentioned in the Qur'an, is given in considerable detail in *Sahih Al-Bukhari*. It appears in a number of overlapping traditions in the hadith, book 15: 9, called *The Anbiya* (Prophets). Number 583 mentions many significant features of the Hagar story as Muslims know it. Its earlier part (which refers to the death of "Ishmael's mother") reads as follows:

> Narrated Ibn 'Abbas: "The first lady to use a girdle was the mother of Ishmael. She used a girdle so that she might hide her tracks from Sarah.[5] Abraham brought her and her son Ishmael while she was suckling him, to a place near the Ka'bah under a tree on the spot of Zam-zam, at the highest place in the mosque. During those days there was nobody in Mecca, nor was there any water. So he made them sit over there and placed near them a leather bag containing some dates, and a small water-skin containing some water, and set out homeward. Ishmael's mother followed him saying, 'O Abraham! Where are you going, leaving us in this valley where there is no person whose company we may enjoy, nor is there anything (to enjoy)?' She repeated that to him many times, but he did not look back at her. Then she asked him, 'Has Allah ordered you to do so? ' He said, 'Yes.' She said, 'Then He will not neglect us,' and returned while Abraham proceeded onwards, and on reaching Thaniya where they could not see him, he faced the Ka'bah, and raising both hands, invoked Allah saying the following prayers: 'O our Lord! I have made some of my offspring dwell in a valley without cultivation, by Your Sacred House (Ka'bah at Mecca) in order, O our Lord, that they may offer prayer perfectly. So fill some hearts among men with love towards them, and (O Allah) provide them with fruits, so that they may give thanks.'" (Surah 14: *Ibrahim*, 37)
> Ishmael's mother went on suckling Ishmael and drinking from the water (she had). When the water in the water-skin had all been used up, she became thirsty and her child also became thirsty. She started looking at him (Ishmael) tossing in agony; she left him, for she could not endure looking at him, and found that the mountain of Safa was the nearest mountain to her on that land. She stood on it and started looking at the valley keenly so that she might see somebody, but she could not see anybody. Then she descended from the Safa and when she reached the valley, she tucked up her robe and ran in the valley like a person in distress and trouble, till she crossed the valley and reached the Marwa mountain where she stood and started looking, expecting to see somebody but she could not see anybody. She repeated that (running between Safa and Marwa) seven times. The Prophet said, "This is the source of the tradition of the walking of people between them (i.e., Safa and Marwa).
> When she reached the Marwa (for the last time) she heard a voice and she asked herself to be quiet and listened attentively. She heard the voice again and said, 'O, (whoever you may be!) You have made me hear your voice; have you got something to help me?' And behold! She saw an angel at the place of Zam-zam, digging the earth with his heel (or his wing), till water flowed

from that place. She started to make something like a basin around it, using her hands in this way, and started filling her water-skin with water with her hands, and the water was flowing out after she had scooped some of it." The Prophet added, "May Allah bestow Mercy on Ishmael's mother! Had she let the Zam-zam (flow without trying to control it) (or had she not scooped from that water) (to fill her water-skin), Zam-zam would have been a stream flowing on the surface of the earth." The Prophet further added, "Then she drank (water) and suckled her child. The angel said to her, 'Don't be afraid of being neglected, for this is the House of Allah which will be built by this boy and his father, and Allah never neglects His people.'

The house (i.e., Ka'bah) at that time was on a high place resembling a hillock, and when torrents came, they flowed to its right and left. She lived in that way till some people from the tribe of Jurhum passed by her and her child, as they (i.e., the Jurhum people) were coming through the way of Kada. They landed in the lower part of Mecca where they saw a bird that had the habit of flying around water and not leaving it. They said, 'This bird must be flying around water, though we know that there is no water in this valley. They sent one or two messengers who discovered the source of water. So they all came (towards the water).'" The Prophet added, "Ishmael's mother was sitting near the water. They asked her, 'Do you allow us to stay with you?' She replied; 'Yes, but you will have no right to possess the water.' They agreed to do that." The Prophet further said, "Ishmael's mother was pleased with the whole situation as she used to love to enjoy the company of the people. So, they settled there, and later on they sent for their families who came and settled with them so that some families became permanent residents there. The child (i.e., Ishmael) grew up and learned Arabic from them and (his virtues) caused them to love and admire him as he grew up, and when he reached the age of puberty they made him marry a woman from amongst them. After Ishmael's mother had died, Abraham came after Ishmael's marriage in order to see his family that he had left before, but he did not find Ishmael there. . . ."[6]

INTERPRETING THE TRADITIONS

Although it may be inferred from the hadith cited above that Sarah did not look kindly upon Hagar, who was fearful of her, it is clear that Abraham's decision to leave Hagar and Ishmael in the desert (believed by Muslims to be in the vicinity of Mecca) was not based on his desire to appease his first wife. Abraham, while not disclosing to Hagar why he was leaving her and her infant son in the wilderness, does respond in the affirmative to her question whether God had commanded him to do so. Abraham's prayer, said when he is out of Hagar's sight, shows that he believes that in order to fulfill the prophetic mission of building the Sacred House of God (which Muslims believe to be the first House of God at Mecca) it was necessary to leave a part of his family in the uninhabited, uncultivated land. His prayer further indicates his faith that this uninhabited, uncultivated land will become populated and fruitful and that God will ensure that those whom he is leaving behind will find sustenance and love in their new environment.

While the biblical narrative in Genesis 21:8–14 tends to leave readers with the impression that Abraham sent Hagar and Ishmael away in order to placate the jealous wrath of Sarah and had nothing more, henceforward, to do with them, the story as told in *Sahih Al-Bukhari* shows that Abraham had a continuing relationship with that part of his family. Muslims believe that Abraham returned periodically to visit Hagar and Ishmael. In the hadith cited earlier, mention is made of a visit to Ishmael's family after the death of "Ishmael's mother."[7] That not only Hagar but also Sarah accepted what Abraham believed to be God's plan for his offspring is brought out in hadith 584, which is a variant of hadith 583.[8] This hadith states that each time Abraham thought of visiting Ishmael, he informed Sarah of his intentions. The figure of Hagar that emerges from the traditions narrated in *Sahih Al-Bukhari* is that of a woman of exceptional faith, love, fortitude, resolution, and strength of character. Once she hears from Abraham that God commands her and her infant son to be left in the desert, she shows no hesitation whatever in accepting her extremely difficult situation. She does not wail or rage or beg Abraham not to abandon her and Ishmael. Instead, surrendering spontaneously and totally to what she believes to be God's will, she says that she is "satisfied to be with Allah," who will never neglect her. She lets Abraham go, without any words of recrimination or sorrow, and returns to her infant son.

With a small supply of food and water, Hagar's major concern is to increase her milk-flow so that she can feed her child adequately. Once out of water she knows that both their lives are imperiled. Unable to endure the sight of her baby son writhing in agony due to dehydration, she undertakes a massive search for help. Running frantically between Safa and Marwa she searches desperately for some sign of hope. Her refusal to give up, to keep running and looking and praying for help demonstrates her determination to fight for her beloved child's life to the last drop of her own strength. Finally, her faith and effort are rewarded and Archangel Gabriel appears to guide her to the spring Zam-zam (whose waters are believed by Muslims to have medicinal or miraculous powers). Through Zam-zam, Hagar is able not only to save her own and Ishmael's life, but also to attract the people of the tribe of Jurhum into becoming her companions and partners in creating a prosperous settlement[9] (154). She raises her son to become a God-conscious man, loved and admired for his many qualities, who becomes his father Abraham's chosen partner in building the first House of God in Mecca.

While Abraham is viewed by the Islamic tradition as the first "Muslim" or true believer in God, Hagar is viewed as the pioneer woman who led the way to the establishment of a new civilization. She is seen not only as "Ishmael's mother" but also as the mother of all Arabs and of those who later became the followers of the Prophet Muhammad, a descendant of the Prophet Ishmael. Hagar, a black slave-girl, rose from the lowliest of positions to the highest place of honor in the Islamic tradition. In Muslim societies the mother is the most highly revered member of the family because, following one of the most popular traditions of the Prophet Muhammad, Muslims widely believe that Paradise lies under the feet of the mother.

The dramatic story of Hagar's life shows that class or color is not a deterrent to any person who has faith in God and is resolutely righteous in action. So Hagar does not see herself as a victim of Abraham and Sarah, or of a patriarchal, class- and race-conscious culture. She is a victor who, with the help of God and her own initiative, is able to transform a wilderness into the cradle of a new world dedicated to the fulfillment of God's purpose on earth. Each year as millions of Muslim pilgrims run or walk between the points that symbolize Safa and Marwa, they pay homage to Hagar, who has become an indestructible emblem not only of a mother's love for her offspring but of a true believer's faith in the saving power of God. Hagar's shadow looms large over the valley where she once stood alone, and her spirit is as inextricably embodied in the Ka'bah as that of her husband Abraham and her son Ishmael.

Finally, Hagar is associated with the idea of "hijrah," or going into exile for the sake of God. While in the Jewish tradition the idea of the diaspora, or the dispersion of the Jewish people in alien lands, inspires feelings of sorrow and nostalgia for a return to homeland and community, according to the Qur'an, the state of hijrah is a blessed one. When one is in the wilderness, without the protection of any familiar framework or faces, one's faith in God and one self is put to a real test. Those who are willing to confront the challenge of hijrah, to leave their place of origin or sojourn in order to live in accordance with the will and pleasure of God, gain merit in the sight of God. Many passages in the Qur'an attest this understanding.[10]

The Prophet Muhammad, himself, becomes an exemplar of hijrah as he left his birthplace Mecca and chose to live in another city so that he could further his prophetic mission of establishing an Islamic society. In doing so he followed in the footsteps of his foremother Hagar who, generations earlier, had chosen to dwell in the desert to which God had directed her, making a home and community out of an unknown land and people. She demonstrated by her faith and actions that for a believer all of God's earth is a sanctified place and that loyalty to God supersedes attachment to terrestrial bonds, be they of place or persons.

ABRAHAM IN THE QUR'AN

Although Hagar's story is recounted in the hadith literature, the symbolic significance of Abraham is underscored in a number of qur'anic passages. It is important to understand how special Abraham is to Muslims. Not only is he the Prophet most often mentioned in the Qur'an after the prophet Muhammad, but he is also the one who broke away from polytheism to become the first "Muslim." The Qur'an repeatedly describes Abraham as "hanif," or one who turns away from all that is not-God to submit to God's law and order[11] (556–557). The Islamic tradition sees Abraham as a unifying figure whom all three Abrahamic traditions—Judaism, Christianity, and Islam—can look back to and claim as their own. The prominence given to Abraham by the Qur'an and by the Islamic tradition is evident throughout the most significant as well as the most spectacular social ritual of the Muslim world: the hajj or pilgrimage. The Qur'an portrays Abraham and his son Ishmael as builders of the Ka'bah and states that God had commanded Abraham to proclaim the first pilgrimage (Surah 21: *Al-Hajj*, 26–29). During the "Hajj," all pilgrims pray at the Station ("Maqam") of Abraham. Then there is commemoration and ritual enactment of the frantic search for water by Hagar as she ran seven times between the hills of Safa and Marwa. The appearance of the Zam-zam is associated with the infant Ishmael beating the earth with his legs. The stoning of the devil and the sacrifice ceremony at the end of the hajj is also associated with Abraham.

According to numerous passages in the Qur'an, Abraham was one of God's chosen ones. He was blessed both in this world and in the hereafter:

> And who, unless he be weak of mind, would want to abandon Abraham's creed, seeing that We have indeed raised him high in this world, and that, verily, in the life to come he shall be among the righteous? (Surah 2: *Al Baqarah*, 130)
>
> Verily, Abraham was a man who combined within himself all virtues, devoutly obeying God's will, turning away from all that is false, and not being of those who ascribe divinity to aught beside God: (for he was always) grateful for the blessings granted by Him who had elected him and guided him onto a straightway. And so We vouchsafed him good in this world; and, verily, in the life to come (too) he shall find himself among the righteous. (Surah 16: *An Nahl*, 120–122)
>
> And (as for Abraham) We bestowed upon him Isaac and (Isaac's son) Jacob, and caused prophethood and revelation to continue among his offspring. And We vouchsafed him his reward in this world; and, verily, life to come (too) he shall find himself among the righteous. (Surah 29: *Al-Ankubat*, 27)

The Qur'an refers to Abraham as the friend of God:

> And who could be of better faith than he who surrenders his whole being unto God and is a doer of good withal, and follows the creed of Abraham, who turned away from all that is false—seeing that God exalted Abraham with His love? (Surah 4: *An-Nisa'*, 125)

Surah 37: *As-Saffat*, 83–84 points out that Abraham approached God with a heart and mind in total accord with the Will of the Creator. Further, the Qur'an states that God recognized and rewarded the faith of Abraham and his righteous progeny:

> And call to mind Our servants Abraham and Isaac and Jacob, all of them endowed with inner strength and vision: for verily, We purified them by means of a thought most pure: the remembrance of the life to come. And, behold, in Our sight they were indeed the elect, the truly good! (Surah 38: *Sad*, 45–47)

In his poetry, Muhammad Iqbal—modern Islam's most outstanding poet-philosopher, frequently pictures Abraham as an iconoclast who is shown breaking his father's idols. The background to Iqbal's image is this qur'anic narrative:

And, indeed, long before (the time of Moses) We vouchsafed unto Abraham his consciousness of what is right; and We are aware of (what moved) him when he said unto his father and his people, "What are these images to which you are so intensely devoted?"

They answered: "We found our forefathers worshiping them."

Said he: "Indeed, you and your forefathers have obviously gone astray!"

They asked: "Hast thou come unto us (with this claim) in all earnest—or art thou one of those jesters?"

He answered: "Nay, but your true Sustainer is the Sustainer of the heaven and the earth—He who has brought them into being: and I am one of those who bear witness to this (truth)!"

And (he added to himself) "By God, I shall most certainly bring about the downfall of your idols as soon as you have turned your backs and gone away!"

And then he broke those (idols) to pieces, (all) save the biggest of them so that they might (be able to) turn to it.

(When they saw what had happened,) they said: "Who has done this to our gods? Verily, one of the worst wrongdoers is he!"

Said some (of them): "We heard a youth speak of these (gods with scorn): he is called Abraham."

(The others) said: "Then bring him before the people's eyes, so that they might bear witness (against him)!"

(And when he came,) they asked: "Hast thou done this to our gods, O Abraham?" He answered: "Nay, it was this one, the biggest of them, that did it: but ask them (yourselves)—provided they can speak!"

And so they turned upon one another, saying, "Behold, it is you who are doing wrong." (Surah 21: *Anbiya'*, 51–64)

To Iqbal it is necessary to negate all that is not-God before God's existence can be affirmed. Negation is signified by the "la" in the phrase "la ilaha illa Allah" (there is no God but God) in the Islamic Shahadah or Confession of Faith. Iqbal's poetry captures the spirit of the qur'anic epithet *hanif*, which refers to one who believes in the One God, but also to a complete refusal to associate anything or anyone with God. Abraham is *hanif* precisely because he upheld the Oneness and Allness of God in the face of all opposition and obstacles. The following passages describe this belief.

And they say, "Be Jews"—or, "Christians"—"and you shall be on the right path." Say: "Nay, but (ours is) the creed of Abraham who turned away from all that is false, and was not of those who ascribe divinity to aught beside God." (Surah 2: *Al-Baqarah*: 135)

Say: "God has spoken the truth: follow, then, the creed of Abraham, who turned away from all that is false, and was not of those who ascribe divinity to aught beside God." (Surah 3: *Al-'Imran*, 95)

Say: Behold, my Sustainer has guided me onto a straight way through an ever-true faith—the way of Abraham, who turned away from all that is false, and was not of those who ascribe divinity to aught beside Him." (Surah 6: *Al-An'am*, 161)

And lastly, We have inspired thee, (O Muhammad, with this message:) "Follow the creed of Abraham, who turned away from all that is false, and was not one of those who ascribe divinity to aught beside God." (Surah 16: *An-Nahl*, 123)

From the afore-cited qur'anic passages it becomes evident that the prominence given to Abraham by the Islamic tradition is grounded in the very revelation upon which Islam is founded. But though the Qur'an stresses the point that Abraham was "neither a Jew nor a Christian" (thus a symbol of unity rather than division), it also repeats with force and clarity that Islam is a confirmation and a continuation of the message given by God to all the prophets before the time of Muhammad. The following passages underscore this point.

> Say: "We believe in God, and in that which has been bestowed from on High upon Abraham and Ishmael and Isaac and Jacob and their descendants, and that which has been vouchsafed to Moses and Jesus, and that which has been vouchsafed to all the (other) prophets by their Sustainer: we make no distinction between any of them." (Surah 2: Al-Baqarah, 136)
>
> Step by step has He bestowed upon thee from on high this divine writ, setting forth the truth which confirms whatever there still remains (of earlier revelations): for it is He who has bestowed from on high the Torah and the Gospel aforetime, as a guidance unto mankind. (Surah 3: Al-'Imran, 3–4)
>
> Say: "We believe in God, and in that which has been bestowed from On high upon us, and that which has been bestowed upon Abraham, and Ishmael and Isaac and Jacob and their descendants, and that which Has been vouchsafed by their Sustainer unto Moses and Jesus and All the (other) prophets: we make no distinction between any of them." (Surah 3: Al-'Imran, 84)
>
> Behold, We have inspired thee (O Prophet) just as We inspired Noah and all the prophets after him—as We inspired Abraham, and Ishmael, and Isaac, and Jacob, and their descendants, including Jesus and Job, and Jonah, and Aaron, and Solomon; and as We vouchsafed unto David a book of divine wisdom; and as (We inspired other) apostles whom We have mentioned to thee ere this, as well as apostles whom We have not mentioned to thee; and as God spoke His word unto Moses." (Surah 4: An-Nisa', 163)
>
> In matters of faith, He has ordained for you that which He had enjoined upon Noah—and into which We gave thee (O Muhammad) insight through revelation—as well as that which We had enjoined upon Abraham, and Moses, and Jesus. (Surah 42: Ash-Shura, 13)

PRAYING TOWARD MECCA

In view of the linkage between Islam and the Hebrew prophets, it is hardly surprising that the early Muslims prayed facing Jerusalem, the "holy" city revered by both Jews and Christians. The hijrah (migration) of the Prophet and the Muslims occurred in 622 CE and was followed by years of conflict and bitterness between Muslims and Jews in Medina. In 624 CE, a qur'anic revelation decreed that the direction of prayer be changed from Jerusalem to Mecca. A number of non-Muslim writers explain this change by saying that it was due to the growing tension between the Jews of Medina and Muhammad or that it was motivated by a desire to break away from the religious tie with the Jewish-Christian heritage and establish a national state. These explanations offend Muslims mainly because the underlying implication is that the Qur'an is not the Word of God but the work of Muhammad, who at different times issued statements designed to meet different political needs or expediencies. From an Islamic standpoint any suggestion that Muhammad manipulated the revelation in any way is tantamount to casting doubt upon the authority of Islamic tradition in toto.

If one looks at the question of the change in Qibla (in the direction for prayer) from the point of view of a Muslim who accepts that the directive came not from Muhammad but from God, how is one to understand the reasons for and meaning of this change? An examination of the relevant qur'anic passage provides significant insights:

> The weak-minded among people will say, "What has turned them away from the direction of prayer which they have hitherto observed?"
>
> Say: "God's is the east and the west; He guides whom He wills onto a straight way."
>
> And this have We willed you to be a community of the middle way, so that (with your lives) you might bear witness to the truth before all mankind, and that the Apostle might bear witness to it before you.
>
> And it is only to the end that We might make a clear distinction between those who follow the Apostle and those who turn about on their heels that We have appointed (for this community) the direction of prayer which thou (O Prophet) hast formerly observed: for indeed it was a hard test for all but those whom God has guided aright. But God will surely not lose sight of your faith—for, behold, God is most compassionate towards man, a dispenser of grace.
>
> We have seen thee (O Prophet) often turn thy face towards heaven (for guidance): and now We shall indeed make thee turn in prayer in a direction which will fulfill thy desire. Turn, then, thy face towards the Inviolable House of Worship; and wherever you all may be, turn your face towards it (in prayer).
>
> And, verily, those who have been vouchsafed revelation aforetime know well that this (commandment) comes in truth from their Sustainer; and God is not unaware of what they do.
>
> And yet, even if thou wert to place all evidence before those who have been vouchsafed earlier revelation, they would not follow thy direction of prayer; and neither mayest thou follow their direction of prayer, nor even do they follow one another's direction. And if thou shouldst follow their errant views after all the Knowledge that has come to thee, thou wouldst surely be among the evildoers.
>
> They unto whom We have vouchsafed revelation aforetime know it as they know their own children: but, behold, some of them knowingly suppress the Truth—the truth from thy Sustainer!
>
> Be not, then, among the doubters: for, every community faces a direction of its own, of which He is the focal point. Vie, therefore, with one another in doing good works. Wherever you may be, God will gather you all unto Himself: for verily, God has the power to will anything.
>
> Thus, from wherever thou mayest come forth, turn thy face (in prayer) towards the Inviolable House of Worship—for, behold, this (commandment) comes in truth from thy Sustainer; and God is not unaware of what you do. Hence, from wherever thou mayest come forth, turn thy face (in prayer) towards the Inviolable House of Worship; and wherever you all may

be, turn your faces towards it, so that people should have no argument
against you unless they are bent upon wrongdoing. And hold not them in
awe, but stand in awe of Me, and (obey Me,) so that I might bestow upon
you the full measure of My blessings, and that you might follow the right
path.

Even as We have sent unto you an apostle from among yourselves to convey unto you Our messages, and to cause you to grow in purity, and to
impart unto you revelation and wisdom. And to teach you that which you
know not: so remember Me. And I shall remember you; and be grateful unto
Me, and deny Me not. (Surah 2: *Al-Baqarah*, 142–152)

As pointed out earlier, "Qibla" may be understood as the direction in which
Muslims turn their faces when they pray, and in this sense the aforementioned
qur'anic passage decrees a change in Qibla commanding Muslims to turn in the
direction of the Sacred Mosque when they pray. But "Qibla" also represents the
focal point of the aspirations and ideals of the Islamic community and in this
sense there was no change in Qibla, since the House of God built by Abraham
who founded the "Din" of Islam was, from the first, the intended center and unifying symbol of the Muslim *ummah* (or community).

An idea that finds frequent expression in the Qur'an is that God will test the
faith of all who profess to believe in God. For instance, Surah 21: *Al-Anbiya'*, 35
points out:

"And every human being is bound to taste death; and We test you (all)
through the bad and the good (things of life) by way of trial."

According to the Qur'an, God designated the Ka'ba at Mecca as the Qibla in
order to "test those who followed the Apostle." The Qur'an recognizes that this
"change" would cause all "except . . . those guided by God" to turn their backs
on the Islamic faith even though the appointment of the Qibla at the Ka'bah
is a "favor" done to Muslims by God since that was the "Qibla to which thou
wast used."

The question arises: why should the change in the direction of prayer be so
"momentous" and why should it be regarded as a test of faith? It is hardly likely
that Jerusalem was so important to the early Muslims that the instituting of the
Qibla at the Ka'bah (which had been sacred to the Arabs since antiquity) would
bring about a serious moral dilemma, nor does it seem probable that the problem of the coexistence of Muslims and Jews in Medina would have been much
affected, either positively or negatively, by the change in the Muslim's Qibla. In
my judgment, what the qur'anic passage about the Qibla is pointing at is that
the Muslim *ummah* has come—both historically and spiritually—to the end of
one phase of development and is about to enter a new one, and that in order to
enter the new phase an act of faith, of accepting the Will of God, is required, and
this is where the test lies. (It is also of interest to observe here that at the time
when the Ka'bah at Mecca was appointed the Qibla, it was in the possession of
the pagan Quraish who were determined to wipe out Islam. It took an act of faith

to believe that the Ka'bah would be purged of its profanities and delivered into the hands of Muslims to be resanctified by them.)

From the beginning, Islam had been proud of its Abrahamic heritage, and the early Muslims had turned their faces towards Jerusalem as they prayed in order to affirm their linkage with the People of the Book, just as the early Christians had insisted upon their connection with Israel. However, with the establishment of the first Islamic society in Medina came the time and the necessity to stress not only the link of Islam with Abraham and Jerusalem but the link of Abraham to all humanity. Jerusalem, the Qibla of the People of the Book, had become associated with the exclusivism characteristic of many Jews and Christians. The former regarded themselves as the Chosen People, while the latter also made special claims to salvation through their belief in Jesus Christ. By turning the attention of the Muslim *ummah* from Jerusalem to the Qibla in Mecca, the Qur'an was, in fact, bringing about a profound change in perspective. The conflict underlying the need for this change was not the localized antagonism between Muslims and Jews in Medina, as is frequently suggested by non-Muslim writers, but a much wider opposition between the principles of exclusivism and universalism.

UNIVERSAL IDEALS

Anyone who has read the Qur'an without bias is aware that Islam is truly universal in its ideals. In this context it is interesting to note that whilst the Old Testament frequently talks of the God of Abraham, Isaac, and Jacob, the Qur'an never does. It describes Islam as the *"Deen"* (or core belief system) of Abraham and the other prophets but does not describe God as the God of Abraham or the God of Muhammad. In *Surah Fatihah*, the opening chapter of the Qur'an, God is described as *"Rabb al-'alamin"* (or "God of all the peoples and universes"). As the following passages show, the Qur'an testifies that the message it contains is meant for all creatures:

> Hallowed is He who from on high, step by step, has bestowed upon his servant the standard by which to discern the true from the false, so that to all the world it might be a warning. (Surah 25: *Al-Furqan*, 1)
>
> And (thus it is:) We have not imparted to this (Prophet the gift of) poetry, nor would (poetry) have suited this (message): it is but a reminder and a (divine) discourse, clear in itself and clearly showing the truth, to the end that it may warn anyone who is alive (of heart), and that the word (of God) may bear witness against all who deny the truth. (Surah 36: *Yasin*, 69–70)
>
> This (divine writ) behold, is no less than a reminder to all the worlds. (Surah 38: *Sad*, 87)
>
> This (message) is no less than a reminder to all mankind—to every one of you who wills to walk a straight way. (Surah 81: *At-Takwir*, 27–78)

The inclusive spirit of Islam also comes through the oft-repeated teaching of the Qur'an contained in verses such as the following:

Verily, those who have attained to faith (in this divine writ), as well as those who follow the Jewish faith, and the Christians, and the Sabians—all who believe in God and the last Day and do righteous deeds—shall have their reward with their Sustainer; and no fear need they have, and neither shall they grieve. (Surah 2: *Al-Baqarah*, 62)

And they claim, "None shall ever enter paradise unless he be a Jew"—or "a Christian." Such are their wishful beliefs! Say: "Produce an evidence for what you are claiming, if what you say is true!"

Yea, indeed: everyone who surrenders his whole being unto God, and is a doer of good withal, shall have his reward with his Sustainer; and all such need have no fear, and neither shall they grieve. (Surah 2: *Al-Baqarah*, 111–112)

And be conscious of the Day on which you shall be brought back unto God, whereupon every human being shall be repaid in full for what he has earned, and none shall be wronged. (Surah 2: *Al-Baqarah*, 281)

And (both) the Jews and the Christians say, "We are God's children, and His beloved ones." Say: "Why, then, does He cause you to suffer for your sins? Nay, you are but human beings of His creating. He forgives whom He wills, and He causes to suffer whom He wills: for God's is the dominion over the heavens and the earth and all that is between them, and with him is all journeys' end." (Surah 5: *Al-Ma'idah*, 18)

[V]erily, those who have attained to faith (in this divine writ), as well as those who follow the Jewish faith, and the Sabians, and the Christians—all who believe in the Last Day and do righteous deeds—no fear need they have, and neither shall they grieve. (Surah 5: *Al-Ma'idah*, 69)

[O]ne Day We shall raise up within every community a witness against them from among themselves. (Surah 16: *An-Nahl*, 89)

To Muslims, Abraham is an embodiment of the universalism implicit in Islam, and it is the Abrahamic spirit that enables Muslims to become "witnesses for humanity":

And strive hard in God's cause with all the striving that is due to Him; it is He Who has elected you (to carry His message), and has laid no hardship on you in (anything that pertains to) religion, (and made you follow) the creed of your forefather Abraham.

It is He who has named you—in bygone times as well as in this (divine writ)—"those who have surrendered themselves to God," so that the Apostle might bear witness to the truth before you, and that you might bear witness to it before all mankind. (Surah 22: *Al-Hajj*, 78)

It is of importance to note that the qur'anic verses that refer to the Ka'bah (which Abraham built) relate the Ka'bah to all humanity and not to any specific group of people:

And lo! We made the Temple a goal to which people might repair again and again, and a sanctuary: take, then, the place whereupon Abraham once stood as place of prayer.

And thus did We command Abraham and Ishmael: "Purify My Temple for those who will walk around it, and those who will abide near it in meditation, and those who will bow down and prostrate themselves in prayer." (Surah 2: *Al-Baqarah*, 125)

Behold, the first Temple ever set up for mankind was indeed the one at Bakkah: Rich in blessing, and a (source of) guidance unto all the worlds, full of clear messages. (It is) the place whereon Abraham once stood; and whoever enters it finds inner peace. Hence, pilgrimage unto the Temple is a duty owed to God by all people who are able to undertake it. And as for those who deny the truth—verily, God does not stand in need of anything in all the worlds. (Surah 3: *Al-'Imran*, 96–97)

God has laid down that the Ka'bah, the Inviolable Temple, shall be a symbol for all mankind; and (so, too,) the sacred month (of pilgrimage) and the garlanded offerings (are symbols) meant to make you aware that God is aware of all that is in the heavens and all that is on earth, and that God has full knowledge of everything. (Surah 5: *Al-Ma'idah*, 97)

In my judgment, on the basis of the above-mentioned verses, a clear case can be made for making Mecca an open city. The government of Saudi Arabia should allow non-Muslims access to Mecca in view of the unambiguous qur'anic statements asserting that the Ka'bah is a sanctuary for all humankind.

SACRIFICE OF ISHMAEL

The "sacrifice of Ishmael" plays an important part in Islamic traditions about Hagar and her family. Although in the Jewish and Christian traditions the son Abraham was about to sacrifice is Isaac, in the Islamic tradition it is Ishmael. From the perspective of the latter, since the son whom God commanded Abraham to sacrifice was his "only" son, the son in question had to be Ishmael who was Abraham's first son. The Jewish and Christian traditions have ignored Ishmael in favor of Isaac because they do not accord to Hagar the same status of being Abraham's "wife" as they do to Sarah. The Islamic tradition does not, however, distinguish between the status of Hagar and Sarah, or Ishmael and Isaac.

The qur'anic narrative that begins with a reference to the time when Abraham prayed for a son reads as follows:

(And he prayed:) "O my Sustainer! Bestow upon me the gift of (a son who shall be) one of the righteous!"—whereupon We gave him the glad tiding of a boy-child gentle (like himself).

And (one day,) when (the child) had become old enough to share in his father's endeavors, the latter said: "O my dear son! I have seen in a dream that I should sacrifice thee: consider, then, what would be thy view!"

(Ishmael) answer: "O my father! Do as thou art bidden: thou wilt find me, if God so wills, among those who are patient in adversity!"

But as soon as the two had surrendered themselves to (what they thought to be) the will of God, and Abraham had laid him down on his face, We called out to him: "O Abraham. Thou hast already fulfilled (the purpose of) that dream-vision!"

Thus, verily, do We reward the doers of good: for, behold, all this was indeed a trial, clear in itself.

And We ransomed him with a tremendous sacrifice, and left him thus to be remembered among later generations: "Peace be upon Abraham!"

Thus do we reward the doers of good—for he was truly one of our believing servants. (Surah 37: *As Saffat*, 100–111)

In the above-cited narrative the "son" is not named. However, unlike Isaac in the biblical narrative, the son in this story does know that God has commanded his father to sacrifice him. The qur'anic narrative, therefore, lacks the suspense of disclosure found in the biblical story. This narrative stresses the obedience to God of both Abraham and Ishmael, who symbolize what it means to be "Muslim." While Abraham and Ishmael do not show the slightest hesitation in accepting God's command, God also does not show any hesitation in offering immediate ransom for the son. Thus, while the story illustrates the faith of Abraham and Ishmael, it also shows the mercy and compassion of God toward those who remain steadfast in their resolve to live and die in accordance with the will and pleasure of God. That one cannot enter Paradise without being tested is clearly stated in the Qur'an, which also points out that, oftentimes, what we have, particularly our children and material possessions, distract us from our highest goals. The test put to Abraham and Ishmael was of the most difficult kind imaginable. That they came through shows that it is possible for "Muslims" to overcome the bondage of attachment to all that is not-God.

Abraham's struggle against various forms of idolatry in his quest for the Ultimate are highlighted in the Qur'an. This struggle ranges from rejection of natural phenomena such as the stars, moon, and sun[12] as God, to his dissociation from his idol-worshiping father once he realized that his father was an enemy of God.[13] The challenge of idolatry did not exist only at the time of Abraham. Idolatry exists today in subtler forms that pervade virtually every aspect of the consciousness of contemporary humanity. The struggle of Abraham, first to find God and then to remain faithful to God in the face of powerful material distractions and obstructions as well as natural affections and inclinations, is profoundly relevant to us.

The story of Abraham, Hagar, and Ishmael, which is commemorated and celebrated by Muslims on the occasion of 'Eid al-Adha (Feast of Sacrifice) remains an undying source of strength and courage, hope and faith, not only for Muslims but also for Jews, Christians, and others who can understand its symbolism and what it can mean for those who consider themselves seekers and servants of God.

The story of Hagar is important not only for Muslim daughters of Hagar but for all women who are oppressed by systems of thought or structures based on ideas of gender, class, or racial inequality. Like her, women must have the faith and courage to venture out of the security of the known into the insecurity of the unknown and to carve out, with their own hands, a new world from which the injustices and inequities that separate men from women, class from class, and race from race, have been eliminated.

Notes

1. Portions of this chapter were published in *Commitment and Commemoration: Jews, Christians, Muslims in Dialogue*, ed. André LaCocque (Chicago: Explo-

ration Press, Chicago Theological Seminary, 1994), 131–50, and are used with permission.

2. Muhammad Asad, trans. and expl., *The Message of the Qur'an* (Gibraltar: Dar Al-Andalus, 1980). All translations of the qur'anic verses are from this translation.

3. Muhammad Muhsin Khan, trans., *Sahih Al-Bukhari* (Lahore: Kazi Publications, 1983), vol. 3, bk. 34: *Buyu' (Bargains)*, chap. 102, no. 420, 230–231. Another version of the story is given in bk. 55: *The Anbiya (Prophets),* chap. 9, no. 578, which reads as follows:

> Narrated Abu Hurairah: "Abraham did not tell a lie except on three occasions. Twice for the sake of Allah when he said, 'I am sick,' and he said, 'I have not done this but the big idol has done it.' (The pagans invited Abraham to join them in their celebrations outside the city, but he refused, claiming that he was sick. When he was left alone, he came to their idols and broke them into pieces. When the pagans questioned him, he claimed that he had not destroyed their idols but the chief idol had, which Abraham left undisturbed and on whose shoulder he had put an axe to lay the accusation on it). The third was that while Abraham and Sarah (his wife) were going (on a journey) they passed by (the territory of) a tyrant. Someone said to the tyrant, 'This man (i.e., Abraham) is accompanied by a very charming lady.' So he sent for Abraham and asked him about Sarah saying, 'Who is this lady? Abraham said, 'She is my sister.' Abraham went to Sarah and said, 'O Sarah! There are no believers on the surface of this earth except you and I. This man asked me about you and I have told him that you are my sister, so don't contradict my statement.' The tyrant then called Sarah and when she went to him, he tried to take hold of her with his hand, but (his hand got stiff and) he was confounded. He asked Sarah, 'Pray to Allah for me, and I shall not harm you.' So Sarah asked Allah to cure him and he got cured. He tried to take hold of her for the second time, but (his hand got as stiff as or stiffer than before and) was more confounded. He again requested Sarah, 'Pray to Allah for me, and I will not harm you.' Sarah asked Allah again and he became alright. He then called one of his guards (who had brought her) and said, 'You have not brought me a human being but have brought me a devil.' The tyrant then gave Hajar as a girl-servant to Sarah. Sarah came back (to Abraham) while he was praying. Abraham, gesturing with his hand, asked, 'What has happened?' She replied, 'Allah has spoiled the evil plot of the infidel (or immoral person) and gave me Hajar for service.'" (Abu Hurairah then addressed his listeners saying, "That (Hajar) was your mother, O Bani Ma'-is-Sama' (i.e., the Arabs, the descendants of Ishmael, Hajar's son)." (4:368–70)

A partial reference to the story is also found in bk. 85: *The Book of Ikrah (Coercion)*, chap. 7, no. 82, which reads,

> Narrated Abu Hurairah: Allah's Apostle said, "(The Prophet) Abraham migrated with his wife Sarah till he reached a town where there was a king or a tyrant who sent a message to Abraham, ordering him to send Sarah to him. So when Abraham had sent Sarah, the tyrant got up, intending to do evil with her, but she got up and performed ablution and prayed and said, 'O Allah! If I have believed in You and in Your Apostle, then do not empower this oppressor over me.' So he (the king) had an epileptic fit and started moving his legs violently." (9:67–68)

4. 'Abdul Hamid Siddiqi, trans., *Sahih Muslim* (Lahore: Shaikh Muhammad Ashraf, 1975), vol. 9, bk. 28: *Kitab Al-Fada 'il (Excellent Qualities of the Prophet and his Companions)*, chap. 989, no. 5848, 1262–63.

5. Muhammad Muhsin Khan, trans., says in the footnote, "When Abraham married Hajar and she conceived Ishmael, Sarah, Abraham's first wife, became jealous of

her and swore that she would cut three parts from her body. So Hajar tied a gir-
dle round her waist and ran away, dragging her robe behind her so as to wipe out
her tracks lest Sarah should pursue her. 'Allah knows better'" (*Sahih Al-Bukhari*
4:372).

6. *Sahih Al-Bukhari* 4:372–76. A partial reference to the story is made in the preceding hadith (no. 582) which reads, "Narrated Ibn 'Abbas: The Prophet said,
"May Allah bestow His Mercy on the mother of Ishmael! Had she not hastened
(to fill her water-skin with water from the Zam-zam well), Zam-zam would have
been a stream flowing on the surface of the earth." Ibn 'Abbas further added,
"(The Prophet) Abraham brought Ishmael and his mother (to Mecca) and she
was suckling Ishmael, and she had a water-skin with her" (372).

7. The fact that Hagar is referred to as "Ishmael's mother" or as "the mother of Ishmael" should not be interpreted to mean that Hagar's identity as a person/woman
is being subsumed in her identity as a mother, or that she is seen as nothing more
than the mother of a son. In Arab culture, it is customary to refer not only to
women but also to men as being "mother" or "father" of so-and-so. No discrimination is thus implied by this form of address.

8. This hadith reads as follows:

Narrated Ibn 'Abbas: "When Abraham had differences with his wife (Because of her
jealousy of Hajar, Ishmael's mother), he took Ishmael and his mother and went
away. They had a water-skin with them containing some water, Ishmael's mother
used to drink water from the water-skin so that her milk would increase for her
child. When Abraham reached Mecca, he made her sit under a tree and afterwards
returned home. Ishmael's mother followed him, and when they reached Kada she
called him from behind, 'O Abraham! To whom are you leaving us?' He replied, '(I
am leaving you) to Allah (Care)!' She said, 'I am satisfied to be with Allah.' She
returned to her place and started drinking water from the water-skin, and her milk
increased for her child. When the water had all been used up, she said to herself, 'I
better go and look so that I may see somebody.' She ascended the Safa mountain
and looked, hoping to see somebody, but in vain. When she came down to the valley, she ran till she reached the Marwa mountain. She ran to and fro (between the
two mountains) many times. Then she said to herself, 'I'd better go and see the state
of the child, she went and found it in a state of one on the point of dying. She could
not endure to watch it dying and said (to herself), 'If I go and look, I may find
somebody.' She went and ascended the Safa mountain and looked for a long while
but could not find anybody. Thus she completed seven rounds (of running)
between Safa and Marwa. Again she said (to herself), 'I'd better go and see the state
of the child.' But suddenly she heard a voice, and she said to that strange voice,
'Help us if you can offer any help.' Lo! It was Gabriel (who had made the voice).
Gabriel hit the earth with his heel like this (Ibn 'Abbas hit the earth with his heel
to illustrate it) and so the water gushed out. Ishmael's mother was astonished and
started digging. (Abu Al-Qasim, i.e., the Prophet, said, 'If she had let the water flow
naturally without her intervention, it would have been flowing on the surface of the
earth.') Ishmael's mother started drinking from the water and her milk increased
for her child. Afterwards some people of the tribe of Jurhum, while passing through
the bottom of the valley, saw some birds, and that astonished them, and they said,
'Birds can only be found at a place where there is water. They sent a messenger who
searched the place and found the water, and returned to inform them about it. Then
they all went to her and said, 'O Ishmael's mother! Will you allow us to be with you
(or dwell with you)?' (And thus they stayed there.) Later on her boy reached the age
of puberty and married a lady from them. Then an idea occurred to Abraham which
he disclosed to his wife (Sarah), 'I want to call on my dependents I left (at Mecca).

When he went there, he greeted (Ishmael's wife) and said, 'Where is Ishmael?' She replied, 'He has gone out hunting.' Abraham said (to her), 'When he comes, tell him to change the threshold of his gate.' When he came, she told him the same whereupon Ishmael said to her, 'You are the threshold, so go to your family (i.e., you are divorced).' Again, Abraham thought of visiting his dependents whom he had left (at Mecca) and he told his wife (Sarah) of his intentions. Abraham came to Ishmael's house and asked, 'Where is Ishmael?' Ishmael's wife replied, 'He has gone out hunting,' she added, 'Will you stay (for some time) and have something to eat and drink?' Abraham asked, 'What is your food and what is your drink?' She replied, 'Our food is meat and our drink is water.' He said, 'O Allah! Bless their meals and their drink.' Abu' Qasim, i.e., the Prophet, said, "Because of Abraham's invocation there are blessings (in Mecca). Once more Abraham thought of visiting his family he had left (at Mecca), so he told his wife (Sarah) of his decision. He went and found Ishmael behind the Zam-zam well, mending his arrows. He said, 'O Ishmael, Your Lord has ordered me to build a house for Him.' Ishmael said, 'Obey (the order of) your Lord.' Abraham said, 'Allah has also ordered that you should help me therein.' Ishmael said, 'Then I will do so.' So, both of them rose and Abraham started building (the Ka'bah) while Ishmael went on handing him the stones, and both of them were saying, 'O our Lord! Accept (this service) from us. Verily You are the All-Hearing, the All-knowing' (Surah 2: Al-Baqarah, 127). When the building became high and the old man (i.e., Abraham) could no longer lift the stones (to such a high position), he stood over the stone of Al-Maqam and Ishmael carried on handing him the stones, and both of them were saying, 'O our Lord! Accept (this service) from us, Verily You are All-Hearing, All-Knowing (Surah 2: Al-Baqarah, 127)" (379–382). (Translator's footnote reads: "This very stone is still preserved in the Sacred Mosque in Mecca and is situated between the Ka'bah and Zam-zam, and one can see the footmarks of Abraham over it.")

9. In this context, the following observation taken from *Tafsir ul Baidawi*, 424, quoted by T. F. Hughes in *A Dictionary of Islam* (Lahore: Premier Book House, originally printed in 1885), is interesting: "When the tribe of Jurhum saw that there was water in that place, they said to Hajar, 'If you will share with us the water of this spring, we will share with you the milk of our herds and from that time Makkah became a place of importance."

10. As, for instance, Surah 4: *An-Nisa*, 95, 97–100, and Surah 16: *An-Nahl*, 41.

11. G. A. Parwez, *Lughat-ul-Qur'an* (Lahore: Idara Tulu'-e-Islam, 1960), vol. 2.

12. For instance, see the Qur'an, Surah 6: *Al-An'am*, 75–82; Surah 21: *Al-Anbiya'*, 51–70.

13. For instance, see the Qur'an, Surah 6: *Al-An'am*, 74; Surah 9: *At-Tawbah*, 114; Surah 19: *Maryam*, 42–47.

PART THREE
HAGAR AND SARAH
IN CONTINUING
CONVERSATION

Chapter 7

Hagar in African American Biblical Appropriation

Delores S. Williams

For many generations African American Christians have appropriated biblical personalities and events to identify models of faith, courage, and hope as a promise that God participates in the human struggle for freedom. Two African American traditions of biblical appropriation support this idea. One of these traditions, the liberation tradition, has gotten considerable development from black male theologians. They use liberation passages in Exodus 1–15 and Luke 4 to validate their theological positions. The other African American tradition of biblical appropriation, the survival, quality-of-life tradition, is getting its development from black female scholars known as womanist theologians. Considerably younger in its evolutionary process than male work in the liberation vein, the survival, quality-of-life tradition builds on the story of a biblical female figure whom the African American community has appropriated from the time of slavery to the present day. The appropriation lifts up the slave woman Hagar and her story as it appears in the Bible.

The aim of this essay is to contribute to further development of this Hagar-centered tradition of appropriation by exploring its significance for the construction of womanist theology. At the onset I identify several assumptions that guide my effort. First, a womanist theological reflection assumes a theological task committed to the survival of a whole people: women, men, and children. Second, the primary audience for womanist theological work is the African American community. But like the poets who believed the artist should leave enough space in his or her work so that different ideas can thunder in, the womanist theologian invites nonblack audiences into dialogue. After all, womanists are not separatists, except when women's health is at stake. Third, womanist theologians search for the African American community's understanding of womanhood and God's relation to it. Thus the womanist theologian assumes that she has the license to create new language and new categories and to develop analytical tools appropriate for conveying the results of her research to the community.

This is not a new practice in the development of the Christian theological tradition. Paul Tillich—convinced of the present ineffectiveness of conventional religious language—had to devise a new vocabulary. And this new vocabulary helped him speak with a theological voice that made a powerful impact upon intellectuals and Christian laypersons. In our own time we know of the great contribution some feminists have made in this area of creating new vocabulary and new meaning. Some of the work of Mary Daly, Rosemary Ruether, and Letty Russell comes to mind. Womanists are, indeed, in good company when they take the license to create fresh language and ideas in order to convey the meanings their research has yielded. That said, I can advance to the major concern of this essay.

ENTER HAGAR

For more than two hundred years, African Americans have appropriated the biblical figure Hagar. She has appeared in many different contexts, supporting a variety of meanings. In literary, social scientific, historical, anthropological, and theological sources Hagar appears. The wide range of this appropriation catalogues easily. Edmonia Lewis, a nineteenth-century African American sculpter, who finally lived in Italy, carved a famous statue she named "Hagar in the Wilderness." Ex-slave woman Susie King Taylor, in her narrative, tells of her grandmother who named one of her children Hagar Ann. In her novel *Iola Leroy*, first published in 1892, Frances Harper describes an ex-slave mother who "like Hagar of old, went out into the wide world to seek a living for herself and her child." The poet Paul Lawrence Dunbar, whose writing career extended from 1898 to 1906, wrote about "the members of the Afro-American Sons of Hagar Social Club." Novelist Richard Wright referred to the African American family as Hagar's children. When he wrote *The Negro Family in the United States*, sociologist E. Franklin Frazier titled one chapter "Hagar and Her Children." Francis P. Reid's book of poetry *Given to Time* contains a long poem entitled "Hagar."[1] African American anthropologist John Langston Gwaltney dedicated his collection of urban narratives, *Drylongso*, to "Lucy and all the other flowers in Aunt Hagar's garden." In the glossary to this book Gwaltney describes Aunt Hagar as a "mythical apical figure of the core black American nation."[2]

Maya Angelou's poem "The Mothering Blackness" alludes to the woman as "black yet as Hagar's daughters." Nobel Prize novelist Toni Morrison named a female character Hagar in her novel *Song of Solomon*.[3] Black preachers have also participated in the community's tradition of appropriating Hagar and therefore her story in the Bible. At a conference on black women in ministry held at Princeton Theological Seminary in the 1980s the Reverend Arlene Churn preached a sermon entitled "Hagar, What Ailest Thee?"[4]

The stories in the biblical book of Genesis seem to be the context from which these African American appropriations of Hagar have derived. Many of the themes from these Genesis stories course through the range of the catalogue listed above. There is the theme of sexual exploitation. In Genesis 16:1–16, Hagar is a sexual victim exploited by members of a family more prominent and more powerful than she. Toni Morrison's novel features a character named Hagar who is also sexually exploited by a member of a family more prominent and powerful than she.[5] There is the theme of destitution and single parentage. In the Genesis 21:9–21 story Hagar and her child Ishmael are cast out into the world alone and destitute. Hagar, now a single parent, must make a way for herself and her child. In Frances Harper's *Iola Leroy*, Iola is cast out into the world following the Civil War, and she too, as a single parent, must make a way for herself and her child. Harper refers to Iola as "like Hagar of Old."[6]

The theme of survival struggle involving children or family appears in the two Genesis passages featuring Hagar. Survival struggle is also suggested in some of the African American sources in which Hagar appears. Novelist Richard Wright and sociologist E. Franklin Frazier portray the black family as a female-guided structure with the black mother, like Hagar, focusing on the survival needs of children or family.[7]

There is also the theme in the stories of a poor, oppressed woman having an encounter with God. In Genesis 16:7–13, Hagar meets the angel of the Lord (interpreted as a face-to-face encounter with God) in the wilderness. In Genesis 21:17–19 Hagar communicates with God, who again gives attention to her and her child's situation. The sermon of the Reverend Arlene Churn ("Hagar, What Ailest Thee?") makes parallels between Hagar's meetings with God and African American women's understanding of their encounters with God.[8] Just as African American anthropologist John Langston Gwaltney recognized "Aunt Hagar as the mythical apical figure of the core black American nation," the Genesis 16 and 21 stories contain God's promise that Hagar, through her son, would be the mother of a great nation.[9] Thus the theme of women's agency in the development of nation building presents itself in both Hagar's and African American women's experience.[10] Just as the biblical Hagar (Genesis 16:1, 15) was a slave when her child was named Ishmael, Susie King's grandmother was a slave when her child was named Hagar Ann. Thus the theme of naming under duress appears in both women's situations. The theme of dark skin translates from Hagar's African heritage in Egypt to African American women's heritage from West Africa. Therefore Maya Angelou can refer to African American women as "black yet as Hagar's daughter."

A talented black female student at Union Theological Seminary has carried the interpretation of the Hagar appropriation a bit further. Valerie Ellis calls attention to the significance of African American people's appropriation of Hagar's child Ishmael. According to Ellis, the correlation here is between Ishmael and African American youth. Ishmael is an abandoned child. He is abandoned by the home context in which he was born and raised. He is abandoned by Abraham his father. He is briefly abandoned by Hagar, who turns her back on the child. She could not bear to see him die. However, in Ellis's formulation we get from Hagar and Ishmael to Jesus on the basis of the abandoned son Jesus on the cross crying to his father-God: "My God, My God, why have you abandoned me?" Ellis's point is that many African American children have been abandoned in all the ways Ishmael was abandoned. She concludes that the church can communicate better with African American youth today through a theological understanding of the many dimensions of this historic experience of abandonment.[11]

The appropriation of Hagar by African Americans and the presence of her themes in black people's sources raise the question of the significance of the appropriation for the construction of womanist theology. I identify and explicate what I see to be three areas of theological import. First, the Hagar appropriation establishes *a continuity of tradition about God* significant for the African American Christian community's understanding of its faith. Second, for the explication of its meaning in the deposits of African American culture, the Hagar appropriation spawns *a new methodological level of interpretation* complementary to (but different from) traditional exegetical methods employed in the interpretation of biblical texts. By traditional methods I mean those historical-critical ways of extracting meaning from a biblical text through analysis of language and the use of methods that give attention to the origin and form of the text as well as to redactional problems.

The third area of theological import associated with the African American appropriation of Hagar is the connection of *faith and politics*. When viewed through the lens of African American women's experience, Hagar's actions yield a certain politic also present in African American women's history. In both Hagar's story and African American women's stories, this politic results in confessions of faith. And these confessions of faith testify to God's involvement in women's struggle for life and well-being.

Later in this essay, I provide support for the claim of the third area of theological import associated with the African American appropriation of the biblical Hagar. Suffice it to say at this point that all three areas of theological import indicate the significance of the Bible for the formation of some African American cultural deposits (e.g., poems, novels, narrative literature, art, socio-scientific works, etc.). And these biblically informed cultural deposits communicate important messages about the community's understanding of its faith and its response to black womanhood.

It is important to indicate what I *am not* declaring here. I am not declaring that traditional historical-critical methods are obsolete. I am suggesting, however, that, for a theological interpretation of what this Hagar appropriation can mean for the African American Christian community, a level of interpretation is needed prior to historical-critical analysis. This essay does not demonstrate how a traditional exegesis of the biblical texts follows and functions in relation to this *prior level of cultural interpretation*. If this study were to be extended, a thorough discussion about the connection between this cultural level and the historical-critical level would be provided. In that case, I would assume that the results of the work of cultural interpretation and those of historical-critical analysis of the Hagar texts would yield insights that can be brought into dialogue. From this dialogue exciting views could emerge, expanding the community's historic understanding of God's relation to its life. This essay, however, explicates only the three areas of theological import identified above: continuity of tradition about God, methodological level of interpretation, and connection of faith and politics.

ESTABLISHING A CONTINUITY OF TRADITION

Establishing a continuity of tradition about God means examining the patterns of a community's culture and faith so that the community can understand what and how it has passed along (from generation to generation) its beliefs about God's relation to its life. For the womanist theologian, establishing a continuity of tradition about God involves uncovering female-centered traditions buried beneath the layers of androcentric cultural traditions. Once uncovered by the theologian, this buried tradition gets its name and provides tools for theological interpretation of data. The newly exposed tradition enters into dialogue with the prevailing and prominent androcentric cultural patterns or traditions and becomes a source for enlarging the community's understanding of the many ways God does and has related to the world—including the many ways God relates to the particular community itself.

At this point, additional reflection upon the Hagar-centered appropriation in the African American context can demonstrate how the womanist theologian uncovers buried tradition and helps to establish the community's continuity of tradition about God. Two analytical moments are involved: the moment of memory and scholarly intention and the moment of reasoning and naming. Memory (of some past situation) dimly recognizes a partially visible pattern and/or practice on the surface of the culture that seems to have roots buried beneath the cultural soil. As the result of what memory has intuited, scholarly intention crafts certain queries it brings to the examination of data. From this relation of memory, scholarly intention, and data, discovery happens.

Let me illustrate this first moment on the basis of my own experience. As a child growing up in the segregated southern United States, I heard Hagar's name mentioned many times in the black community. I had a dim recollection that this name had something to do with black American women, but I had forgotten the name as I traveled through the ranks of academia. Then one day, at a meeting of the American Academy of Religion, I was walking down a corridor in the hotel. Suddenly I heard a resonant male voice behind me belt out the words "Ma Hagar!" Instantly I whirled around. I felt the voice was calling me, and it was. A family friend, Professor Riggins Earl, and I were facing each other. At that moment he had called something deep in my cultural memory that recognized the name Hagar was associated with African American women. This cultural memory was the first step in the birth of a scholarly intention associated with Hagar. The next step came when, upon my expressing dismay at black women's absence from black and feminist liberation theologies, one of my professors advised me to reread African American sources from many disciplines. As I read, I was to keep in the forefront of my mind this sentence: "I am a black WOMAN!" I followed his advice and I discovered, in African American sources, this vast, vast appropriation of the biblical figure Hagar!

The second analytical moment in this process of uncovering buried tradition and establishing continuity of tradition about God involves reasoning and naming. Let me again provide an example from my own scholarly experience. On the basis of such widespread and long-term appropriation of Hagar by African Americans and on the basis of the parallels between Hagar's experience recorded in the Bible and African American women's experience portrayed in the black sources, I did some reasoning. I reasoned that Hagar was not a random, disconnected pattern floating in the fluidity of the African American cultural stream. Rather this appropriation of Hagar and intimations of her story were a tradition trying to deliver an important message to the community. Since her name and story had been passed to so many generations of black Americans, I also reasoned that Hagar was an analogue for African American womanhood. Inasmuch as this Hagar appropriation was rooted in biblical story, I further reasoned that it must have religious significance for the black community. Unlike the liberation tradition of African American biblical appropriation, the Hagar tradition was unnamed and its meaning for the community was not clear.

However, as a womanist theologian with some intellectual roots in feminist presuppositions, I concluded that my theological task was to name this Hagar-centered tradition of African American biblical appropriation. If what I reasoned about Hagar being an analogue for black womanhood was true, then the appropriation, as a tradition, must be given a visible and viable place in the community's understanding of its experience and God's relation to it.

Though the concept of naming came from feminist presuppositions, insights about the process of naming came from a traditional way in which many African American Christians used the Bible. They interpreted God's relationship to their lives on the basis of the way God was reported in the Bible to deal with situations like theirs. Especially during slavery, they did not accommodate themselves to the Bible. They accommodated the Bible to the urgent necessities of their lives. God's deliverance of the Hebrews from slavery indicated that God would liberate African American slaves. I knew that in their way of appropriating from the Bible, the black American religious community had not traditionally put final emphasis upon the hopelessness of the painful aspects of black history. Rather, they used the Bible to put primary emphasis upon God's response to the community's situation of pain and bondage.

A careful reading of Genesis 16:1–16 and Genesis 21:9–21 reveals that Hagar's predicament involved slavery, poverty, ethnicity, sexual and economic exploitation, surrogacy, domestic violence, homelessness, single parenting, and radical encounters with God. African American women's historic predicament in society resembles Hagar's in the biblical stories. By appropriating Hagar, I concluded that black Americans wanted to keep this female experience alive in the memory of the community. But what about God in this Hagar-black-American-woman scenario? Was there something about God's response to Hagar's situation that correlated with African American people's understanding of God's response to the historic situation of black American women?

It was obvious to me that God's response to Hagar in Genesis was not liberation. Rather, God participated in Hagar and her child's survival on many occasions. When she was a runaway slave, God met her in the wilderness and told her to return to Sarai and Abram's domicile. Then, when Hagar and her child were finally cast out of the home of their oppressors and were not given proper resources for survival, God provided Hagar with a resource. She received new vision to see survival resources where she had seen none before. Thus it seemed to me that God's response to Hagar's (and her child's) situation was survival and involvement in their development of a quality of life appropriate to their situation and their heritage (e.g., Gen. 21:20).

Many black women have testified that "God helped them make a way out of no way." They believe God is involved not only in their survival struggle, but also that God supports their struggle for quality of life, which making a way suggests. I concluded that this female-centered tradition of African American biblical appropriation could be named the survival, quality-of-life tradition of African American biblical appropriation. In black consciousness, God's survival and quality of life response to Hagar is God's response of survival and quality of life to African American women and mothers of slave descent struggling to sustain their families with God's help.

It is reasonable, then, to conclude that this survival, quality-of-life tradition of African American biblical appropriation involving Hagar expands the community's knowledge of God's activity in the world. While the androcentric dominance in African American culture has, for generations, passed along faith in a liberator God, the Hagar-centered survival tradition of African American biblical appropriation passes along a God involved in the daily survival and quality-of-life struggle of black American women. The emergence of this cultural interpretation helps to establish a continuity of tradition about God that the community can see as open and extending rather than as petrified into a single liberation emphasis.

My point is not to suggest that the liberation tradition of African American biblical interpretation lacks relevance and meaning in the context of Afro-Christian experience. The liberation appropriation of biblical events and persons is consistent with some aspects of that experience and has brought the theological voice of the black Christian community into wider areas of theological discourse. But the point here is that the survival, quality-of-life tradition of African American biblical appropriation strengthens the black theological voice and affirms God's freedom to act in many different ways in response to a community's life and faith.

To reiterate, establishing a continuity of tradition about God involves two analytical moments: the moment of memory and scholarly intention leading to discovery and the moment of reasoning and naming leading to broader visions of God's action in the world. Of course, it is the survival, quality-of-life tradition of African American biblical appropriation that has resulted from the work of the two analytical moments.

A NEW METHODOLOGICAL LEVEL OF INTERPRETATION

Following continuity of tradition about God, the second area of theological import is a new methodological level of interpretation. Coming before traditional historical-critical methodologies used in the interpretation of the biblical texts, this new womanist method is informed by some of the theological work of JoAnne Terrell. In her book *Power in the Blood? The Cross in the African-American Experience*, Terrell coins the term "proto-womanist" to indicate perspectives and interpretations earlier than today's womanism but definitely contributing to womanist meanings in our time.[12]

Like Terrell, I point to a level of interpretation (with regard to Hagar's appearance in African American culture) that can be applied to black American culture and can influence the historical-critical exegesis of the text. In womanist terminology this type of interpretation is named *proto-gesis*. It employs methodologies that analyze all the African American deposits of culture in which the Hagar references appear from slave-time to the present day. Proto-gesis is a womanist theologian's way of leading the community into cultural self-study. The study not only focuses on the significance of the biblical appropriation for revealing issues and questions vital to the community's daily life and sustenance; it also provides issues and questions from the culture that the theologian can use in the dialogue between the results of both proto-getical analysis and historical-critical exegesis of the Hagar text.

Conceptually, proto-gesis is loosely informed by some of the insights from discussions about meaning in the area of Cultural Studies. I use the term "loosely informed" to indicate similarities between proto-gesis and Cultural Studies, despite the differences. As one way of defining Cultural Studies, Richard Jones has provided a help for understanding what proto-gesis involves. He advocates that Cultural Studies "be seen as . . . an alchemy for producing useful knowledge about the broad domain of human culture"[13] For purposes of this essay, I would add something more specific to what Jones offers. Proto-gesis produces useful knowledge about the broad range of meanings projected in African American culture when biblical imagery is also used to shape cultural deposits reflecting the faith, life, and gender issues in the community.

Stuart Hall's understanding of the goal of Cultural Studies resonates, in part, with the aim of proto-gesis. He writes that a central goal of Cultural Studies is to "provide ways of thinking, strategies for survival and resources for resistance."[14] But proto-gesis must also go beyond this goal to assert that while survival and resistance are primary womanist concerns, meaning must be extracted from the culture unencumbered by the ideologies to which the interpreter might want the meaning to conform. However, there is no denying that meaning will be partly influenced by the nature of the questions the interpreter asks.

Proto-getical analysis in the work of cultural self-study must be done by using interpretative strategies appropriate to the genre of the cultural deposit in which the biblical appropriation is lodged. If the appropriation appears in a poem, novel, or play, the tools of literary criticism must also be employed. Thus the theologian-interpreter might ask how the biblical appropriation affects the resolution of the plot. If the biblical appropriation is used in character development, she might explore how this characterization advances the themes that the author uses to structure the novel. Or the womanist theologian-interpreter might seek to discover the message about community, identity, religion, God, and worldview the artist is trying to communicate through his or her method of characterization, through the juxtaposition of themes, through the nature of the language, through the use of figures of speech (metaphor, simile, etc.), and through processes of symbolization. These are only a few of the literary-critical theological questions the womanist theologian might ask of the cultural deposit featuring biblical appropriations.

As far as the Hagar appropriation is concerned, the object of proto-gesis is not only to discover how the formation of culture has contributed to the development of ideas about religion and gender in the community, but it also gives attention to the way the appropriation of Hagar's story contributes to changing the cultural deposit in which Hagar is located. Whether Hagar in the African American context appears in a novel, poem, social-scientific treatise, sculptured art, or sermon, we can assume that she brings religious or spiritual connotations to whatever meanings the cultural deposit communicates to the community.

As an example of the way proto-gesis works, Toni Morrison's novel *Song of Solomon* makes an apt subject. All the major female characters have names derived from the Bible. Thus Pilate, Hagar, Magdalene, Ruth, and First Corinthians appear in the text. The women are kin and have the surname "Dead" derived from the family patriarch Macon Dead. A proto-getical analysis, using literary-critical strategies, would explore such questions as follow: Do these biblically derived female names (all with the surname Dead) have symbolic value in the text? If so, how does this symbolism freight the themes through which the author conveys meanings? What do the relationships between these women (as well as their names) tell us about the worldview of the community in the novel? Does the characterization of these biblically appropriated females suggest issues peculiar to black women's culture? If so, what? What are the religious and gender issues for black women and for the black community that emerge from Morrison's portrayal of the life world of Pilate, Hagar, Ruth, and First Corinthians?

However, an examination of Morrison's work does not complete the proto-getical task related to African American "cultural self-study." Before definite statements can be made about the religious and gender issues emerging from African American culture, there must be a proto-getical analysis of all the cultural deposits in which the Hagar appropriation is contained. And methodological strategies must be used that are appropriate to the genre containing the appropriation. For instance, the social-scientific treatise by sociologist E. Franklin Frazier entitled "Hagar and Her Children" must be interpreted with strategies appropriate for sociology. One of the questions of proto-getical analysis would be this: in the use of Hagar, what is Frazier communicating about the African American understanding of the place and role of women in the black family? Are religious innuendoes threaded throughout Frazier's sociological analysis that suggest a connection between religion and gender in his work? Certainly many more questions can be posed to Frazier's work.[15]

The point here is that a proto-getical analysis of all these cultural deposits, using the methdological strategies appropriate to the genre of the deposit, will unearth issues and questions from African American culture about religion and gender. Also, the work of proto-gesis can bring womanist theologians into dialogue with scholars from other disciplines. For instance, conversation with literary critics can help the womanist theologian discern what can be reasonably concluded from her analysis of literary texts. Some of the issues resulting from this dialogue can be used to shape the questions the womanist theologian brings to the historical-critical analysis of the biblical texts in which Hagar appears.

In summary, then, womanist theologians engaging the interdisciplinary methods of proto-gesis arrive at a more scientific way of determining some of the ideas and beliefs about women and religion that African American culture has carried in its stream over time. When a biblical figure like Hagar becomes a cultural icon (cf. Gwaltney's declaration: Aunt Hagar as a "mythical apical figure of the core black American nation"), something is being insinuated about veneration related to the African American female figure. And this veneration has gained momentum as women like Hagar passed through many stages of African American culture. One of the tasks of womanist theology, then, is to uncover the meaning of this veneration in terms of the connection between African American people's religious beliefs and what might be their cultural understanding of the characteristics and roles of "the ideal" black woman. Thus the dialogue between the results of proto-gesis and the results of the historical-critical interpretation of the Hagar texts can provide a firm foundation upon which womanist theologians can construct their proposals about the community's faith regarding God's relation to women.

FAITH AND POLITICS

The third area of theological import associated with the African American appropriation of Hagar is the connection of faith and politics. Historians Darlene Clark Hine and Kathleen Thompson surveyed African American women's history and concluded that "it is more than a story of oppression and struggle . . . it is a story of hope."[16] My own research has shown that this hope is supported by a connection between black women's religious faith and their political ways of acting in the world. This action has involved endurance. It has involved resistance that is sometimes aggressive, sometimes subtle. And it has involved the verbal expression of a triumphant faith grounded in the belief that God is a coworker with black women in their life struggle.

Hagar's story also shows this connection between faith and her political way of acting in the world. Thus it is not difficult to understand why the faith and political dimension of Hagar's story can be so attractive to African American women. Hagar endured when endurance yields suffering and sacrifice. Obeying God's command for her to return to slavery after escaping, Hagar again endures bondage at the cruel hands of her owner Sarai. Inasmuch as resistance can be expressed by a hostile countenance, Hagar subtly looked with contempt upon Sarai when she (Hagar) discovers she is pregnant by Sarai's husband Abram. Like African American slave women, Hagar did not have the resources to win in an attack on the law that allowed her owner Sarai to use her (Hagar's) body to gain a child. Nuzi law in ancient Mesopotamia, which the Hebrews may have followed, allowed barren upper-class women to gain children by commanding their slave women to cohabit with a man the slave owner selected. Sarai was barren. Hagar could not say "no" when Sarai demanded that Abram, Sarai's husband, cohabit with Hagar so that a child could be produced. But in the midst of her defiance Hagar met God in the wilderness and received God's promise: "I [God] will so greatly multiply your descendants that they cannot be numbered for multitude." Then, in response, Hagar makes a triumphant faith statement: "Thou art a God of seeing" (Gen. 16:13, RSV).

Like Hagar, some African American slave women experienced upper-class white women taking their children away from them. The slave Sarah Debro said, "I was kept at the Big House to wait on Miss Polly, to tote her basket of keys and such as that. The day she took me my mammy cried, 'cause she knew I would never be allowed to live at the cabin with her no more."[17] Also like the slave Hagar, African American slaves experienced violence at the hands of their owners. Historians Hine and Thompson claim that on these American slave plantations "discipline was swift and often cruel . . . southern plantations had their share of outright sadists. Without constraints of law or social disapproval, these people [i.e., the slave owners] women and men, were free to commit extremes of physical violence on even the youngest slaves. . . ."[18]

Theologically, the significance of the union of faith and politics is that it gave birth to triumphant confessions of faith uttered by black women, as indeed by Hagar. Many African American women have expressed the belief that "God helped them make a way out of no way." This confession of faith has been passed along in the African American oral tradition for many generations. It is impossible to determine precisely when black women's words actually crystallized into this faith statement supported by their ways of acting in the world. The story of a nineteenth-century black woman named Nancy Prince contains ideas that suggest such a confession of faith and related politics.[19]

Incorporated in her naming of God is Hagar's confession of faith: "Thou art a God of seeing" (Gen. 16:13). Then in amazement she asks, "Have I really seen God and remained alive after seeing him?" (Gen. 16:13). Rather than an expression of doubt, this question registers Hagar's awe that God could pay attention to a lowly slave like herself. Obviously this faith of Hagar, told in the biblical story, has passed through many generations of readers. It is no wonder that black women can declare from generation to generation, "God helped us make a way out of no way." And they can easily resonate with Hagar's faith statement—i.e., "Thou art a God of seeing."

We cannot deny that the Bible, Christian religion, Euro-centric American culture, and African American culture have played a large role in shaping African American women's faith and politics. But it is also true that strands of non-Christian religions and culture have threaded through this faith and these politics from the seventeenth century to the present day. Hagar and African American women have a heritage rooted in Africa. It is not far-fetched, then, to view their faith, politics, and confessions of faith through the lens of an imagination informed by African culture. However, such a task is beyond the scope of what this essay can accomplish. It is enough at this point to emphasize that, in a Christian context, African American women have found in Scripture and culture a point of connection and a point of departure from which an authentic womanist theology can be launched.

THEOLOGICAL DESIGN UNDER CONSTRUCTION

This essay has attempted to demonstrate that new interpretative tools are needed to open wider the gates of African American culture, and these will help the Christian community obtain a realistic view of God and "woman-related" themes that the culture has carried over time. The process of uncovering androcentric biases and naming different possibilities (e.g., establishing a continuity of tradition about God) direct attention to new visions of the many ways God has acted and does act in human history. Relational experience in a sociohistorical context (e.g., faith and politics) yields insight about God and female agency working together, ultimately yielding confessions of faith that affirm women's beliefs about God's care in their daily lives.

Many theological designs can be constructed on the basis of the African American appropriation of the biblical Hagar story. The birth of the *survival, quality-of-life tradition of African American biblical appropriation* provides new interpretative possibilities. When survival and quality of life function hermeneutically, the theologian is directed to other biblical stories and traditions beyond Hagar and beyond liberation, traditions that have meaning for a variety of Christians. For instance, the theme of survival brings the biblical covenant tradition into focus and with it the association of an economic motif related to the promises of God. Quality-of-life themes, associated with survival, point to the wilderness tradition and yield insights about the kind of life and religious orientation God ordains for God's people. They show what is involved in the making of a people, a message significant for the African American effort to hold a black peoplehood together. Further, this molding of survival and quality-of-life issues can help the theologian to interpret divine insights and divine participation in diasporic situations similar to the Babylonian captivity. Such interpretation would be important for those Christians in the African diaspora in the West trying to live a Christian life.

Womanist theologians will no doubt continue to take seriously the role African American biblical appropriation has had in shaping the black community's consciousness about God and ethnic women. This kind of focus will perhaps urge black theologians, male and female, not to fixate on one hermeneutical possibility but to interpret God's changing Word in the context of an inquiring faith. In such an endeavor, the story of Hagar and her children plays no small role.

Notes

1. Delores S. Williams, *Sisters in the Wilderness: The Challenge of Womanist God-Talk* (Maryknoll, NY: Orbis Books, 1993), 245.
2. John Langston Gwaltney, *Drylongso* (New York: Random House, 1980), glossary.
3. Toni Morrison, *Song of Solomon* (New York: Alfred A. Knopf, 1977).
4. Williams, *Sisters in the Wilderness*, 245.
5. Morrison, *Song of Solomon*.
6. Frances Ellen Watkins Harper, *Iola Leroy, or Shadows Uplifted*, 2nd ed. (Philadelphia: Garrignes Brothers, 1893).
7. E. Franklin Frazier, *The Negro Family in the United States* (Chicago: University of Chicago Press, 1939).
8. Williams, *Sisters in the Wilderness*, 245.
9. Gwaltney, *Drylongso*.
10. Williams, *Sisters in the Wilderness*, 245.
11. Presentation in a seminar conducted by Delores Williams on "Women's Experience as a Resource for Worship," by Valerie Ellis, Union Theological Seminary, New York, 2001.
12. JoAnne Terrell, *Power in the Blood: The Cross in the African-American Experience* (Maryknoll, NY: Orbis Books, 1998).
13. Richard Jones, "What Is Cultural Studies Anyway?" *Social Texts* 16 (1986/7): 38f.

14. Stuart Hall, "The Emergence of Cultural Studies and the Crisis of the Humanities," *October* 53 (1990): 11.
15. Frazier, *The Negro Family in the United States*.
16. Darlene Clark Hine and Kathleen Thompson, *A Shining Thread of Hope: The History of Black Women in America* (New York: Broadway Books, 1998), 6.
17. Ibid., 70.
18. Ibid.
19. Nancy Prince, "The History of Nancy Prince, A West Indian Slave," in *Six Women's Slave Narratives*, ed. William L. Andrews (New York: Oxford University Press, 1988), 6. First published in London by F. Weatley and A. H. Davis, 1831.

Chapter 8

Children of Struggle

Letty M. Russell

The story of Hagar, Sarah, and their children is a story of struggle—struggle with each other and against patriarchal oppression. As we study the story and the trajectory of its interpretation through history and into the twenty-first century, we see the seeds of conflict and struggle we have inherited. The question for us now seems to be: How can we get the women and their children back together? Is there any way to overcome the hidden and not-so-hidden injuries of class, race, gender, economics, and politics that use our faith traditions to excuse continuing conflict?

This may be the wrong question, however. When we look at the Genesis story and its interpretation by Phyllis Trible, we see that we can't get the women and children back together because they never were together. Hagar and Sarah were divided from the beginning. Born of these different mothers, Ishmael and Isaac only came together to honor their father Abraham at his burial (Gen. 25:7–10). This observation might lead us to join many interpreters, both ancient and modern, to ask, How can we rewrite the story so that the two women are reconciled? Yet that question may not work well either, because the patriarchal writers get rid of both women as soon as the sons are safe. In the story, Sarah's last words are her command to "cast out this slave woman and her son . . ." (Gen. 21:10). She disappears from the story in death soon after the sacrifice of Isaac (Gen. 21:1–2) As

Trible points out, Hagar also disappears after securing a wife for Ishmael from Egypt without even a report of her death and burial (Gen. 21:20–21).

There is a long tradition of interpretation through rewriting. For instance, the church fathers followed Paul in using allegory to look for a deeper meaning of the story relevant to issues in their own times. Jewish writers made use of midrash in order to interpret the story with a new story. Claiming descent from Abraham and Ishmael for the tribes of the Arabian peninsula, the hadith or collected sayings of Muhammad and his companions emphasized Hagar's role as pioneering woman and mother of the faith. Similar patterns of retelling the story are used by feminists of all three faiths as they reflect on their own faith traditions, seeking ways to reconcile their two mothers.

Another approach might be to focus on the two women's common struggle for what Delores Williams calls "survival and quality of life," rather than on their struggle against each other. Recognizing ourselves in the predicaments of the story we could ask, What drives the women apart? What clues does the story provide for dealing with the enmity that continues today in our life and world? If we study the struggles of Sarah and Hagar, we may discover many of our own struggles and failings and the ways they prevent our coming together. The daily struggles of our own living teach us that a search for solidarity in struggle may engage the trajectory of the story more directly than rewriting the unhappy ending.

No doubt, there are many other questions to ask as well, each of which can lead us in a search for God's welcome in a world of difference. Here, however, I want to reflect on this last question by focusing on the relationship of Sarah and Hagar and what their enmity seems to be teaching us. Even though the question and my theological reflections come out of my own white, feminist, Protestant tradition, the question can lead us into conversation with the Muslim, Jewish, and Christian writers in this book. Along with all the writers I want to continue the conversation that has been going on throughout the ages about this cautionary tale, in the expectation that we will keep finding ways the text reads our lives and points us to an alternative future.

In this invitation to conversation I will reflect on three aspects of the relationship of Hagar and Sarah that are discussed in this book. The first relates to the theme of motherhood and fertility that is so much the perspective of the patriarchal traditions in Genesis and in the dominant interpretations in all three faiths. Much of the interpretation is related to sorting out the way the story of these two mothers constrains patriarchal expectations by putting the possibility of a male heir at risk.

A second aspect of their relationship heightens the crisis of fertility by emphasizing the competition of the two mothers and their descendants over ownership of God's promise of blessing. Interpreters in all three traditions believe that theirs reflects the true inheritance of God's covenant with Abraham and election to God's favor. The competition of the two women to be part of the covenant through the birth of their sons is reflected over and over, even through the religious ideologies of the present-day wars in the Middle East and the anti-Jewish and anti-Muslim bias in North America and Europe.

A third aspect of their relationship involves the wilderness and wandering motif in these particular stories. Abraham and Sarah first move from their homeland in Mesopotamia to Canaan. In time of famine they move to Egypt and then return to Canaan. Twice Hagar moves to the wilderness, at first through her own flight and at last through expulsion. The experience of Abraham and Sarah as strangers who were welcomed and blessed by God might have taught them to welcome strangers, but it did not. There is little consideration of Hagar, the stranger in their midst, whose difference includes her female status as slave and as Egyptian foreigner. These three aspects of the relationship by no means exhaust the many dimensions of the story of Hagar, Sarah, and their children, but they can guide us in our struggles with the trajectory of their story as it continues to be lived out in our lives.

MOTHERHOOD CONSTRAINED BY PATRIARCHY

In the Genesis account the mothers are caught in a dualistic struggle against each other in a patriarchal context. The account has frozen each mother into an opposing role and ignored the roles they share as subordinates, seeking the approval of Abraham and God. Although the survival struggle dramatizes the conflict between the two, it is important to refuse a dualistic, either/or view of their relationship. They are part of a broader picture of power dynamics in which patriarchy constrains their motherhood. Each in her own context is trying to make "a way out of no way."

Constrained by Patriarchy

The predicament of patriarchy that Hagar and Sarah represent is that women's ability to bear children and to love and nurture them is a powerful biological tool that has been constructed socially to support the "rule of the father" over the mother and over all slaves, dependent persons, and property in the household. The dualistic and hierarchical structure of this household is reinforced by an understanding that a free woman's identity is dependent on the father, husband, and son to whom she belongs. The slave woman is inferior because of her subordinate social location. Her identity also includes her bodily access as sexual partner and mother.[1]

Over time patriarchy has taken many different social configurations that include gender, class, race, and whatever differences are considered of importance in a particular society. In order to make it clear that patriarchy refers to many different concrete and complex social arrangements and not just to gender relations, Elisabeth Schüssler Fiorenza prefers to speak of *kyriarchy*, "rule of the lord," in family, state, and social institutions in communities that are male dominated. Thus she contrasts kyriarchy to communities that are more egalitarian and less hierarchical, practicing what she calls a discipleship of equals.[2]

Although in the story of Hagar and Sarah the household of Abraham and the culture of the writers can be understood to be patriarchal, the term "patriarchy" or "kyriarchy" is also used in feminist interpretation to refer to any social construction of reality or thinking that is based on the domination of women and of all groups considered inferior because of race, gender, class, sexual orientation, disability, and the like. Abraham is the father of a patriarchal household, and the relationships in the story reflect both a social reality of male domination, class division, and a way of thinking that is hierarchical and dualistic.

Ability to Bear an Heir

This way of thinking establishes the role of women as dependents whose main source of identity is their ability to bear an heir to carry on the lineage of the patriarchal family. In fact, the women's struggles are used in the story to heighten the major issue at hand. How can Abraham become the father of a great nation when he has no sons? This issue of motherhood and sonship is echoed in Paul's allegory and in the interpretations from Christianity, Judaism, and Islam (Gal. 4:21–31). The possibility of Sarah bearing an heir is repeatedly in jeopardy as Abraham pretends to Pharaoh that his beautiful wife is his sister and as Ishmael becomes the firstborn son (Gen. 12:10–16; 17:18).

Because of the power relations in the crowded marriage, both Sarah and Hagar compete with each other for the validation of their motherhood through Abraham and through God. Fertility is understood not only as the basis of a woman's identity but also as a sign of divine approval. This view is not so dissimilar from many cultures in our world. A woman in Ghana or in Korea, for instance, is not considered a woman until she bears a child, particularly a son.[3] In the United States as well, women are expected to become mothers in order to be "somebody" and to fulfill social expectations of what it means to be a woman.

In this marriage of three the competition is a matter of life and death. For Sarah there is the pressure to live up to the divine mandate of God's promise to Abraham that he would become a great nation. According to Delores Williams, the possibility is that she may be replaced and left out of the family if Ishmael is to inherit first place as head of the patriarchal household.[4] For Hagar there is the desire for freedom that is denied by God's command to return to slavery in order to give birth to Ishmael. Later, her need is to survive in the wilderness and establish a new family for her son.

A Way Out of Enmity

It is not only the women who seek a way out of this situation of enmity but also the men who subsequently comment on the stories in their faith traditions. Some of them, like Paul, seek a resolution of the power instability by declaring that Sarah is the winner. In turn, she becomes a model for winning against various opponents. Elizabeth Clark tells us that the church fathers follow suit, applying

Paul's allegory to condemn their gnostic, Jewish, Donatist, and Manichean opponents. Many rabbis, on the other hand, focus on the problem of Sarah's infertility, which undermines her social status in relation to Hagar. According to Adele Reinhartz and Miriam-Simma Walfish, some medieval Jewish interpreters are also concerned with the immorality of Sarah's treatment of Hagar. They discuss at length whether or not Hagar is to blame for her expulsion.

The early interpreters who seem to get beyond the competition of Hagar and Sarah are those cited by Riffat Hassan. Coming at the beginning of the seventh century, Muhammad's teachings in the Qur'an and the collection of his sayings in the hadith include parts of Jewish and Christian Scriptures to show how Islam is the true form of the religion of Abraham. Although the Qur'an mentions neither Sarah nor Hagar by name, the hadith portray Hagar setting up a new household for Ishmael and becoming the Mother of Islam. In one story Abraham continues to visit both of his wives and even works with Ishmael to rebuild the Ka'bah, the first house of God in Mecca. As Hassan reminds us, Hagar is not a victim of power struggles in Islam. She is a victor, "the pioneer woman who led the way to the establishment of a new civilization."[5]

Certainly both Sarah and Hagar found their motherhood constrained by the social realities of the patriarchal culture in which they lived. Similarly many male interpretations of that tradition have reinforced those constraints. The question for the children of the two women is whether there is a way to change this paradigm of patriarchal thinking and action in order to honor motherhood as well as the many other gifts that women bring to their families and world.[6] Alternative models of family and community life require changes in our view of social reality and our thought patterns so that all persons are equally valued. In this way we could see that we are related to one another, not just as children of Hagar or Sarah, but as children of God who are partners in the struggle for quality of life in our global society.[7]

PROMISE CONSTRAINED BY COMPETITION

Patriarchal constraints are not the only tension in our traditions about Hagar, Sarah, and their children. In Genesis the horizontal violence between the two women as they compete for Abraham's and God's favor is portrayed on a larger screen that displays their competition and that of their children for God's promise of blessing. This is no small competition. Their eyes are on the prize, and so are the eyes of the children's children in all three faith traditions. Jews, Muslims, and Christians alike claim the promise to Abraham of God's special blessing.

Promise to Abraham

In Genesis 12:2 the call of Abraham includes the promise "I will bless you, and make your name great, so that you will be a blessing." This promise contains the gift of progeny, prosperity, and a new home. In chapter 17 the promise is confirmed by God's everlasting covenant with Abraham, Isaac, and their descendants. It is sealed through the promise of Isaac's birth, Sarai's name change to Sarah, and the command to circumcise all the males in Hebrew households. God's choice of Abraham and his descendants calls for a response of faithfulness. This faithfulness of Abraham, believing that he could have a son and being willing to offer him up in sacrifice at God's command, becomes the source of repeated divine blessing (Gen. 17:17–19; 22:15–19). His faithfulness is held up again and again as an example for his many children.

This blessing promised to Abraham signifies every good gift that God could offer the faithful community. The tradition originates, however, from a people who know that all is not blessing. They claim this blessing in their written traditions only after they have experienced slavery, exodus, and wandering. The covenant offers both blessing and liberation and speaks of God's intention to bless all nations through the Hebrew people (Gen. 12:2–3). This conviction of God's steadfast love and faithfulness upholds the covenant in spite of the people's unfaithfulness, disaster, and despair as "hope against hope." As Psalm 85:10–11 declares,

> Steadfast love and faithfulness will meet;
> righteousness and peace [*shalom*] will kiss each other.
> Faithfulness will spring up from the ground,
> and righteousness will look down from the sky.
> Yea, the LORD will give what is good,
> and our land will yield its increase.

Constrained by Competition

In the biblical tradition we also see this conviction repeatedly deformed when it is interpreted through the lens of patriarchy, whereby the promise becomes a privilege that belongs only to those who have the truth. It is constrained by competition with other nations and peoples and by the denial of the possibility of God's blessing for all. This process of deformation can be seen in all three faiths. They agree that this is the promise to Abraham, but they often deform the promise by claiming it as their own inheritance to the exclusion of others.

Jewish theologian Judith Plaskow points out that this claim yields a cycle in which the oppressed become the oppressors.[8] We see Paul and other Christian writers claiming that Abraham's righteous faith makes him the father of all Christians who live according to God's gracious gift of faith and salvation. In Galatians 4:25, Paul reinforces this conviction by again casting out Hagar, now understanding her to represent those who consider circumcision to be an indispensable mark of the promise.

Making exclusive claims to salvation is a particular temptation for Christians because, according to Rosemary Radford Ruether, early Christianity synthesized Jewish Messianic universalism and Greco-Roman imperialist universalism.[9] The conviction that Jesus Christ already fulfilled the Jewish expectation of God's final reign and replaced the rule of Caesar by the rule of Christ as Lord over all led Christians to claim that their faith was the one true universal religion and not just the religion of a particular people. Over the years the idea of election became a way of showing how Abraham's faith and God's covenant with Israel were now inherited by those who had faith in Jesus Christ.

The Qur'an also asserts that the Abrahamic faith founded in Mecca was universal (Surah 2:122–131).[10] For Muhammad, Abraham was the first Muslim or true believer in God. In Islam his wife Hagar led the way to a new civilization as the mother of all Arabs. Abraham was the father of the true faith that had been perverted by idolatry among the Arab tribes and by the interpretations that Jews and Christians give to that faith. God was not the God of Abraham or Muhammad, but " God of all peoples and universes."[11] Over the centuries this universal vision was also deformed into a claim of priority, blessing, and truth by followers of the Prophet Muhammad. Not unlike Jewish and Christian believers, they see Abrahamic faith assuring their own salvation while they deny a similar promise to those outside their religion.

Truth Still to Be Fully Revealed

One alternative way of approaching the universal claims of all three monotheistic faiths is to stress that each way of understanding God is an anticipation of God's truth that is still to be fully revealed. This *proleptic* or anticipatory aspect of our traditions points us to God's intention to mend the creation but leaves open the future expectation of a new heaven and a new earth. According to Ruether, each religion can also be understood as a *paradigm* of God's self-revelation.[12] Our particular faith tradition is a way of understanding reality and God's presence in and through our lives, but this way does not need to exclude the possibility that God is known to others in different ways.

It would seem that, as long as insights into God's care and presence in our lives are interpreted through the lens of patriarchal faiths, the deformation and constraint of the promise of God will happen over and over. When God is imaged as an all-powerful Father at the top of the universe, then those who see themselves as representing God will draw the conclusion that others cannot also have a true understanding of God.

If, instead, God's power is understood as the power of love and not of domination, then God can be present to us and to all people as the one who cares for us all. God as creator allows nature to work in the way God has created it and calls human beings to responsibility for the care of one another and of the earth. The power of God's love is expressed in solidarity with all who struggle for justice, peace, and integrity of creation. God's partiality is seen in God's care for those who have been denied access to the fullness of life and are marginalized in their societies. God's care is highlighted in our Genesis texts where God stands with the tiny struggling family of Abraham, as well as with the family of Hagar and Ishmael in their wilderness experience. Although Hagar and Ishmael are not included in God's covenant with Abraham, Sarah, and Isaac, they most certainly were included in God's blessing as those who were specially in need of care. A clue here is the possibility that God's promise is for everyone. As Plaskow asserts, "It is not in the chosenness that cuts off but in the distinctiveness that opens itself to difference that we find the God of Israel and of each and every people."[13]

HOSPITALITY CONSTRAINED BY DIFFERENCE

Hagar and Sarah are strangers caught in the dualistic and hierarchical social structures and thought patterns of the original storytellers and later interpreters; yet they themselves are examples of courage and of faith struggle. We think of Hagar as "archetypal stranger." Her survival skills are to be greatly prized in our postmodern world of hybridity, mixture, and constant struggle to combine one's roots and one's new reality as cultures change and we move from one part of the globe to another. But Sarah is not so different. She is also a stranger, living in both Egypt and Canaan, searching for a way to live out the promise of blessing to many nations. Such stories encourage us to remember our own histories of wandering and struggle and to honor the stranger and person in need. By such actions we honor our mothers of long ago, who were strangers in a strange land, in the expectation that the *God of Seeing* may also be in our midst.

Welcoming the Stranger

Reflecting the experience of difficult travel and the dependence of strangers on the hospitality along the way, all three faiths include injunctions to offer hospitality to the stranger. The classic image of this hospitality is the story of Abraham and Sarah at the oaks of Mamre. In both Genesis and the Qur'an Abraham provides hospitality to his guests, who turn out to be messengers from God (Gen. 18:1–15; Surah 51:25–30). In Christian tradition Jesus promises to be present among the broken and marginalized people whom he came to make welcome (Matt. 25:31–46). Luke 24:13–35 has a similar theme of unexpected divine presence at Emmaus as the Risen Christ is known in the breaking of bread.

The injunctions to welcome the stranger are also based on the experience of God's welcome and deliverance. Thus the Hebrew Scriptures exhort the community not to oppress the stranger, because the Israelites were once strangers in Egypt (Exod. 23:9). Having been delivered from slavery and oppression, they are to care for the stranger, the widow, and orphan, those in need of God's special care because they do not have a family to care for them.

In the early Christian communities hospitality was to be practiced among church members and with itinerant missionaries who came to visit. Hospitality implied a delight in a guest-host relationship which was one of give and take.[14] This mutual reaching out to others was a catalyst for community or partnership on which Paul depended as he encouraged his small, struggling churches to live in harmony with one another in order to overcome such disagreements as highlighted in Galatians 4. In Romans 15:7 he concludes a discussion of disputes over eating together by urging the church members to "[w]elcome one another, therefore, just as Christ has welcomed you, for the glory of God." Hospitality included table fellowship and was a catalyst for partnership in the hybrid church communities whose members came from different classes, religious backgrounds, genders, races, and ethnic groups.

Constrained by Difference

A major difficulty for all the communities of faith, in their origin as well as among their many children around the globe, is the way in which patriarchal social structures constrain differences by turning gifts of creativity into instruments of exclusion and oppression. Difference and hospitality are interlocked because it is the challenge of difference, strangeness, and "otherness" that calls for the practice of hospitality. Hospitality responds to difference through reciprocity and solidarity with strangers rather than through fear and exclusion of "otherness."[15] Fear and exclusion characterize the challenge of Sarah and Hagar. Of different nationality and social status, their competition for the favor of Abraham and God turned differences into weapons for exclusion and oppression rather than opportunities to share the many gifts of difference created by God in the rainbow variety of our world. As Audre Lorde has said in *Sister Outsider*,

> Certainly there are real differences between us of race, age, and sex. But it is not those differences between us that are separating us. It is rather our refusal to recognize those differences, and to examine the distortions which result from our misnaming them and their effects upon human behavior and expectation.[16]

In Galatians, Paul's use of Sarah's words and actions in casting out Hagar shows inhospitality at work. We can also see the result of this misuse of stereotyped difference in many of the other writings cited in this book. *Where difference is feared*, hospitality is denied and the dominant group justifies actions of inhospitality and oppression by blaming the more vulnerable members of the community. *Where difference is respected and valued*, hospitality becomes a catalyst of community like that of the baptismal liturgy in Galatians 3:28–29.

> There is no longer Jew or Greek, there is no longer slave or free, there is no longer male and female; for all of you are one in Christ Jesus. And if you belong to Christ, then you are Abraham's offspring, heirs according to the promise.

Survival and Quality of Life

In biblical understanding God's hospitality to those who are marginalized and excluded involves justice. Divine hospitality, expressed through believers, involves actions to put things right in our communities and world. This justice of God includes concern for the fundamental well-being of persons through access to food, water, shelter, work, and community, as well as for human dignity and self-determination in community.[17] It includes resistance to oppression, a putting things right in people's lives, and not just the presence of distributive rights.

Amazingly enough, when we look beyond the Hagar and Sarah story line of enmity and competition, we see in Hagar this very struggle for "survival and quality of life" in the wilderness. As Delores Williams recounts,

> [I]t seemed to me that God's response to Hagar's (and her child's) situation was survival and involvement in their development of quality of life appropriate to their situation and their heritage (Gen. 21:20).[18]

Searching for basic well-being and life itself, Hagar also showed her claim for human dignity and self-determination in her first bid for freedom and in her care for her son's future. Out of the wilderness experience we gain a basis for discussion of the meaning of justice that pushes all three of our religious traditions to say how they serve a God whose hospitality is seen in solidarity with the stranger, the social and religious outcast. Hospitality and justice belong together in our practice of God's welcome by reaching across difference to participate in God's actions of bringing justice and healing to our world in crisis.

Both Hassan and Williams have called attention to the importance of searching for an understanding of God's welcome in our lives through the wilderness story of Hagar. Hassan does this by reminding us that the Qur'an and the hadith do not divide the Abrahamic family. Instead, they report that Abraham continued to live with both women and to respect both sons. Nevertheless, in Islam Ishmael and Hagar receive the most attention as the direct ancestors of Muhammad and all Arabs. Hagar's courage in the wilderness when she searches for water for Ishmael is remembered in the annual pilgrimage or hajj to Mecca, the holy site of the spring at Zam-zam, between the two mountains of Safa and Marwa. As Hassan says, the pilgrims "pay homage to Hagar who has become an indestructible emblem not only of a mother's love for her offspring but of a true believer's faith in the saving power of God."

In her contribution to the book *Daughters of Abraham*, Hibba Abugideiri writes that Hagar's "God-consciousness" made her worthy to receive divine revelation, to see the "God of Seeing" and live, and strong enough in her struggles to "carve out an active female role within Islam."[19] Commenting on Genesis 16:9–12, which reports on Hagar's relationship to God, Trible points out that this Egyptian maid is the first person in the Bible to be visited by a divine messenger who speaks directly to her by name. She is the only woman in the Bible to receive a promise of future descendants, the only woman to receive an annunciation that she will bear a son, whom she is to name Ishmael (God hears), "for God has heard your affliction."

Williams describes this story of faith and struggle as one in which the God of Seeing gives Hagar the ability to see the resources she needs for survival.[20] She shows how Hagar's story has been appropriated as the basis of insight and faith in the African American cultural tradition and for the construction of womanist theology. It has become a lens, what Williams calls "proto-gesis," through which African Americans interpret the Bible based on their experience of wilderness and struggle to survive. She shows us that the presence of God is not only found with those who declare themselves to be the "winners." God is present to Hagar, the outcast, in surprising actions of solidarity and in actions that do not necessarily deliver her but instead provide her with resources to make her own way. As many African American women know so well, the wilderness experience continues despite repeated declarations of independence and freedom. In that wilderness the presence of God, as One in solidarity with the marginalized, gives them the strength to live each day in the hope that God intends things to be made right in the world and in their lives.

We could say that God is on the side of Abraham and Abraham's heir in our story and that God appears to Hagar to bid her return to slavery in Abraham's household. But, at the same time, God takes special care to provide Hagar with what she and her son need for survival. In the lives of those struggling for survival and quality of life, God's presence with them makes the difference between life and death. It is not in the dramatic victory but in the daily discovering of grace and love that we find God's hospitality in the African American womanist tradition, and in every tradition that seeks to see God in the midst of daily struggles. Beyond the story of enmity between two women, we can see a story of God's hospitality as accompaniment in the wilderness. This insight gives hope to those who, like Hagar and Sarah, live in the "already, not yet" of God's intention of *tikkun olam*, repair of the world (cf. Eccl. 7:13).[21]

In the biblical text Hagar and Sarah appear because the writers have what Trible calls "genealogy with a flaw." Sarai was barren (Gen. 11:30). As Clark points out, "their interpretive fate" is that women are good "to think with" as the male interpreters develop the stories.[22] The two mothers disappear when they are no longer needed for the story line of patriarchal lineage. Sarah dies after the "sacrifice" of Isaac when it is clear that Isaac is saved (Gen. 21:1–2). Hagar simply disappears from the story as soon as Ishmael becomes safely married and able to father many tribes (Gen. 25:12–18).

Even without a happy resolution in the biblical text or in later interpretations, the story of Hagar and Sarah endures, not only as a cautionary tale of inhospitality, competition, and patriarchal domination, but also as a story of blessing in which God's welcome is discovered in the wilderness. Many generations of children continue to find that their lives are read by the story as they seek to move beyond the enmity and constraints that flow from the misuse of difference to welcome the stranger.

I have often found myself conflicted and guilty over this story from Genesis and the enmity it has symbolized through the ages. I could see the way that Sarah and Hagar were trapped into competition because of oppressive patriarchal social structures. Yet I also knew that Sarah's actions in casting out Hagar mirror many of the ways that I, as a white, North American, Christian woman have shared in patterns of privilege that use stereotypes of difference to oppress my sisters of color as well as my Jewish and my Muslim sisters.

In rereading Genesis and these articles, I have come to see that there is more to the story than my own complicity and guilt. There is a story of "survival and quality of life"; a story of blessing that comes to us as children of struggle seeking the courage and faith we need to share God's peace and justice together as one human family. As Muslims, Jews, and Christians we are all *children of struggle* even to the thousandth generation. One discovery we can make as we reflect together on the enmity between Hagar and Sarah is that the struggle between us will not cease unless we become *children who struggle* for the wider gift of God's justice, peace, and wholeness in our lives and in the whole creation.

Notes

1. Sheila Briggs, "Slavery and Gender," in *On the Cutting Edge: The Study of Women in Biblical Worlds*, ed. Jane Schaberg, Alice Bach, and Esther Fuchs (New York: Continuum, 2004), 176–77.

2. Elisabeth Schüssler Fiorenza, "Discipleship of Equals"; Rosemary Radford Ruether, "Patriarchy," in *Dictionary of Feminist Theologies*, ed. Letty M. Russell and J. Shannon Clarkson (Louisville, KY: Westminster John Knox Press, 1996), 70–71, 105–6.

3. Mercy Amba Oduyoye, "Coming Home to Myself: The Childless Woman in the West African Space," in *Liberating Eschatology: Essays in Honor of Letty M. Russell*, ed. Margaret A. Farley and Serene Jones (Louisville, KY: Westminster John Knox Press, 1999), 105–20; Choi Hee An, *Korean Women and God* (Maryknoll, NY: Orbis Books, 2005), 159.

4. Delores S. Williams, *Sisters in the Wilderness: The Challenge of Womanist God-Talk* (Maryknoll, NY: Orbis Books, 1993), 28.

5. See chap. 6, p. 154.

6. Saʿdiyya Shaikh, "Transforming Feminisms: Islam, Women, and Gender Justice," in *Progressive Muslims: On Justice, Gender and Pluralism*, ed. Omid Safi (Oxford: One World, 2003), 157.

7. Marjorie Hewitt Suchocki, "In Search of Justice: Religious Pluralism from a Feminist Perspective," in *The Myth of Christian Uniqueness: Toward a Pluralistic Theology of Religions*, ed. John Hick and Paul F. Knitter (Maryknoll, NY: Orbis Books, 1998), 149–61.

8. Judith Plaskow, *Standing Again at Sinai: Judaism from a Feminist Perspective* (San Francisco: Harper and Row, 1990), 116–17. Cf. Letty M. Russell, *Church in the Round: Feminist Interpretation of the Church* (Louisville, KY: Westminster John Knox Press, 1993), 164–75.

9. Rosemary Radford Ruether, "Feminism and Jewish-Christian Dialogue: Particularism and Universalism in the Search for Religious Truth," in *Myth of Christian Uniqueness,* ed. Hick and Knitter, 138.

10. Riffat Hassan, "'Eid al-Adah' (Feast of Sacrifice) in Islam: Abraham, Hagar and Ishmael," in *Commitment and Commemoration: Jews, Christians and Muslims in Dialogue*, ed. André LaCocque (Chicago: Exploration Press, 1994), 143.

11. Hassan, "'Eid al-Adah,'" 143.

12. Rosemary Radford Ruether, *To Change the World: Christology and Cultural Criticism* (New York: Crossroad, 1981), 42–43.

13. Plaskow, *Standing Again at Sinai*, 107.
14. John Koenig, *New Testament Hospitality: Partnership with Strangers as Promise and Mission* (Philadelphia: Fortress Press, 1985), 8; Henri J. M. Nouwen, *Reaching Out: The Three Movements of the Spiritual Life* (New York: Doubleday, 1975), 79–100.
15. Iris Marion Young, *Intersecting Voices: Dilemmas of Gender, Political Philosophy, and Policy* (Princeton, NJ: Princeton University Press, 1997), 39–41; Jodi Dean, *Solidarity of Strangers: Feminism after Identity Politics* (Berkeley: University of California Press, 1996), 3.
16. Audre Lorde, *Sister Outsider: Essays and Speeches* (Trumansburg, NY: Crossing Press, 1984), 115.
17. Suchocki, "In Search of Justice," in *The Myth of Christian Uniqueness,* ed. Hick and Knitter, 154–55.
18. See chap. 7, p. 177.
19. Hibba Abugideiri, "Hagar: A Historical Model for 'Gender Jihad,'" in *Daughters of Abraham: Feminist Thought in Judaism, Christianity, and Islam,* ed. Yvonne Yazbeck Haddad and John L. Esposito (Gainesville: University Press of Florida, 2001), 84.
20. Catherine Keller, "Delores Williams: Survival, Surrogacy, Sisterhood, Spirit," *Union Seminary Quarterly Review* 58, nos. 3–4 (2004): 84–88.
21. Plaskow, *Standing Again at Sinai*, 217–20.
22. See chapter 5, p. 143.

Selected Bibliography

Berlin, Adele, Marc Zvi Brettler, and Michael A. Fishbane. *The Jewish Study Bible: Jewish Publication Society Tanakh Translation.* Oxford: Oxford University Press, 2004.

Carroll, James. *Constantine's Sword: The Church and the Jews, A History.* Boston: Houghton Mifflin Company, 2001.

Fletcher, Richard. *The Cross and the Crescent: Christianity and Islam from Muhammad to the Reformation.* New York: Viking, 2003.

Frankel, Ellen. *The Five Books of Miriam: A Woman's Commentary on the Torah.* New York: G. P. Putnam's, 1996.

Fredriksen, Paula, and Adele Reinhartz, eds. *Jesus, Judaism, and Christian Anti-Judaism: Reading the New Testament after the Holocaust.* Louisville, KY: Westminster John Knox Press, 2002.

Frymer-Kensky, Tikva. *Reading the Women of the Bible.* New York: Schocken Books, 2002.

Gottlieb, Lynn. *She Who Dwells Within: A Feminist Vision of a Renewed Judaism,* 1st ed. San Francisco: HarperSanFrancisco, 1995.

Haddad, Yvonne Yazbeck, and John L. Esposito, eds. *Daughters of Abraham: Feminist Thought in Judaism, Christianity, and Islam.* Gainesville: University Press of Florida, 2001.

Hick, John, and Paul F. Knitter, eds. *The Myth of Christian Uniqueness: Toward a Pluralistic Theology of Religions.* Maryknoll, NY: Orbis Books, 1998.

Hine, Darlene Clark, and Kathleen Thompson. *A Shining Thread of Hope: The History of Black Women in America.* New York: Broadway Books, 1998.

Horsley, Richard A. *Paul and Politics: Ekklesia, Israel, Imperium, Interpretation: Essays in Honor of Krister Stendahl.* Harrisburg, PA: Trinity Press International, 2000.

Hyman, Naomi M. *Biblical Women in the Midrash: A Sourcebook.* Northvale, NJ: Jason Aronson, 1998.

Kraemer, Shephard, and Mary Rose D'Angelo, eds. *Women and Christian Origins.* New York: Oxford Unversity Press, 1999.

Kwok, Pui-lan. *Post-Colonial Imagination and Feminist Theology.* Louisville, KY: Westminster John Knox Press, 2005.

LaCocque, André, ed. *Commitment and Commemoration: Jews, Christians and Muslims in Dialogue.* Chicago: Exploration Press, 1994.

Levine, Amy-Jill, ed., with Marianne Blickenstaff. *A Feminist Companion to Paul*. Cleveland: Pilgrim Press, 2004.

McAuliffe, Jane Dammen, Barry Walfish, and Joseph Ward Goering. *With Reverence for the Word: Medieval Scriptural Exegesis in Judaism, Christianity, and Islam*. New York: Oxford University Press, 2003.

Meyers, Carol L., Toni Craven, and Ross Shepard Kraemer. *Women in Scripture: A Dictionary of Named and Unnamed Women in the Hebrew Bible, the Apocryphal/ Deuterocanonical Books, and the New Testament*. Grand Rapids: Wm. B. Eerdmans Publishing Co., 2001.

Peters, F. E. *The Children of Abraham: Judaism, Christianity, Islam*. Princeton, NJ: Princeton University Press. 2004.

Plaskow, Judith. *Standing Again at Sinai: Judaism from a Feminist Perspective*. San Francisco; Harper and Row, 1990.

Pobee, John S., and Barbel von Wartenberg-Potter, eds. *New Eyes for Reading: Biblical and Theological Reflections by Women from the Third World*. Geneva: World Council of Churches, 1986.

Reimer, Gail Twersky, and Judith A. Kates, eds. *Beginning Anew: A Woman's Companion to the High Holy Days*. New York: Simon & Schuster, 1997.

Ruether, Rosemary Radford. *Faith and Fratricide: The Theological Roots of Anti-Semitism*. New York: Seabury Press, 1974.

Safi, Omid. *Progressive Muslims: On Justice, Gender and Pluralism*. Oxford: One World, 2003.

Sakenfeld, Katharine Doob. *Just Wives? Stories of Power & Survival in the Old Testament and Today*. Louisville, KY: Westminster John Knox Press, 2003.

Sawyer, Deborah F., and Diane M. Collier, eds. *Is There a Future for Feminist Theology?* Sheffield: Sheffield Academic Press, 1999.

Schaberg, Jane, Alice Bach, and Esther Fuchs, eds. *On the Cutting Edge*. New York: Continuum, 2004.

Schottroff, Luise. *Lydia's Impatient Sisters: A Feminist Social History of Early Christianity*. Louisville, KY: Westminster John Knox Press, 1995.

Schüssler Fiorenza, Elisabeth. *Rhetoric and Ethic: The Politics of Biblical Studies*. Minneapolis: Fortress Press, 1999.

———. *Searching the Scriptures*, Vol. 2, *A Feminist Commentary*. New York: Crossroad, 1994.

Solomon, Norman. *Judaism: A Very Short Introduction*. Oxford: Oxford University Press, 1996.

Steinmetz, Devora. *From Father to Son: Literary Currents in Biblical Interpretation*. Louisville, KY: Westminster/John Knox Press, 1991.

Thompson, John L. *Writing the Wrongs: Women of the Old Testament among Biblical Commentators from Philo through the Reformation*. Oxford: Oxford University Press, 2001.

VanderKam, James C. *An Introduction to Early Judaism*. Grand Rapids: Wm. B. Eerdmans Publishing Co., 2001.

Wadud, Amina. *Qur'an and Woman: Rereading the Sacred Text from a Woman's Perspective*. New York: Oxford University Press, 1999.

Weems, Renita. *Just a Sister Away: A Womanist Vision of Women's Relationships in the Bible*. San Diego: Lura Media, 1988.

Williams, Delores S. *Sisters in the Wilderness: The Challenge of Womanist God-Talk*. Maryknoll, NY: Orbis Books, 1993.

Wire, Antoinette Clark. *The Corinthian Women Prophets: A Reconstruction through Paul's Rhetoric*. Minneapolis: Fortress Press, 1990.

Index of Scripture References

*Verse-by-verse references in Genesis are not listed.

*Verse-by-verse references in Galatians are not listed.

Index of Authors and Editors

Index of Subjects

207

St. Louis Community College
at Meramec
LIBRARY